# BACKCOUNTRY HUTS & LODGES
## *of the*
### ROCKIES & COLUMBIAS

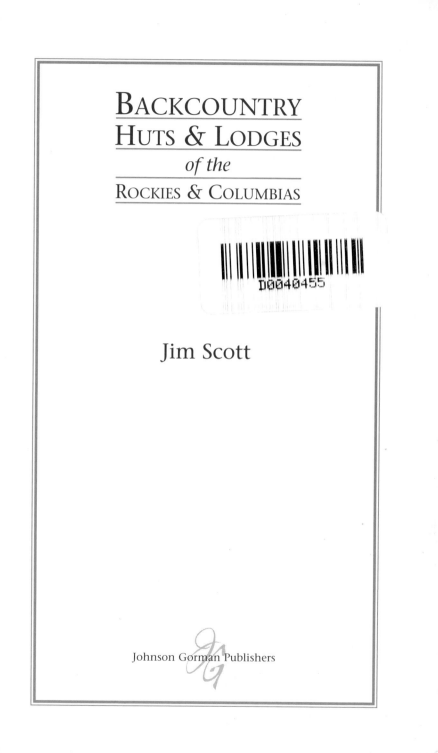

## Jim Scott

Johnson Gorman Publishers

*The Publishers*
Johnson Gorman Publishers
2003 – 35 Avenue SW
Calgary AB Canada T2T 2E2
www.jgbooks.com

*Credits*
Frontcover photo courtesy of Sorcerer Lake Lodge.
Backcover photo of Fairy Meadow Hut courtesy of the Alpine Club
    of Canada.
Cover design by Duncan Campbell.
Text design by Dennis Johnson.
Author photo by Elaire Frenette.
Printed and bound in Canada by Friesens for Johnson Gorman
    Publishers.

*Acknowledgments*
Financial support provided by the Alberta Foundation for the Arts, a
beneficiary of the Lottery Fund of the Government of Alberta.

COMMITTED TO THE DEVELOPMENT OF CULTURE AND THE ARTS

*National Library of Canada Cataloguing in Publication Data*
Scott, James Beresford, 1949–
Backcountry huts & lodges of the Rockies & Columbias
Includes bibliographical references and index.
ISBN 0-921835-58-2
1. Wilderness lodges—Rocky Mountains, Canadian (B.C. and Alta.)*
2. Wilderness lodges—British Columbia—Columbia Mountains.
3. Rocky Mountains, Canadian (B.C. and Alta.)—Guidebooks.*
4. Columbia Mountains (B.C.)—Guidebooks. I. Title.
GV191.46.R62S36 2001    796.5    C2001-911337-4

# Contents

Huts & Lodges by Geographic Sector . . . . . . . . . .7

Introduction . . . . . . . . . . . . . . . . . . . . . . . . . . . .9

South Rockies . . . . . . . . . . . . . . . . . . . . . . . . . .19

Central Rockies . . . . . . . . . . . . . . . . . . . . . . . . .59

North Rockies . . . . . . . . . . . . . . . . . . . . . . . . . .99

South Columbias . . . . . . . . . . . . . . . . . . . . . . . .143

Central Columbias . . . . . . . . . . . . . . . . . . . . . . .197

North Columbias . . . . . . . . . . . . . . . . . . . . . . . .243

British Columbia Forest Service
    Regional & District Offices . . . . . . . . . . . . . . . .274

British Columbia Provincial Parks
    District Offices . . . . . . . . . . . . . . . . . . . . . . . . .277

National Parks Contact Information . . . . . . . . . . .279

Selected Bibliography. . . . . . . . . . . . . . . . . . . . . .280

*In Memoriam:* Recently Defunct Huts . . . . . . . . . .282

Index . . . . . . . . . . . . . . . . . . . . . . . . . . . . . . . . .285

About the Author . . . . . . . . . . . . . . . . . . . . . . . .287

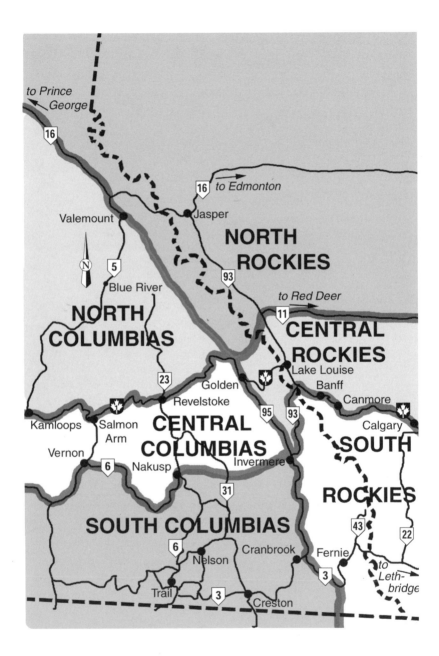

# Huts & Lodges by Geographic Sector

The carving up of the mountains into the 6 sectors used in this book is my own invention, created for the sake of efficiency in the design of maps and the text. There is no official division of these two mountain groups into South, Central, and North. Also, I've been somewhat liberal in the mountain ranges that I've grouped under the rubric "Columbias," for some would argue that the Cariboo Range (northwest of the Big Bend area of the Columbia Valley) is not part of the Columbias. Still, this definition enables me to cover all the high alpine country that lies between the Rockies and the comparatively lower ranges that extend from the southern Okanagan to Prince George.

## SOUTH ROCKIES
- Thunder Meadows Cabin
- Island Lake Lodge
- Lakit Lookout Shelter
- Fish Lake Cabin
- Connor Lakes Cabin
- Tobermory Creek Cabin
- Queen Mary Lake Cabin
- Ralph Lake Shelter
- Mitchell River Shelter
- R.C. Hind Hut
- Naiset Cabins
- Mount Assiniboine Lodge
- Surprise Creek Cabin
- Police Meadows Cabin
- Bryant Creek Cabin
- Sundance & Halfway Lodges
- Egypt Lake Shelter
- Shadow Lake Lodge

## CENTRAL ROCKIES
- Diana Lake Lodge
- Fay Hut
- Neil Colgan Hut
- Castle Mountain Hut
- Lake O'Hara Lodge
- Elizabeth Parker Hut
- Abbot Pass Hut
- Halfway/Ptarmigan Shelter
- Skoki Lodge

### The Wapta Traverse
  - Scott Duncan Hut
  - Balfour Hut
  - Bow Hut
  - Peter & Catharine Whyte (Peyto) Hut
- Stanley Mitchell Hut
- Twin Falls Chalet
- Amiskwi Lodge
- Mistaya Lodge

## NORTH ROCKIES
- Campbell Icefield Chalet
- Chatter Creek Lodge
- Lawrence Grassi (Mt Clemenceau) Hut
- Lloyd MacKay (Mt Alberta) Hut
- Fortress Lake Lodge
- Sydney Vallance (Fryatt) Hut
- Wates–Gibson Hut
- Tonquin Valley Adventures Lodge
- Tonquin Valley Backcountry Lodge
- Shangri-La Cabin
- Shovel Pass Lodge

- Mt Colin Centennial Hut
- Dave Henry Lodge
- Swift Creek Cabins
- Ralph Forster Hut
- Berg Lake Shelter
- West Range Lodge
- Kakwa & Jarvis Lakes Cabins
- North Rockies Ski Tours Lodge

## SOUTH COLUMBIAS
- Char Creek Cabin
- Ripple Ridge Cabin

### The Bonnington Traverse
  - Grassy Hut
  - Steed/Marble Hut
  - Snowwater Hilton Hut
  - Snowwater Lodge
  - Copper Hut
  - Barrett Lake Hut
  - Huckleberry Hut
  - Bonnington Yurts
- Ymir Yurts
- Boulder & Ptarmigan Lodges
- Doctor Creek Cabin
- Powder Creek Lodge
- Woodbury Cabin
- Silver Spray Cabin
- Flint Lake Lodge & Mt. Carlyle Hut
- Slocan Chief Cabin
- Crusader Creek Cabin
- Enterprise Creek Cabin
- Valhalla Lodge
- Evans Lake Cabin
- Wee Sandy Creek (Jules Holt) Cabin
- Ruby Creek Lodge
- Meadow Mountain Lodge

## CENTRAL COLUMBIAS
- Sultana Creek Cabin
- Jumbo Pass Cabin
- Forster Creek Cabin

- Olive Hut
- Dunn Creek Cabin
- Galena Lodge
- Monashee Powder Lodge
- Blanket Glacier Chalet
- Bugaboo Lodge
- Conrad Kain Hut
- Malloy Igloo
- Bobbie Burns Lodge
- International Basin Hut
- Battle Abbey Lodge
- Selkirk Lodge
- McMurdo Creek Cabin
- Glacier Circle Hut
- Sapphire Col Shelter
- Asulkan Cabin
- A.O. Wheeler Hut
- Purcell Lodge

## NORTH COLUMBIAS
- Caribou Cabin
- Eva Lake Cabin
- Durrand Glacier & Mt Moloch Chalets
- Keystone–Standard Basin Hut
- Sorcerer Lake Lodge
- Sunrise, Meadow & Vista Lodges
- Adamants Lodge
- Benjamin Ferris (Great Cairn) Hut
- Fairy Meadow Hut
- Trophy Mountain, Discovery & Fight Meadow Chalets
- Clearwater River Chalet
- Monashee Chalet
- Peter Huser Memorial Chalet
- Cariboo Lodge

# Introduction

This book began with rumors. Rumors about great cabins deep in the backcountry, havens that you could retreat to at the end of a hard day, wet and cold and hungry, and then dry out in front of a fire, sipping a Brandy and eating a hot meal. But these rumors (as rumors always are) were frustratingly vague. "Near Queen Something Lake in the Royal Group, although it might be locked," I was told, or "Somewhere in back of the ski hill at Fernie, but I don't know how you book it."

And then I began hearing about the proliferation of backcountry lodges catering to skiers and hikers who could afford to shell out a bit of extra money for a pampered week amid awesome terrain. But again, I only heard enough about them to be teased ("My cousin heli-ed in to some string of lodges west of Kimberly where it puked snow all night and was sunny all day—I forget their name, though").

All right, I figured, let's pick up a guidebook that tells exactly where all these places are, and go check them out. Actually, that's when the book began. There was no guidebook. So, knowing how Nature abhors a vacuum, I decided to fill the void. You're holding it now.

Having logged quite a few trips into the Rockies and Columbias, I thought as I started this book that I could simply write up all the ones I'd visited and then dig up the info on the dozen or so that I'd heard reports of. A year later, I'd stumbled onto about 60 new (to me) huts and lodges, and every time that I'd complete an absolute, final, totally comprehensive master list—I'd find another one.

And as the number of places began to proliferate, I also found that I would need to establish some clear parameters limiting the sorts of facilities I would include in the book. After a lot of discussion with friends, I eventually came to define "backcountry hut or lodge" as any facility that cannot be reached year-round by vehicles. Thus, a few of the places in this book can be reached by 4x4s in summer but not in winter. I also decided to include only those lodgings that are used, at least in part, by people who like to engage in self-propelled activities in the backcountry. Given that skiing downhill can be seen as a form of self-propulsion, I included heli-ski and snowcat-ski lodges, but I did not include facilities such as fly-in fishing lodges or chalets that cater exclusively to snowmobilers.

This book, then, is my current master list of all such lodgings, but I no longer delude myself into thinking I've found them all. I have, in fact, purposefully left some out. Throughout the Kootenays, for example, there are innumerable old trappers' cabins and mining shacks that aren't identified here, mainly because they are now vermin-condos or else are on the verge of collapse. I had to scrap one cabin just a few months ago when I learned that its roof collapsed last winter, luckily with no one inside.

I have also not included some places whose owners/caretakers made it plain, directly or indirectly, they didn't want to be in this book, no doubt because they fear that their often-unattended building might suffer an increase in vandalism and forced entries. In fact, those of you who remember the General Store cabin in the Forster Creek valley will no longer find it there. After a serious vandalizing last winter, it has been airlifted by its heli-ski owners to a secret locale.

Having said this, I also realize that there are other sites that should be in this book but aren't. If you know of some appalling oversight on my part, please let me know. The nature of this book is such that its information becomes dated within a few years, and thus (heh, heh) new editions with updated and expanded information are called for. I would appreciate learning of any serious omissions (or, of course, any goofs or gaffes in this edition); your contribution would be acknowledged in these subsequent editions. To contact me, see my e-mail address at the end of this introduction.

As for errors, well, I have done everything I could to be accurate. In the process, I discovered that many of the existing guides to hiking and ski trails—and even the professionally done guiding maps—contain errors. The hiking guides, for example, not uncommonly contain sharply conflicting information on distances or geographical features, and when I pursued one oddity with a map company, I discovered that their positioning of a hut on a map was really just a guess (and they guessed in error by over a kilometer).

In a few cases, I found that the guidebooks published over the past 20 years all contained suspiciously identical details, almost as if each successive one just "borrowed" the nuts-and-bolts data (such as topo map grid references) from its predecessors. All of which is fine, of course, except where the original—or even the topo map itself—was inaccurate.

I have happened upon a few such errors and corrected them here, but I cannot claim to have caught them all, nor would I dare maintain that this book is 100 percent free of any borrowed misinformation or any inaccuracies of my own inadvertent making.

I have visited many of the facilities listed here, but not all of them. For one thing, I couldn't afford to go to all the commercial lodges (although I would graciously accept any invitations they might offer me as I prepare the next edition). In those instances where I have not actually been in to the facilities, I have sent the lodge owners draft copies of my material and had them correct any errors or extol more flatteringly their amenities.

I have also worked closely with the Alpine Club of Canada (thank you, Nancy Hansen) to ensure that the descriptions of their 20+ huts and cabins are both accurate and current. I have been in to most of the other noncommercial operations, but in a few cases I have relied on textual material and/or the reports of friends who have actually been there recently.

Still, in the interests of accuracy, let me run through the template in which I've arranged my information, clarifying what my intent was—and throwing in a few cautions or disclaimers about my material (okay, maybe loopholes is the right term).

## GENERAL DESCRIPTION

I set out to present each facility in the most positive light, trying to show why someone would want to go in there in the first place. Obviously, most of the huts and lodges are where they are because of what's around them. I do not provide a great deal of detail about the kind of skiing, hiking or climbing to be had nearby; instead, I generally just mention what sorts of outdoor activities are there to be indulged in. It almost goes without saying that you will find these activities to be exciting and the surrounding terrain to be more than usually beautiful.

As for the facilities themselves, I again tried to emphasize their appeal without being gushy or misleading. Certainly, all the commercial operations offer facilities that are many notches in quality and service above most of the huts; there is, to be sure, quite a spread in their quality, as you might infer from the broad range in prices charged. As a general rule, the level of luxury you can expect is pretty well proportional to the cost.

At the other end of the scale, some of the huts and shelters are little more than enclosures that provide protection from the wind and rain. The Malloy Igloo, for example, would never be the average hiker's vacation destination, but for climbers playing around on the peaks near the Vowell Glacier, it can be a veritable palace during bad weather. You should also read between the lines in the descriptions of a few of the cabins; terms like "a bit dilapidated" or "rustic" or "primitive" should tip you off that you wouldn't want to bring your fussy Aunt Priscilla in there, especially if she has this thing about mice.

## LOCATION

This section gave me the gray hair you see in the back cover photo. Honest. Completing the one line "Specific" sometimes consumed days of my time. As previously mentioned, the guidebooks and maps often contained conflicting information, generally with no way of knowing which, if any, of them was accurate. I went in to many of these buildings with my own GPS in order to get readings, but for all others I had to go with coordinates or GPS readings from reliable sources. I also used some of the map coordinates that seemed standard in the guidebooks, although I did check these for apparent accuracy and had to correct a few.

But these map coordinates—the 6-digit Grid References (GRs) by which a point on a topo map is identified—are frustratingly unclear. As you may know, if you're given a GR, you can then navigate your way to the very spot of land that corresponds to that number. However, in the mid-80s, Canadian cartographers changed the coordinate system used on these maps, which means that we now have two systems. The original system is known as NAD 27 (referring to the North American Datum of 1927), and the new one is NAD 83. The trouble arises when you try to use an old GR on a new map, or vice versa—you could end up more than a kilometer away from where you expect to be. Like the difference between quarts and liters, the discrepancy isn't much, but it could really mess things up for you.

Surprisingly, many guidebooks give GRs with no NAD identifier, which is about as helpful as giving a house address as 16—with no street name. You generally tend to assume that these guidebooks would be using the 1983 datum maps, but some of the books seem to have just "borrowed" the NAD 27 GRs from earlier books. Besides, there are large areas of British Columbia (even popular ones such as the Bugaboos) for which there are no updated maps. I have, then, stipulated the NAD date for all of my specific references. Note that at the bottom of all NAD83 maps, there are directions on how to convert a NAD27 GR.

No doubt, in 20 years' time everyone will be packing GPS units. In fact, I hear that wrist-mounted GPSs are on their way. As you probably know, you can use a GPS to find your way from your living room to your bathroom. However, these units can help you with map navigation only if you program them to use the same datum as your maps. Therefore, since some users of this book will have GPSs, and some won't (and many will never use a map coordinate in their lives), I have indicated specific location in two succinct ways. Where I have a known 6-digit Grid Reference I will give that (such as "NAD27 123456"). Where I have a GPS reading, I will give that, and since the standard GR is always "hidden" in such a reading, I have highlighted in bold type the relevant 6 digits. Here is a sample:

- What appears on a GPS programmed to NAD83 units is:
  11 U 0530240 UTM 5708383.
- The shorthand version used in this book is:
  NAD83 5**302**40 7**083**83.
- The GR to use on your 1983-vintage topo map is:
  **302 083**.

To program a waypoint into your GPS with my shorthand version, be sure to add the numbers and letters that I have omitted (because they are the same for every coordinate in this book).

If you're not sure how to find a GR on a map, here's a quick recap. Once you have a GR number, use the first 3 digits to find your position east–west ("side-to-side") on the map, and then use the final three to find your position north–south ("up and down"). For example, if you want to stand at the spot identified as GR 123456 on the map below, envision a line running up and down at the 12.3 mark, and then another line running sideways at the 45.6 mark. Where they intersect is where you want to be, as shown by the junction of the black lines below:

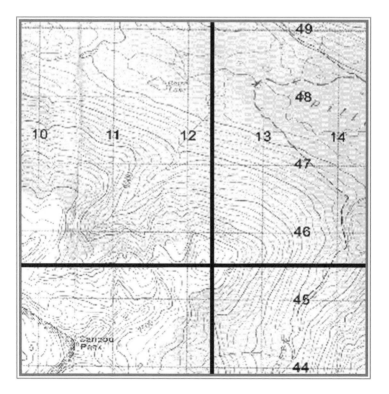

If this seems intimidating, don't worry. Many of the huts and all of the lodges have very clear trails leading to their front door—except where you helicopter in, of course. Even if you have a hard time reading a road map, you should be able to make your way to these huts. As for the ones where good route-finding skills are important, I clearly identify these.

### Free Topo Maps

Want to see every topo map in Canada on your computer screen? Just go to this government website and follow the links: www.toporama. cits.rncan.gc.ca/. With a good color printer, you can select and print off just what you need for your trip, but note that these maps do not give elevations, and they do not name all the features (creeks, mountains) that are named on the print maps.

## AMENITIES

These are as accurate as I can make them. Note, however, that for some of the unmaintained or irregularly maintained cabins, the amenities can change rapidly—and generally for the worse. It does astound me how some people can use a shelter and then wreck it before leaving, but such does happen. Nature, to be sure, is sometimes no less kind. Vermin love to shred foamies, and one pissed-off wolverine can do more damage to a cabin than a dozen drunks. This all means that you cannot be 100 percent certain of finding a stove in good working order or lanterns that actually light. Always pack candles, and bringing along a stove and cookware would often be prudent, as would spare mantles for the lanterns.

## COST

Costs cited were accurate as this book went to press, but it goes without saying that they may change within the year. My intention in including something as variable as cost was to give you a sense of the price range and thus the quality range that you might be looking at. Clearly, an $18-a-night Alpine Club hut will be a different experience from a $40-a-night commercial yurt which will be totally unlike a $300-a-night chalet. Even two years from now, these prices should provide a good basis for comparison shopping. Note also that the cost of access is sometimes, but not always, included in the price. If it isn't (and generally this applies to operations that the hardy can access on foot to save the cost of helicopter or snowcat), I indicate what the extra cost will be. But please do not complain to the lodge owners if their price is higher than what's listed here. Just be pleasantly surprised if it isn't.

Unless otherwise noted, costs shown do not include the federal

Goods and Services Tax (GST), which adds 7 percent to the cost, or the British Columbia provincial sales tax, which, when combined with the GST, brings the total to 15 percent. Visitors from outside of Canada can apply for a rebate on the GST. Alberta does not have a provincial sales tax. And finally, anglers should note that sport fishing licenses are, of course, an additional cost.

## ACCESS

The same cautions and caveats apply here as for map location. I feel sure that my route descriptions will suffice, but I aimed for succinctness rather than explicitness, for three principal reasons (four if you include the cost of paper):

1. I assume that you will want to do something in the backcountry after arriving at your hut or lodge, and thus you probably will have some form of a guidebook with you (if you are not being professionally guided). Whether you plan to climb Mt Sir Sandford or ski in the meadows near Skoki Lodge, any relevant guidebook will, in effect, take you by the hand and get you from your car to your accommodation. My directions are a little less exhaustive, but they certainly should be plain enough to get you there. For really complex routes, such as the access to the climbers' hut 5000 feet up Mount Robson, I simply refer you to maps and details in the climbers' guidebook that you would need to have in order to carry on to the summit.

2. For some of the huts, especially those in the National and Provincial Parks, my directions could simply state: "Get on the well-traveled trail and follow all the signposts to the front door of the hut." That is, even the most hapless of route-finders could not fail to find their way in to such places.

3. Anyone heading in to a comparatively remote cabin along unmarked or nonexistent routes (such as glacier travel) should already be skilled in map reading and visual navigating. Such people, no doubt equipped with good maps, typically need only to be informed of the major landmarks or grid references, for their experience and common sense generally should be adequate to get them safely to their destination. I do, to be sure, point out any important hazards or difficulties or common misdirections.

I should also point out that, except in a few cases where I could bike in and read an odometer, the distances given are approximate. Again, if you read two different guidebooks, you will often find sharply conflicting distances given (such as the 5 km difference between 2 books' descriptions of the same trail into Wates–Gibson Hut). Personally, I have a hard time measuring distance as I walk; after 2 hours along a trail, my guess as to the distance covered could be out by at least a kilometer. Some new guidebooks claim that their trail distances have been measured with a calibrated wheel, and the better commercial maps seem to have measured the distances fairly precisely. Where possible, I have gone with the number that seems most reliable. Still, you should look on the distances as a general indicator of the amount of ground to be covered. Obviously, the quality of the trail itself, more so than its length, will play the major role in determining the amount of time and effort you should expect to expend.

### Time

There are bound to be two kinds of readers of this book: those who think my time estimates are preposterously slow, and those who think my estimates are impossibly fast. As is the case with any guidebook, you should look on these numbers as very rough indicators of the time needed for the trip. Hopefully, with a bit of experience you will soon discover whether you should add or subtract a certain percent to my estimates. Do recognize, of course, that a host of factors—mud, late-season snow, raging creeks, washouts, blistering heat, and blistering feet, to name a few—can radically change the hiking time.

For winter access, I generally don't even bother to try predicting a time. The time difference between gliding along a clear track and trail-breaking through knee-deep snow can easily be a factor of two. For example, on my first venture into Fay Hut, my friends I and skied it in about 5 hours following a clear track. The next time we went, we had to trail-break the last one third of the way, and the journey took us 11 hours. Had we been forced to trail-break all the way from the parking lot, we certainly could not have made it in a day.

### Guidebooks

Quite often, this is only a partial list, especially for the more popular hiking areas. I have tried to list texts that I have found to be very helpful, although I recognize that others could do the job just as well. My intention primarily was to provide you with a good text that could fill you in on the kinds of activities (especially day-trips) that you can engage in once you get to your accommodation. I am a bit sparse in mentioning guides to mountaineering, mainly because those of you into more high-end climbing would almost certainly have detailed climbing guides. If not, a resource such as the book section of the Mountain Equipment Co-op store or website, or any bookstore specializing in wilderness adventure books, would be a good place to find guides to rock and ice climbs for specific geographical sectors of British Columbia and Alberta.

## INFORMATION & BOOKING

This should give you all you need by way of mailing and e-mail addresses, phone and fax numbers, and websites. These do change, of course, (especially websites that tend to disappear quickly without a trace), but hopefully at least one of these forms of contact will work for you.

My goal when I set out to do this book was to create a Bible, the definitive text that would be so thorough and accurate that it would become the standard authority on huts and lodges for decades to come. Okay, maybe that's putting it a little too theatrically, but I certainly did try to create a text that was as comprehensive and accurate—and as genuinely helpful—as I could possibly make it. If you find anything misleading about my info—whether it's just a missing lantern or a hut that's become a heap of ashes—please let me know.

As I said, I decided to do this book only because I wanted to buy one like it but found that no such book existed. In putting this text together, then, I first charted out all that I could possibly need to know if I was planning to go somewhere new to ski or hike or climb and have a roof over my head at day's end. I hope that you find this book to be as handy and informative as I had intended it to be. I'll be continuing to conduct my field research (or that's how I describe it to my wife—playing around in the mountains is more like it) for years to come. So be forewarned—if I see you with this book, I'll pick your brains relentlessly about any great havens that I may have overlooked. This Bible will only get better.

## ACKNOWLEDGEMENTS

To identify everyone who assisted me in the gathering of information for this book would entail another book in itself. Needless to say, my friends and family who accompanied me on a good many of my trips into the huts and lodges have provided invaluable support. Of course, their sharing of my passion for the backcountry and for exploring new terrain had made them important contributors to this project long before I had ever conceived of it. Their faces are sprinkled throughout this book.

I am as well indebted to at least a dozen British Columbia Forest Service Recreation Officers and BC Parks Information Officers. Their patience with my interminable probing and their knowledge of their territory made them extremely helpful to me.

Also, I received a lot of input from quite a variety of outdoor activity clubs which caretake various huts. Where I had feared there might be some opposition to any widespread publicizing of their facilities, I encountered only support and good advice.

I must also thank Red Deer College for all the technical support it has given me in the preparation of this book; in particular, all the folks in the TLTC Centre who helped me learn how to manipulate digital images and draw maps in Photoshop deserve commendation, if only for their patience with me.

Finally, by far my biggest debt of gratitude is to Brian Anderson. He embarked on this project with me and did an enormous amount of research and brainstorming with me in the first half-year of this book's gestation. Without his support and energy, this book may have remained just an idle fantasy of mine.

## PHOTO CREDITS

Except for the shots of most of the commercial lodges and some of the Alpine Club of Canada huts, all of the photos used throughout this book were taken by my friends and me. Unfortunately, because we often exchange photos after our trips, I cannot be fully sure in all cases who took which photo. Rather than try to identify the photographer for each of these shots, then, my friends agreed to a blanket recognition of them as contributors.

So, other than the specific recognitions given below, the principal photographers (and backcountry buddies) are Dave Maclean, Mike Knopp, Brian Anderson, Add and Gail Wilson, Stephen Scott, Rick Price and Marvin Lloyd.

In all cases except where indicated, the photos of the commercial lodges are credited to the lodge owners, and the photos of the Alpine Club of Canada huts are credited to the organization.

Other contributors include Canadian Mountain Holidays, page 211; Therese Roberts, page 226; Roger Laurilla, page 242; and John Bilodeaux, pages 222, 216, 272, 273.

Jim Scott
E-mail: jim.scott@rdc.ab.ca
Red Deer Alberta
August 2001

# South Rockies

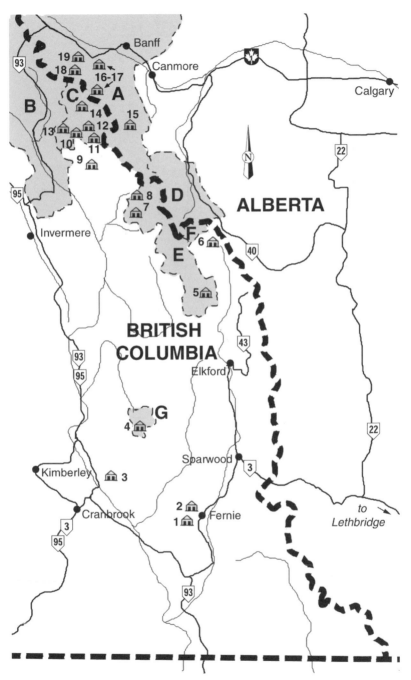

## PROVINCIAL & NATIONAL PARKS

*Map*
*Reference*

A .................Banff National Park

B..................Kootenay National Park

C .................Mount Assiniboine Provincial Park

D .................Peter Lougheed Provincial Park

E..................Height of the Rockies Provincial Park

F..................Elk Lakes Provincial Park

G .................Top of the World Provincial Park

## HUTS & LODGES

*Map*  *Page*
*Reference*  *Number*

1 .................Thunder Meadows Cabin .............................22

2.................Island Lake Lodge .........................................24

3.................Lakit Lookout Shelter .................................26

4.................Fish Lake Cabin ...........................................28

5.................Connor Lakes Cabin .....................................30

6.................Tobermory Creek Cabin .............................32

7.................Queen Mary Lake Cabin...............................34

8.................Ralph Lake Shelter .......................................36

9.................Mitchell River Shelter ................................38

10...............R.C. Hind Hut...............................................40

11...............Naiset Cabins ...............................................42

12...............Mount Assiniboine Lodge............................44

13...............Surprise Creek Cabin ...................................46

14...............Police Meadows Cabin..................................48

15...............Bryant Creek Cabin .....................................50

16–17..........Sundance & Halfway Lodges ........................52

18...............Egypt Lake Shelter .......................................54

19...............Shadow Lake Lodge ......................................56

# Thunder Meadows Cabin

This club hut affords great access to the same terrain and deep powder snow that attracts so many people to the Fernie Alpine Resort Ski Hill and to the cat-skiing at the nearby Island Lake Lodge. Located in an alpine meadow, it also serves as a base for lovely day-hikes and scrambles in the summer. In summer and winter the cabin can be accessed from the lifts at the Ski Hill (if avalanche conditions permit) or from the Cedar Valley Road. Note the conditions of club membership regarding bookings.

## LOCATION

*General* In the Lizard Range about 8 km (5 mi) SW of Fernie BC.

*Specific* 82 G/6 Elko NAD27 632286 482460.

*Other pertinent maps* 82 G/11 Fernie (for terrain N of the cabin). Map of access routes can be requested when reservations are being made.

*Elevation* 1890 m (6200 ft).

*Elevation gain from Cedar Valley Road* 890 m (2789 ft).

## AMENITIES

*Heat* Woodstove (wood flown in; please use sparingly).

*Cooking* Propane stove (guests supply own 1-lb propane bottles); cookware and dishware provided.

*Lighting* Propane lantern (guests supply own 1-lb propane bottles).

*Sleeping* Bunks with foam pads.

*Capacity* 12 (maximum of 8/ group).

**COST** (as of Summer 2001)
$10/person/night or $90/night
for exclusive rental of cabin. Only
members can book the cabin.
(Annual membership is $25, but
only one person in a group need
hold a membership).

## ACCESS

The cabin is closed in May and
June for wildlife protection.
When registering, be sure to ask
for a copy of the map showing
the access routes.

*From Mt Fernie Provincial Park*
   Turn N off Hwy 3 into this
   park just W of Fernie and then
   proceed 5.2 km (3.3 mi) up
   this road to the Cabin Bowl
   trailhead; the trail then climbs
   steadily and at times steeply to
   a pass. The cabin is not far
   below the pass. Alternately, at
   the 2-km (1.2-mi) point on the
   road, head S up the Lizard
   Lake Trail to Liverworst Pass
   and descend to Easy Street Valley and then up NW to the
   cabin.
*Time* 4–5 hours.
*From Fernie Alpine Resort ski area*
   The cabin can be reached in
   summer by a beautiful ridge
   walk from the top of the lifts.
   Access to the ridge is varied
   with some routes having fixed
   cables for aid. In winter, this
   access from the lifts is still
   possible, but when a significant risk of avalanche exists,
   the Ski Hill does not allow
   access from its property.

## INFORMATION & BOOKING

Elk Valley Ski Touring Association
Attention Patrick Gilmar
RR 1 Site 9 Comp 10
Fernie BC V0B 1M0
*Phone* (250) 423-3905
Alternately, try
The Guide's Hut
671 2 Ave
Fernie BC V0B 1M0
*Phone* (250) 423-3650

# Island Lake Lodge

Although accessible by car in summer, these luxurious log lodges in the Lizard Range can be accessed only by ski or snowcat in winter. There are numerous hikes and climbs in the immediate area (guides available), and the powder snow makes for awesome skiing. The lodges cater to your every need, from fresh-baked pastries in the morning to a pre-bedtime soak in the outdoor hot tub. Primarily a cat-skiing operation in winter, the lodges do offer the possibility of guided ski touring after mid-April. A traverse to the Thunder Meadows hut is an option.

## LOCATION

*General* Near treeline in a valley just NW of Fernie BC.
*Specific* 82 G/11 Fernie NAD83 6**320**43 4**856**16.

*Other pertinent maps* 82 G/6 Elko (for terrain to the S, including Thunder Meadows Cabin).
*Elevation* 1372 m (4500 ft).
*Elevation gain from Hwy 3* 372 m (1220 ft).

## AMENITIES

*Heat* Hot water radiant.
*Cooking* All meals provided.
*Lighting* Electric.
*Sleeping* Private bedrooms; linen provided.
*Capacity* 16 in main lodge; 18 in Red Eagle Lodge.
*Features* Gourmet meals, fine wines, large living room with stone fireplace, outdoor hot tub, certified guides, massage, mountain biking, hiking, good fishing.

## COST (as of Summer 2001)

*Summer* Adults $130–$150/person/night; $60–$90 for children. Fees for guided activities extra.

**Winter** From about $1500/person for a 3-day snowcat skiing package in low season to about $2600 for a 4-day package in high season. Visit the website for all the options and booking information.

## ACCESS

Road directions or snowcat transport arrangements provided upon registration.

## GUIDEBOOKS

*Mountain Footsteps: Selected Hikes in the East Kootenays,* Strong.
*Summits and Icefields,* Scott.

## INFORMATION & BOOKING

Island Lake Lodge
Attention Shannon Mercer
Box 1229
Fernie BC V0B 1M0
**Phone** 1-888-422-8754
**Fax** (250) 423-4055
**E-mail** reserve@islandlakelodge.com
**Website** www.islandlakeresorts.com

# Lakit Lookout Shelter

Described by one visitor in the hut register as "a little hotel in the sky," this restored lookout tower provides a dramatic place to spend the night and photograph the alpine sunsets and sunrises. High on a spur ridge running from the summit of Mt Lakit, the views of the Kootenay valley and the southern Rockies are spectacular. Dayhikes up to and beyond the summit are possible, as is a multi-day traverse involving numerous peak-scrambles north to the Stevens Pass area. The shelter is surprisingly snug and has a small woodstove, but it offers few amenities and there is no nearby water supply. It does get some winter use by skiers, but only when avalanche conditions permit.

## LOCATION

*General* Near the summit of Mt Lakit, NE of Cranbrook BC.

*Specific* 82 G/12 Cranbrook NAD83 6**011**01 5**079**74.

*Other pertinent maps* www.for. gov.bc.ca/hfp/rec/maps/nelson/ lakit%20lookout.pdf

*Elevation* 2360 m (7720 ft).

*Elevation gain from end of road* 460 m (1450 ft).

## AMENITIES

*Heat* Small woodstove; no firewood supplied.

*Cooking* None.

*Lighting* None.

*Sleeping* Platform with foam pad for one person.

*Capacity* 6 (5 sleep on floor).

## COST (as of Summer 2001)

Free; no reservations.

## ACCESS

**Summer** From Hwy 93/95 in the community of Fort Steele, turn E onto Fort Steele–Wardner Road and then in 300 m (1000 ft) take the first left onto Wildhorse River Road. Follow this road N for 5 km (3 mi) and take the right fork uphill. Take the left forks uphill at the 6.5- and the 10.3-km marks (4- and 6.4-mi marks)—both of which forks are marked with "Lakit Lookout" signs. Continue up this steep road to the trailhead sign and parking area at the 14.5-km (9-mi) mark; the road can be negotiated by 2WD vehicles, but the surface is quite rough. The trail is very good but persistently steep as it heads up through alpine terrain to open meadows, for a total distance of about 2 km (1.2 mi).

**Time** About 1 hour.

**Winter** Same, but access depends on snow conditions on the roads and avalanche hazard rating. (One winter entry in the hut register describes a tough 5-hour slog to a shelter almost fully buried by snow).

## GUIDEBOOKS

*Mountain Footsteps: Selected Hikes in the East Kootenays,* Strong.

## INFORMATION

To obtain the British Columbia Forest Service road map, contact:
Cranbrook Forest District Office
1902 Theatre Rd
Cranbrook BC V1C 6H3
**Phone** (250) 426-1700
**Website** www.for.gov.bc.ca/nelson/district/cranbrk
**Note** For a 360º view from the lookout, visit www.adventurevalley.com/360/cranbrook_area/lakpan.htm

# Fish Lake Cabin

This roomy log cabin provides a good central base for hiking, climbing, fishing and ski touring in Top of the World Provincial Park. Many of the nearby peaks lend themselves to great scrambling or climbing, and there are good hiking trails in the park. The alpine meadows near the base of Mt Morro are especially attractive, and the lakes within easy hiking distance of the cabin have long been popular with local fishers. The cabin is in very good shape, and will be receiving a new foundation and floor in late 2001. It is permissible to bike into the cabin—an easy ride that takes less than an hour.

## LOCATION

**General** Beside Fish Lake in Top of the World Provincial Park BC in the East Kootenays.

**Specific** 82 G/14 Queen Creek NAD27 6**11**926 5**22**724.

**Other pertinent maps** *Top of the World Provincial Park Map; Backroad Mapbook* or *British Columbia Forest Service Map* of Forest Service road access to trailhead.

**Elevation** 1768 m (5820 ft).

**Elevation gain from parking lot** 92 m (302 ft).

## AMENITIES

**Heat** Woodstove; firewood supplied.

**Cooking** No cookware or dishware provided.

**Lighting** None.

**Sleeping** Bunks, but no foam pads.

**Capacity** 25.

## COST (as of Summer 2001)

$15/person; $30/family; no reservations.

## ACCESS

**Summer** From a few minutes S of Canal Flats on Hwy 93/95, take the well-signposted turnoff to Whiteswan Lake Park. Stay on this road—stopping if you wish at the free roadside hot springs at the entrance to the park—and then turn S at the "Top of the World Park" sign at the 21.3-km (13-mi) mark. Carry on up alongside the Lussier River, bearing right after 29.6 km (18.5 mi) to avoid going up Coyote Creek. All other junctions are clearly signposted. The road reaches the trailhead parking lot after a total of 52 km (32.5 mi), all of which can be traveled in low-clearance vehicles. The wide, well-marked 6-km (3.7-mi) trail to Fish Lake starts here.

**Time** 1.5–2 hours.

**Winter** Same, but the road is usually not plowed beyond the mine site at the 25-km (15-mi) mark.

## GUIDEBOOKS

*Mountain Footsteps: Selected Hikes in the East Kootenays,* Strong.

## INFORMATION

Kootenay District Parks Office
Box 118
Wasa BC V0B 2K0
**Phone** (250) 422-4200
**Fax** (250) 422-3326
**Website** www.elp.gov.bc.ca/
    bcparks/explore/kootney.htm
To obtain the British Columbia

Forest Service road map, contact:
Cranbrook Forest District Office
1902 Theatre Rd
Cranbrook BC V1C 6H3
**Phone** (250) 426-1700
**Website** www.for.gov.bc.ca/
    nelson/district/cranbrk

# Connor Lakes Cabin

This restored log cabin in Height of the Rockies Wilderness Park provides superb shelter in this remote but spectacular sector of the Rockies. Many come here for the good fishing in the two Connor Lakes, although there are some good ridge scrambles near the cabin, and the hike up Forsyth Creek to the meadows near the Mt Abruzzi Glacier is lovely. The cabin is small but very secure and vermin-proof. Note that the trailhead is reached by 73 km (45 mi) of gravel road.

## LOCATION

**General** On South Connor Lake at the southern end of Height of the Rockies Provincial Park, about 75 linear km (47 mi) N of Sparwood BC.

**Specific** 82 J/6 Mt Abruzzi NAD27 6**363**13 5**763**10.

**Other pertinent maps** *Height of the Rockies Provincial Park Map; Backroad Mapbook* or *British Columbia Forest Service Map* of Forest Service road access to trailhead; see small map in *Hikes Around Invermere.*

**Elevation** 1815 m (5950 ft).

**Elevation change from trailhead** 410 m (1345 ft) gain to Maiyuk Pass, then 125 m (410 ft) drop to lake.

## AMENITIES

**Heat** Woodstove (wood usually provided).

**Cooking** No cookstove, but cookware and dishware for 2–3 provided (also a sink).

**Lighting** None.

**Sleeping** Bunks, but no foam pads.

**Capacity** 5 (crowded with 6).

COST (as of Summer 2001)
Free; no reservations.

## ACCESS

*From the west* Caution: be atten-
tive to road maps, signs and
the yellow roadside kilometer
markers, for there are numerous junctions along the 73-km
(45-mi) length of the road
(which can be traveled in a
2WD vehicle). From a few minutes S of Canal Flats on Hwy
93/95, take the well-marked
turnoff to Whiteswan Lake
Park. Stay on this White River
Road as it passes the lake and
carries on E, noting especially
to bear right at km 44 (avoiding the North White River
Road) and to bear left at km 45
(avoiding the East White River
Road). This latter junction is
marked with a "Height of the
Rockies" signpost, as are all of
the following junctions (the
later ones reading "Maiyuk
Creek Trail"). The road ends in
a large cut-block with a prominent trailhead sign. Follow the
generally clear trail SE up the
Maiyuk Creek Valley, noting
these possibly misleading junctions: bear right after about 1
km (0.6 mi) (6**326**93 5**783**39,
NAD27), and bear left in
Maiyuk Pass (635538 576246).
Upon reaching the creek join-
ing the lakes, bear left
(upstream) for about 50 m (160
ft), cross the creek on a bridge,
turn right and carry on to the
cabin on the N end of the

main lake. The total hike is
about 7 km (4 mi). Note that
on the trail there is a creek that
must be forded (risky at high
water) or crossed on a small log
(risky when wet).
*Time* 2–3 hours.

*From the south* Head N up the
main Elk River Road from Elkford for about 30 km (18 mi)
and take the turnoff on the
rough road to the Forsyth Creek
campground. Follow the trail
(sometimes used by outfitters)
that starts on the N side of the
creek and then parallels the
creek for about 13 km (8 mi) to
the main lake. Carry on along
the W side of the lake to the
cabin.
*Time* 5–7 hours.

## GUIDEBOOKS

*Hikes Around Invermere,* Cameron
and Gunn.

## INFORMATION

Kootenay District Parks Office
Box 118
Wasa BC V0B 2K0
*Phone* (250) 422-4200
*Fax* (250) 422-3326
*Website* www.elp.gov.bc.ca/
bcparks/explore/kootney.htm
To obtain the British Columbia
Forest Service road map, contact:
Invermere Forest District Office
Box 189
625 4 St
Invermere V0A 1K0
*Phone* (250) 342-4200
*Website* www.for.gov.bc.ca/
nelson/district/invermer

# Tobermory Creek Cabin

This small but cosy shelter just east of Elk Lakes Park is used by both skiers and snowmobilers in winter and by hikers in summer. Although it can be reached from the south by car in summer, it entails in winter a long snowmobile ride from the Elkford area or a ski-tour over Elk Pass from Peter Lougheed Park in Alberta. It provides few amenities, but with a new insulated roof, it is very warm and secure. The cabin serves as a good base from which to do day-trips into the park or to tour along the Elk Valley.

## LOCATION

*General* Near the northern end of the Elk River, a short distance S of the main entrance to Elk Lakes Provincial Park BC.

*Specific* 82 J/11 Kananaskis Lakes NAD83 6**408**15 5**986**80

*Other pertinent maps* Backroad Mapbook or British Columbia Forest Service Map of Forest Service road access to cabin.

*Elevation* 1950 m (6410 ft)

*Elevation change from Elk Pass Trailhead* 230 m (760 ft) gain to Elk Pass and then same drop to cabin.

## AMENITIES

*Heat* Woodstove (no wood provided).

*Cooking* No cookware or dishware provided.

*Lighting* None.

*Sleeping* Platforms with mattresses.

*Capacity* 3–4.

## COST (as of November 2000)

Free, no resevations.

## ACCESS

*From the south* Turn N off Hwy 3

at Sparwood and follow Hwy 43 N to Elkford. Carry on along the Elk River Forest Service Road to the roadside cabin at Tobermory Creek (beside the yellow "161" kilometer post).

*From the north* Follow the paved Kananaskis Lakes Trail off Hwy 40 for 12 km (7.5 mi) to the clearly marked Elk Pass trailhead parking lot. The route initially follows the powerline road for 2 km (1.2 mi), at which point there are two options. The clearly marked hiking trail (the right-hand branch) leads to Elk Pass and then carries down to the Elk Lakes Park main entrance. This route is more scenic, but the powerline road over the Pass and down to the park entrance is shorter and, for bikers, the only permissible route into BC. From the park entrance, the cabin is about 5 km (3 mi) farther down the Forest Service Road. The net distance from the trailhead is about 15 km (9 mi). This is one of the few facilities in this book to which bike access is both easy and permissible.

*Winter* Same, but the Forest Service road may not be plowed.

## INFORMATION

To obtain the British Columbia Forest Service road map, contact:
Cranbrook Forest District Office
1902 Theatre Rd
Cranbrook BC V1C 6H3

*Phone* (250) 426-1700
*Website* www.for.gov.bc.ca/nelson/district/cranbrk

# Queen Mary Lake Cabin

This new and well-appointed log cabin provides a lovely base for hiking or mountaineering in the chain of 8 glaciated peaks that make up the Royal Group. In fact, since the cabin is set in a lakeshore meadow at treeline with glaciated peaks and a 1000-foot waterfall in the near distance, a great day could be had just lounging on the small grassy beach. Although rather remote, with the access involving 60 km (37 mi) of gravel road, the rewards for making it in to this postcard setting are substantial. The trail to the cabin is distinct and well maintained, but does involve 8 fords of the creek—normally quite safe. The cabin is spacious, clean and very comfortable.

## LOCATION

**General** On the S shore of Queen Mary Lake in the basin W of Mt Prince Edward in Height of the Rockies Provincial Park BC.

**Specific** 82J/11 Kananaskis Lakes NAD83 6**101**96 6**075**20.

**Other pertinent maps** *Height of the Rockies Provincial Park Map; Backroad Mapbook* or *British Columbia Forest Service Map* of Forest Service road access to trailhead; see small map in *Hikes Around Invermere.*

**Elevation** 2090 m (6850 ft).

**Net elevation gain from Palliser River** 820 m (2700 ft).

## AMENITIES

**Heat** Woodstove (wood provided).

**Cooking** Coleman stove; cookware and dishware provided (but only cutlery for 4).

**Lighting** Coleman lantern.

*Sleeping* Bunks with foam pads.
*Capacity* 8.

COST (as of Summer 2001)
Free; no reservations.

ACCESS

*Summer* Turn from Hwy 93 onto
the Settlers Road 18 km (11
mi) NE of Radium. Note the
yellow roadside kilometer
markers. At the Kootenay Park
boundary, take the left fork
over the bridge and within 2
km (1.2 mi) take the right
fork; follow the "Palliser
River" signs at both junctions.
Continue S until reaching the
Palliser River Road just beyond
the bridge over the Palliser
River. Head E alongside the
river, taking care not to turn
left onto the Albert River
Road. Near the 54-km marker
is a "Queen Mary" sign point-
ing left. Follow this road over
the river and on for another 4
km (2.5 mi) to the trailhead
on your right (watch for the
big signs). The clear trail leads
through logged-off terrain and
then carries on up alongside
Queen Mary Creek (crossing it
10 times, 8 of which are fords)
to the cabin on the S shore of
the lake—*not* the private outfitter's shack on the NW corner.
Total distance from the trailhead is about 12 km (7 mi).
*Time* 5–8 hours.

*Winter* The hut register shows no
winter use, although it could
be reached by snowmobiling

to the park boundary and
then skiing from there if the
creek is frozen.

GUIDEBOOKS
*Hikes Around Invermere,* Cameron
and Gunn.

INFORMATION
Kootenay District Parks Office
Box 118
Wasa BC V0B 2K0
*Phone* (250) 422-4200
*Fax* (250) 422-3326
*Website* www.elp.gov.bc.ca/
bcparks/explore/kootney.htm
To obtain the British Columbia
Forest Service road map,contact:
Invermere Forest District Office
625 4 St
Box 189
Invermere BC V0A 1K0
*Phone* (250) 342-4200
*Website* www.for.gov.bc.ca/
nelson/district/invermer

# Ralph Lake Shelter

This rustic, dirt-floored shelter on the shores of Ralph Lake provides some protection from the weather, but if you value hygiene you may prefer the extra weight of packing in a tent. There is good fishing in the lake, and nearby are many opportunities for hiking and mountaineering, including scrambles up onto high ridges that afford great views of Mt Assiniboine. Road access from the west is the fastest, but multi-day hikes from Banff and Kananakis parks also can provide access. If doing a traverse that includes Queen Mary Cabin, you may find it easiest to start at the southern (Queen Mary Creek) end because the ascent up Ralph Creek is very grueling.

## LOCATION

**General** On the S shore of Ralph Lake in Height of the Rockies Park, about 50 km (31 mi) due E of Radium Hot Springs BC.

**Specific** 82J/11 Kananaskis Lakes NAD83 **6076**90 **6115**98.

**Other pertinent maps** *Backroad Mapbook* or *British Columbia Forest Service Map* of Forest Service road access to trailhead; see small map in *Hikes Around Invermere.*

**Elevation** 2160 m (7100 ft).

**Elevation gain from Albert River** 820 m (2700 ft).

## AMENITIES

**Heat** None.

**Cooking** None.

**Lighting** None.

**Sleeping** Rough platform made from halved logs; no foam pads.

*Capacity* 5–7.

**COST** (as Summer 2001)
Free; no reservations.

**ACCESS**
Follow the road directions for
Queen Mary Cabin, except turn
left off the Palliser Road at the
well-marked Kootenay–Albert
Road until reaching a dirt track
leading to the right at km 57 (mi
35.6). There is a parking area at
the trailhead 400 m(1300 ft) up
this track (GR 041127 NAD83).
The route initially follows an old
road and then turns into a trail
that soon bends left, angling high
above the creek that drains Ralph
Lake. The trail, extremely rigorous
and at times not plainly marked,
reaches the lake after a total of
about 5 km (3 mi). If doing a traverse from the S (the easiest way
to do the traverse), see the access
description for Queen Mary
Cabin. From there, head up the
first slide path W of the outfitter's
cabin. When you reach the goat
trail, follow it right up to the ridge
N of the lake. Proceed along the
ridge to the far eastern end
(beyond the little pinnacle) where
a cairn marks the start of an easy
ramp—the only safe route—down
through the cliffband. From here,
find your own way across the
open basin and then through the
col that leads to Ralph Lake. This
trip is for very experienced and fit
hikers only.
*Time* 3–5 hours from Albert River
or from Queen Mary Lake.

**GUIDEBOOKS**
*Hikes Around Invermere,* Cameron
and Gunn.

**INFORMATION**
Kootenay District Parks Office
Box 118
Wasa BC V0B 2K0
*Phone* (250) 422-4200
*Fax* (250) 422-3326
*Website* www.elp.gov.bc.ca/
bcparks/explore/kootney.htm
To obtain the British Columbia
Forest Service road map, contact:
Invermere Forest District Office
625 4 St
Box 189
Invermere BC V0A 1K0
*Phone* (250) 342-4200
*Website* www.for.gov.bc.ca/
nelson/district/invermer

# Mitchell River Shelter

Although most often accessed by those on horseback (because of the river crossings), this rustic cabin could be a good place to pass the night while on a hike into Mt Assiniboine Park. It is, however, rather dark and run-down at present; in good weather in summer, it may be preferable to camp in the nearby meadows. It lies outside the parks and is maintained irregularly by outfitters, who use it mainly in hunting season.

## LOCATION

*General* On the Mitchell River, near the southern edge of Mt Assiniboine Park BC, accessed by about 50 km (31 mi) of gravel roads.

*Specific* 82 J/13 Mt Assiniboine NAD83 877388.

*Other pertinent maps* 82 J/12 Tan-gle Peak (for Mitchell River Road); *Banff & Mt Assiniboine*, Gem Trek; *Backroad Mapbook* or *British Columbia Forest Service Map* of Forest Service road access to trailhead.

*Elevation* 1616 m (5300 ft).

*Elevation gain from end of road* Approximately 340 m (1115 ft).

## AMENITIES

*Heat* Woodstove.

*Cooking* No gas stove, cookware or dishware provided.

*Lighting* None.

*Sleeping* Bunks, no foam pads.

*Capacity* 4–6.

## COST (as of Summer 2001)
Free; no reservations.

## ACCESS
From Radium Hot Springs, travel 18 km (11 mi) NE on Hwy 93

and take the turnoff S onto the Settlers Road. Follow this gravel road for about 14 km (9 mi) until you cross the Kootenay River near the Natural Bridge. Turn E here and follow the Forest Service road up the Cross River for about 30 km (19 mi) until reaching a junction at the Mitchell River. Take the left fork here and follow the road along this river until the road ends shortly after the Baymag Mine site. The trail starts here and carries on NW up alongside the river for about 14.2 km (9 mi). Although the trail crosses the Mitchell River in numerous locations it is not necessary to make all the crossings, as they are connected by short bushwhacks. The shelter lies W of Mt Watson,

near where the river begins a long curl to the right around the base of this mountain.

**Time** About 5 hours from parking lot (more if river crossings are difficult).

## GUIDEBOOKS
*Canadian Rockies Trail Guide,* Barton and Robinson.

## INFORMATION
To obtain the British Columbia Forest Service road map, contact:
Invermere Forest District Office
Box 189
625 4 St
Invermere BC V0A 1K0
**Phone** (250) 342-4200
**Website** www.for.gov.bc.ca/
nelson/district/invermer

# R.C. Hind Hut

This is primarily a shelter for those climbing nearby Mt Assiniboine or any of 5 other peaks, although well-equipped scramblers may wish to get up onto the top of the headwall on which the hut rests just for the great view of Lake Magog and the meadows—not to mention the massive horn of Assiniboine. However much appreciated this hut is for the shelter it affords, it has few luxuries. Reservations can now be made. Heli access (or just gear transport) to the Assiniboine Lodge area is an option.

## LOCATION

*General* On a headwall above Lake Magog, not far from the base of Mt Assiniboine in Mt Assiniboine Park BC.

*Specific* 82 J/13 Mt Assiniboine NAD83 946373.

*Other pertinent maps* Banff & Mt Assiniboine, Gem Trek (note that the hut is not accurately located on this map).

*Elevation* 2710 m (8900 ft).

*Elevation gain from Naiset Cabins* 510 m (1673 ft).

*Features* Radio link with Assiniboine Lodge.

## AMENITIES

*Heat* None.

*Cooking* Propane stove; cookware and dishware provided.

*Lighting* None.

*Sleeping* Platforms with foam pads.

*Capacity* 12–15.

COST (as of Summer 2001) $15/person.

## ACCESS

See description of access routes to Naiset Cabins. From here, follow the W side of Magog Lake to its S end. Formerly, the principal route entailed heading up the center of the obvious large couloir above the lake; most guide books now discourage this because of the danger of breaking through to the waterfall beneath the snow. Preferably, then, scramble up over the two ledges about 330 m (1000 ft) to the right (some may appreciate a belay here). Experienced scramblers should be able to find their own way up the ledges, but see the Dougherty or the Cameron and Gunn books for photos of this route. Follow the top ledge across to the top of the large couloir and move up onto flatter terrain above. Cross a rough boulder field up to the hut on the black outcrop. This hut is seldom visited in winter; access can be very risky.

*Time* 2–3 hours from the end of Lake Magog.

## GUIDEBOOKS

*Canadian Rockies Trail Guide,* Patton and Robinson.

*Selected Alpine Climbs,* Dougherty.

*Hikes Around Invermere,* Cameron and Gunn.

See also www.ualberta.ca/~gbarron/route/ass.html for descriptions of climbs up Assiniboine.

## INFORMATION & BOOKING

Kootenay District Parks Office
Box 118
Wasa BC V0B 2K0
*Phone* (250) 422-4200
*Fax* (250) 422-3326
*Website* www.elp.gov.bc.ca/bcparks/explore/kootney.htm

*Reservations & heli-flights*
*Phone* (403) 678-2883
*Fax* (403) 678-4877
*E-mail* assinilo@telusplanet.net
*Website* www.canadianrockies.net/assiniboine/naiset.html

# Naiset Cabins

Located amid the beautiful alpine terrain of the Mt Assiniboine area, these 4 cabins are popular with hikers, climbers, skiers and wildflower admirers. With trails to numerous lakes, meadows, ridges and peaks, it could be easy to spend a week without running out of things to do in any season of the year. It is a long trudge in, but heli-access is possible. In winter, the huts may be reserved, but in summer they are available on a first-come basis (and thus may be full).

## LOCATION

**General** In the center of Mt Assiniboine Park BC just W of the Continental Divide, about 33 linear km (20 mi) S of Banff townsite.

**Specific** 82 J/13 Mt Assiniboine NAD83 973402.

**Other pertinent maps** *Banff & Mt Assiniboine,* Gem Trek; 82 J/14 Spray Lakes Reservoir (for Bryant Creek access); 82 O/4 Banff (for Sunshine Ski Area access).

**Elevation** 2180 m (7152 ft).

**Elevation gain** Varies for each of the 5 main access trails.

## AMENITIES

**Heat** Woodstove, Presto firelogs sold at main lodge or packed in.

**Cooking** No stove, cookware or dishware provided.

**Lighting** None (no gas lights or candles allowed in cabins).

**Sleeping** Two layers of bunks with foam pads.

**Capacity** 2 cabins for 5; 2 cabins for 8.

## COST (as of Summer 2001)

**Summer** $15/person.

**Winter** $30/cabin (family rate).

**Heli-flight** Approximately $100/person, one way.

## ACCESS

For more detailed descriptions of trails and the park, visit www.elp.gov.bc.ca/bcparks/explore/park pgs/mtassini/trails.htm

**Summer from Spray Lake (Smith–Dorrien Road)** See the description for the route in to Bryant

Creek Shelter. From here follow the clearly marked trail through Assiniboine Pass to Lake Magog for a total distance about 25 km (16 mi) from the parking lot. The route past Marvel Lake and through Wonder Pass is much more scenic but involves more elevation gain.

*Time* 6–8 hours.

**Summer from Sunshine Village Ski Area** With Mt Assiniboine as a visible destination, follow the trail for 29 km (19 mi) via Quartz Ridge, Citadel Pass, Golden Valley and Valley of the Rocks. The ski area can be accessed by gondola.

*Time* 7–9 hours from the ski area.

**Summer from roads in BC** The park can also be reached by longer (usually multi-day) hikes from Hwy 93 in Kootenay Provincial Park. For the Simpson River route, see the description for Surprise Creek and Policeman Meadow cabins. For the Mitchell River route, use the British Columbia Forest Service road map or the *Backroad Mapbook* to get as far up the Mitchell River valley as current logging and mining in the area allows; the trail follows the Mitchell River to the Wedgewood Lake area and then on to Lake Magog, with a total hiking distance of about 30 km (19 mi) and an elevation gain of about 1100 m (3600 ft).

*Time* 8–9 hours.

**Winter** All routes are possible, but the BC access may require snowmobile use, where permitted. The most direct winter route is via Bryant Creek, where avalanche risk is usually slight and where there is the option of an overnight stay at the Bryant Creek Shelter.

## GUIDEBOOKS

*Selected Alpine Climbs,* Dougherty.
*Hikes Around Invermere,* Cameron and Gunn.
*Canadian Rockies Trail Guide,* Barton and Robinson.
*Ski Trails in the Canadian Rockies,* Scott.

## INFORMATION & BOOKING

Kootenay District Parks Office
Box 118
Wasa BC V0B 2K0
*Phone* (250) 422-4200
*Fax* (250) 422-3326
*Website* www.elp.gov.bc.ca/
   bcparks/explore/kootney.htm
*Reservations & heli-flights*
*Phone* (403) 678-2883
*Fax* (403) 678-4877
*E-mail* assinilo@telusplanet.net
*Website* www.canadianrockies.net/
   assiniboine/naiset.html

# Mount Assiniboine Lodge

In its dramatic alpine setting, this Matterhorn of the Rockies amply deserves its designation as a UNESCO World Heritage Site. Both rustic and comfortable, this historic log lodge serves as a great base for numerous day-trips through lake-side meadows, onto ridges and up mountains. Casual hikers, technical climbers and ski-tourers all find ample terrain to captivate them for many days. Accessed by foot, ski or helicopter, the lodge offers various packages that include all meals, lodging and guiding.

## LOCATION

*General* In the center of Mt Assiniboine Park BC just W of the Continental Divide, about 33 linear km (20 mi) S of Banff townsite.

*Specific* 82 J/13 Mt Assiniboine NAD83 971407.

*Other pertinent maps* Banff & Mt Assiniboine, Gem Trek; 82 0/4 Banff (for northern end of park); 82 J/14 Spray Lakes (for eastern access).

*Elevation* 2180 m (7152 ft).

*Elevation gain from Mt Shark parking lot* 520 m (1700 ft).

## AMENITIES

*Heat* Propane stove.

*Cooking* All meals provided.

*Lighting* Propane (12-volt electrical in bedrooms).

*Sleeping* Private bedrooms: linen provided.

*Capacity*
Main Lodge: 6 double bedrooms
Private cabins: 3 2-person cabins; 3 cabins sleeping 3–5 people.

*Features* Certified guides for hiking and skiing, ski rentals, sauna/shower house (separate shower for men and women).

**COST** (as of summer 2001)
All rates based on a minimum of double occupancy for 2 nights.
*Summer* Main lodge or 5-person cabin: $155/person/night; 2-person cabin: $205/person/ night.
*Winter* Main lodge or 5-person cabin: $140/person/night; 2-person cabin: $175/person/ night.
*Children 12 & under* $110/ child/night in all cases.

## ACCESS
Information on heli-access can be provided on registration. For access by foot or ski via 5 different trails, see description of Naiset Cabins. Note that you can hike or ski in and have your gear flown in.

## GUIDEBOOKS
*The Canadian Rockies Trail Guide*, Patton and Robinson.
*Ski Trails in the Canadian Rockies*, Scott.
*Selected Alpine Climbs*, Dougherty
*Banff–Assiniboine: A Beautiful World*, Beers.

## INFORMATION & BOOKING
Mount Assiniboine Lodge
Attention Sepp and Barb Renner
Box 8128
Canmore AB T1W 2T8
*Phone* (403) 678-2883
*Fax* (403) 678-4877

*E-mail* assinilo@telusplanet.net
*Website* www.canadianrockies. net/assiniboine

# Surprise Creek Cabin

A former outfitter's cabin, this rustic log structure could afford shelter to those hiking towards the Assiniboine area by following trails along either the Simpson River or Surprise Creek. The cabin, however, is rather dark and dreary, offering few amenities beyond sleeping platforms, a table (no benches) and an old wood cookstove. Except in bad weather, hikers may prefer to tent in the meadows. Also, since it is only 2–3 hours from the highway, hikers may prefer to make their day's destination farther in.

## LOCATION

*General* On the Simpson River just inside the western boundary of Mt Assiniboine Park BC, accessed from Hwy 93 in Kootenay National Park.

*Specific* 82 J/13 Mt Assiniboine NAD83 5**825**10 6**469**95.

*Other pertinent maps* Kootenay Park & Radium, Gem Trek (note that the cabin is not precisely at the location indicated on this map).

*Elevation* 1450 m (4750 ft).

*Elevation gain from parking lot* 205 m (672 ft).

## AMENITIES

*Heat* Woodstove (no wood provided).

*Cooking* Wood cookstove with oven; no cookware or dishware provided.

*Lighting* None.

*Sleeping* Two layers of bunks, no foam pads.

*Capacity* 8.

## COST (as of Summer 2001)

Free; no reservations.

## Access

**Summer** The trailhead is at the Simpson River parking lot on Hwy 93, 57 km (35.6 mi) NE of Radium Hot Springs or 36.5 km (22.8 mi) SE of the BC–Alberta border. Follow the clear, well signposted trail for about 10.6 km (7 mi) up the N side of the river to a suspension bridge at the junction with the trail that heads E up Surprise Creek. The cabin is just across the bridge.

**Time** 2–3 hours from hwy.

**Winter** Same.

## Guidebooks

*Canadian Rockies Trail Guide,* Barton and Robinson.

*Ski Trails in the Canadian Rockies,* Scott.

## Information

Kootenay District Parks Office
Box 118
Wasa BC V0B 2K0

**Phone** (250) 422-4200

**Fax** (250) 422-3326

**Website** www.elp.gov.bc.ca/
bcparks/explore/kootney.htm

# Police Meadows Cabin

Now used most often as an outfitter's cabin, this old log building affords good shelter but it offers little to attract hikers bound for the Assiniboine area. Access to the cabin involves a 6 km (4 mi) return trip off the main Simpson River trail from an unmarked junction. Also, the river must be forded, which can be risky in high water if not on horseback. Hikers may prefer to tent at the sites on the main trail. The building itself is rather dark, and has few amenities.

## LOCATION

**General** In Mt Assiniboine Park BC, near the headwaters of the Simpson River.

**Specific** 82 J/13 Mt Assiniboine NAD83 908475.

**Other pertinent maps** 82 O/4 Banff (for middle section of Simpson River trail); *Banff & Mt Assiniboine,* Gem Trek.

**Elevation** 1953 m (5400 ft).

**Elevation gain from Hwy 93** 708 m (2320 ft).

## AMENITIES

**Heat** Woodstove (no wood provided).

**Cooking** No stove, cookware or dishware provided.

**Lighting** None.

**Sleeping** Two layers of bunks, no foam pads.

**Capacity** 6.

## COST (as of Summer 2001)
Free; no reservations.

## ACCESS

See the description for access to Surprise Creek Shelter. At the suspension bridge over the river at Surprise Creek, stay on the W side of the river (the E side is the horse trail, which has no bridges over the creeks and rivers). For the first 7 km (4 mi), the trail is bit indistinct and is strewn with a lot of deadfall—not recommended for novice hikers. It becomes clearer for the next 6 km (3.5 mi) up to a junction with the side trail leading W to the cabin. This junction is not signposted, although the trail generally is marked by heavy horse traffic; the map coordinate for the junction is NAD83 5**9044**4 6**5045**8. About 500 m (1600 ft) along is a ford of the river—take care here. The cabin is a further 2.5 km (1.5 mi) beyond the river.

*Time* About 8 hours from Surprise Creek; 11 hours from hwy.

## GUIDEBOOKS

*Canadian Rockies Trail Guide,* Barton and Robinson.

*Ski Trails in the Canadian Rockies,* Scott.

## INFORMATION

Kootenay District Parks Office
Box 118
Wasa BC V0B 2K0
*Phone* (250) 422-4200
*Fax* (250) 422-3326
*Website* www.elp.gov.bc.ca/ bcparks/explore/kootney.htm

# Bryant Creek Cabin

This easily accessed cabin is often used as an overnight way-station by those on their way in to the Mt Assiniboine area, although some will want to use it as a comfortable base for day-trips in any of three different directions. It is close to Marvel Lake, and a hike or ski up to the Assiniboine meadows makes for a good day's outing. A more rigorous, but more spectacular day-trip involves a circle tour past Marvel Lake and on through Wonder and Assiniboine Passes. The cabin is on the edge of a meadow well below treeline.

## LOCATION

*General* Halfway up the Bryant Creek Valley, W of Spray Lake and about 50 linear km (31 mi) S of Banff AB.

*Specific* 82 J/13 Mt Assiniboine NAD83 6**04**196 6**395**29.

*Other pertinent maps* 82 J/14 Spray Lakes (for the first few km of the trail, but the trail is very distinct and well signposted); *Banff & Mt Assiniboine*, Gem Trek.

*Elevation* 1860 m (6100 ft).

*Net elevation change from parking lot* 90 m (300 ft) drop to Spray River, then 135 m (450 ft) gain to the cabin.

## AMENITIES

*Heat* Woodstove.

*Cooking* No cookstoves, cookware or dishware provided.

*Lighting* None.

*Sleeping* Platforms, but no foam pads.

*Capacity* 18 (maximum of 10 booked through one reservation).

**COST** (as of Summer 2001)
$11/person/night, inclusive of
Wilderness Pass.

## ACCESS

From Canmore, follow the
Spray Lakes/Smith–Dorrien
Road 38 km (24 mi) to the
Mount Shark turnoff sign and
follow this road 5 km (3 mi)
to its end at the trailhead
parking lot. Get on the trail
marked by the "Watridge Lake
Trail" signs. The trail crosses
the Spray River after 5.6 km
(3.5 mi) and then carries on
up the gently sloping Bryant
Creek Valley to the shelter, for
a total distance of about 14
km (9 mi). All junctions are
well signposted, and the trail
is broad and smooth.
*Time* 3–4 hours.

## GUIDEBOOKS

*Selected Alpine Climbs,* Dougherty.
*Canadian Rockies Trail Guide,* Patton and Robinson.
*Ski Trails in the Canadian Rockies,* Scott.

## INFORMATION & BOOKING

Make reservations up to 90 days
in advance through the Parks
Canada Information Office in
Banff.
*Phone* (403) 762-1550
*Calgary* (403) 292-4401
For general park Information,
contact:
Banff National Park
PO Box 900
Banff, AB T0L 0C0

*Phone* (403) 762-1550
*Fax* (403) 762-1551
*E-mail* banff_vrc@pch.gc.ca
*Website* www.worldweb.com/
    ParksCanada-Banff

# Sundance & Halfway Lodges

Located at the base of the Sundance Range next to Brewster Creek, these historic lodges offer a superb destination for hikers or cross-country skiers who wish to enjoy the trails and alpine terrain north of Mt Assiniboine. The lodges in summer cater especially, but not exclusively, to those on horseback. The main lodge (Sundance) is a two-story log structure with ten guest rooms, while the Halfway Lodge further south up the valley offers more rustic lodging for those on a multi-day tour of the trails in southern Banff National Park.

## LOCATION

**General** About 11 km (7 mi) SW of Banff AB in the upper Brewster Creek basin, along the century-old trail from Banff to Mt Assiniboine.

**Specific** Sundance: 82 O/4 Banff NAD83 593518 661477; Halfway: 82 J/13 Mt Assiniboine NAD83 599462 649774.

**Other pertinent maps** *Banff* & *Mt Assiniboine,* Gem Trek; follow the links on the website for a detailed access map.

**Elevation** 1590 m (5220 ft).

**Elevation gain from Healy Creek parking lot** Sundance: 170 m (560 ft); Halfway: 520 m (1710 ft).

## AMENITIES

**Heat** Sundance: wood and propane; Halfway: woodstove.

**Cooking** All meals provided, including afternoon tea.

**Lighting** Sundance: solar electric; Halfway: propane lanterns and candles.

**Sleeping** Sundance: 10 private rooms; Halfway: dorm-style

**Capacity** Sundance: 20; Halfway: 14.

**Features** Sundance: indoor washrooms, showers, large dining and lounging areas, private rooms, bedding provided; Halfway: single beds; bedding provided.

## COST (as of Summer 2001)

**Summer** Lodges are used primarily for guided horseback tours, and rates vary from $301/person for a 2-day stay in low season to $1022/person for a 6-day stay in high season.

**Winter** Sundance Lodge: $98/person/night (Halfway Lodge is closed).

## ACCESS

Visitors on horseback are guided along a 16 km (10 mi) trail from Banff townsite. Hikers can shave 8 km (5 mi) off the trip by taking the Sunshine exit off Hwy 1 just W of Banff and then parking at the Healy Creek trailhead located 400 m(1600 ft) along this road. The trail is clear and has well-signposted junctions at the 0.6- and 3.1-km (0.3- and 2-mi) marks. At the second junction, the trail picks up the horse route, an old fire road that leads to the lodge; the total distance from the parking lot is just over 8 km (5 mi). The trail usually is trackset in winter, and the horse route may be biked.

**Time** 2–3 hours from Healy Creek trailhead.

## GUIDEBOOKS

*The Canadian Rockies Trail Guide,* Barton and Robinson.

*Rocky Mountain Retreats: Recommended Accommodation in the Canadian Rockies,* Schmaltz.

*Ski Trails in the Canadian Rockies,* Scott.

## INFORMATION & BOOKING

Warner Guiding &Outfitting
Box 2280
Banff AB T0L 0C0
**Phone** 1-800-661-8352
**Fax** (403) 762-8130
**E-mail** warner@horseback.com
**Websites** www.xcskisundance.com *and* www.horseback.com

# Egypt Lake Shelter

L ocated near the Egypt Lake campground in Banff National-al Park, this shelter affords a good base for hikes or ski-tours into various nearby lakes and high ridges. Easily reached by an old fire road, it is a popular destination for those who want nonrigorous access to some striking alpine vistas. It is at the midpoint of the mini-traverse from the Sunshine Gondola base over Healy Pass and down along Redearth Creek to Hwy 1. Some good turns can be had in winter in the glades near Healy Pass.

## LOCATION

**General** On Egypt Lake, about 20 km (12 mi) up a fire road from Hwy 1 W of Banff AB.

**Specific** Banff 82 O/4 NAD83 5**771**56 6**624**51.

**Other pertinent maps** *Banff & Mt Assiniboine,* Gem Trek.

**Elevation** 1996 m (6550 ft).

**Elevation gain from parking lot** 595 m (1950 ft).

## AMENITIES

**Heat** Woodstove (wood provided).

**Cooking** No cookstove, cookware or dishware provided.

**Lighting** None.

**Sleeping** 2 rooms with sleeping platforms, no foam pads provided.

**Capacity** 18 (maximum of 10 booked through one reservation).

## COST (as of Summer 2001)

$11/person/night, including Wilderness Pass.

## ACCESS

**From Hwy 1** From the Redearth Creek parking lot 20 km (12 mi) W of Banff townsite, follow the signs onto the fire road and then the trail that leads for a total of 20 km (12 mi) to Egypt Lake. The first 11 km (7 mi) can be biked and are usually trackset in winter. Alternately, after 11 km (7 mi) at the Shadow Lake junction, turn right and follow the longer, more scenic route over Whistling Pass and down to the lake.

*Time* 5–7 hours.

***From Sunshine Ski Hill Gondola Base***
Start up the ski-out trail, but after 1 km (0.6 mi) stay on the clearly marked Healy Creek trail when the ski-out and gondola turn left up a tributary valley. Once reaching Healy Pass, take almost any line down to the valley floor and, after crossing the creek onto the main trail, turn left and carry on for a few hundred meters to the shelter. The total distance is about 13 km (8 mi).

*Time* 4–6 hours.

## GUIDEBOOKS

*Canadian Rockies Trail Guide,* Patton and Robinson.

*Ski Trails in the Canadian Rockies,* Scott.

## INFORMATION & BOOKING

Make reservations up to 90 days in advance through the Parks Canada Information Office in Banff.

***Phone*** (403) 762-1550
***Calgary*** (403) 292-4401
For general park Information, contact:
Banff National Park
Box 900
Banff, AB T0L 0C0
***Phone*** (403) 762-1550
***Fax*** (403) 762-1551
***E-mail*** banff_vrc@pch.gc.ca
***Website*** www.worldweb.com/
ParksCanada-Banff

# Shadow Lake Lodge

Originally built by the CPR as part of its campaign to showcase the Rockies, this log lodge has been totally refurbished, and 12 more cabins have been added for private accommodation. It is a popular destination for hikers and skiers, as it provides a good base for exploring numerous alpine lakes and passes, as well as some nearby ice caves. The lodge is open from late June to early October and mid-December to early April (subject to snow and trail conditions).

## LOCATION

**General** Near Shadow Lake in Banff National Park, about 27 km W of Banff AB.

**Specific** 82 O/4 Banff NAD83 5**736**75 6**690**19.

**Other pertinent maps** *Banff & Mt Assiniboine*, Gem Trek.

**Elevation** 1829 m (6000 ft).

**Elevation gain from parking lot** 440 m (1450 ft).

## AMENITIES

**Heat** Propane in cabins; large wood fireplace in main lodge.

**Cooking** All meals provided, including afternoon tea.

**Lighting** Propane and kerosene in cabins.

**Sleeping** 12 private cabins; linen and down duvets provided.

**Capacity** 32.

**Features** Private cabins, luxury meals.

**COST** (as of Summer 2001) Prices range from $135/person (double occupancy) in low season to $160/person (single occupancy) in high season. (Third person in some cabins: $120).

## ACCESS

From the Redearth Creek parking lot 20 km (19 mi) W of Banff townsite, follow the fire road that leads up the creek valley. After 11 km (7 mi), turn right at the well-marked junction onto the 3.4-km (2-mi) trail in to the lodge. The first 11 km (7 mi) can be biked and are usually trackset in winter.

*Time* 3–5 hours.

## GUIDEBOOKS

*The Canadian Rockies Trail Guide,*
   Barton and Robinson.
*Ski Trails in the Canadian Rockies,*
   Scott.

## INFORMATION & BOOKING

Brewster's Shadow Lake Lodge
Attention Alison Brewster
Box 2606
Banff AB T0L 0C0
*Phone* (403) 762-0116
*Calgary direct phone* 262-2070
*Fax* (403) 760-2866
*E-mail* shadow@telusplanet.net
*Website* www.brewsteradventures.
   com/ShadowLake/index.html

*Wildflowers in the Petain Basin in Elk Lakes Provincial Park*

*The cabin on South Connor Lake*

# Central Rockies

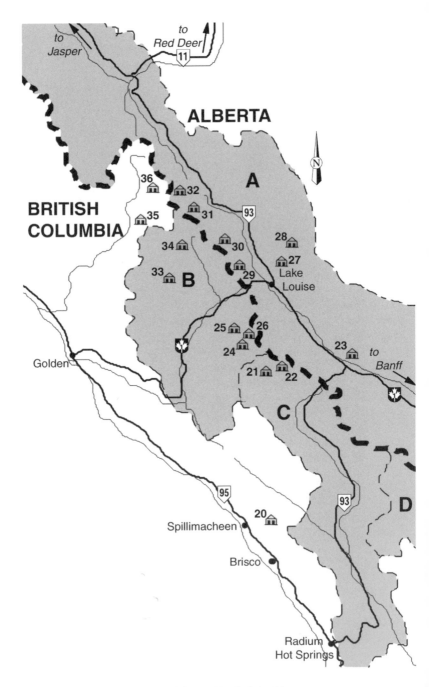

## Provincial & National Parks

*Map*
*Reference*

A .................Banff National Park

B.................Yoho National Park

C .................Kootenay National Park

D .................Mt Assiniboine Provincial Park

## Huts & Lodges

*Map*                                                    *Page*
*Reference*                                              *Number*

20.................Diana Lake Lodge .........................................62

21.................Fay Hut......................................................64

22.................Neil Colgan Hut............................................66

23.................Castle Mountain Hut ....................................70

24.................Lake O'Hara Lodge.......................................72

25.................Elizabeth Parker Hut .....................................74

26.................Abbot Pass Hut............................................76

27.................Halfway/Ptarmigan Shelter...........................78

28.................Skoki Lodge .................................................80

### The Wapta Traverse

29.................Scott Duncan Hut .........................................82

30.................Balfour Hut ..................................................84

31.................Bow Hut .......................................................86

32.................Peter and Catharine Whyte (Peyto) Hut......88

33.................Stanley Mitchell Hut.....................................90

34.................Twin Falls Chalet ..........................................92

35.................Amiskwi Lodge..............................................94

36.................Mistaya Lodge...............................................96

# Diana Lake Lodge

Situated near treeline at the base of Mt Norman, this lovely lakeside retreat affords easy access to wildflower-rich meadows and high ridges in an otherwise remote corner of the Rockies. The fishing in nearby lakes often yields 5lb trout and there is a lot of wildlife in the alpine meadows and subalpine terrain beyond the lodge. The cabin itself and all its amenities (including fully prepared meals) will provide with rustic luxury (it was once Bette Midler's mountain getaway). This meadow can be accessed by a summer hiking trail, although most guests take a helicopter ride from heliports near Banff or Golden. The lodge is open only from July to mid-Sept and must be booked well in advance.

## LOCATION

**General** Near the headwaters of Pinnacle Creek, just W of Kootenay National Park, about 40 linear km (25 mi) N of Radium Hot Springs BC.

**Specific** 82 K/16 Spillimacheen NAD83 537387; see small map in *Hikes Around Invermere*.

**Elevation** 2140 m (7020 ft).

**Elevation gain from end of road** 600 m (1970 ft).

## AMENITIES

**Heat** Propane heater and wood fireplace.

**Cooking** All meals provided.

**Lighting** Solar electric.

**Sleeping** Private cabin; bedding provided.

**Capacity** Maximum of 6

**Features** Shower, certified guide available, good fishing.

**COST** (as of Summer 2001) $250/person/night with a minimum 2-night stay; children 5–10: $170.

***Heli-flight from Banff*** $550/person each way, based on a full helicopter (4 or 6 seats)—may be more depending on the number of passengers.

***Certified Mountain Guide*** Check with Pure West Expeditions.

## ACCESS

Most guests helicopter in, although those who wish to hike in to the lodge on the trail that climbs through the Pinnacle Creek Valley will be guided. The trailhead is reached by 20 km (12 mi) of rough gravel road, and the hike is fairly rigorous and at times steep, for there is a 600 m (1970 ft) gain in elevation. Arrangements for air or ground access are made when registering.

## GUIDEBOOKS

*Hikes Around Invermere,* Cameron and Gunn.

## INFORMATION & BOOKING

Pure West Expeditions & Tours
***Phone*** 1-877-894-9378
***Fax*** (403) 932-0591
***E-mail*** info@purewest.com
***Website*** www.dianalake.com

# Fay Hut

A cozy and recently refurbished log cabin, this hut no longer serves its original purpose as a base for climbs in the Ten Peaks overlooking Moraine Lake (Neil Colgan Hut now serving that purpose much better). Still, it is a good destination for hikers or skiers wishing to do day-trips onto the open terrain and glaciers higher up. Skiers (and, less commonly, summer climbers) bound for the Colgan Hut may choose to overnight here. Several of the Ten Peaks can be summited in a day from the hut. Perched on a treed bench, the views across to the peaks of Kootenay Park are very striking.

## LOCATION

*General* 18 km (11 mi) S of Lake Louise in Prospectors Valley, Kootenay National Park BC.

*Specific* 82N/8 Lake Louise NAD83 553791.

*Other pertinent maps* 82 N/1 Mt Goodsir (for the trail along Tokumm Creek, but not really necessary); *Lake Louise & Yoho*, Gem Trek.

*Elevation* 2108 m (6915 ft).

*Elevation gain from parking lot* 610 m (2000 ft).

## AMENITIES

*Heat* Woodstove (wood provided).

*Cooking* Coleman stoves (guests supply own fuel); cookware and dishware provided.

*Lighting* Coleman lanterns.

*Sleeping* Two layers of bunks with foam pads.

*Capacity* 12.

**COST** (as of Summer 2001) Alpine Club Class A hut: $15 for members; $22 for nonmembers; $17 for group members.

## ACCESS

*Summer* From the Marble Canyon parking lot on the Banff–Radium Hwy 93, follow the broad and well-marked trail along the E side of Tokumm Creek for about 10 km (6 mi) and then turn right at the trail sign indicating the hut route. The trail gains elevation more steeply and after about 1.5 km (1 mi) ascends a steep incline. A rope hanging from the top of the incline provides some help in the steepest section. The hut is only a few hundred meters E of the top of the rope. Note that you gain 450 m (1480 ft) vertically while covering the last 2 km (1.2 mi).

*Time* 4–5 hours.

*Winter* Same route as summer, but route-finding after leaving Tokumm Creek can be difficult, especially going up the steep incline to the rope. After crossing the small bridge at about the 10-km (6-mi) mark, watch for the signpost directing you into a drainage to the E. Head up alongside or on top of the small creek and, about 50 m (160 ft) after encountering a small ice wall on the right, start the steep slog up. There is a fixed rope to help with a short steep section, and although all or part of it may be buried by snow, it usually is not needed as it is fairly easy to kick steps up this section. At the top, the hut is a few hundred meters to your right, but without a defined track or a GPS, you may have to spread out to find it.

*Time* As little as 5 hours if there is a clear track, but up to 11 hours if breaking trail (many groups have had to bivy near the headwall).

## GUIDEBOOKS

*The Canadian Rockies Trail Guide,* Patton and Robinson

*Selected Alpine Climbs in the Canadian Rockies,* Dougherty

*Ski Trails in the Canadian Rockies,* Scott

*Rocky Mountains of Canada–South,* Boles

## INFORMATION & BOOKING

The Alpine Club of Canada
Box 8040
Canmore AB T1W 2T8
*Phone* (403) 678-3200
*Fax* (403) 678-3224
*E-mail* alpclub@telusplanet.net
*Website* www.alpineclubof canada.ca

# Neil Colgan Hut

Set amidst a wide array of alpine climbs of all difficulty levels, this hut is the highest permanent building in Canada. From here, it is not uncommon to climb and/or scramble up several of the Ten Peaks in a day. The ice routes up nearby Mt Fay are classics, but much of the rock is too rotten for climbing. The nearby views down onto Moraine Lake are some of the most spectacular in the Rockies. Note that travel to and beyond the hut entails crossing glaciers. In winter, an overnight stay at Fay Hut may be needed on the way in.

## LOCATION

**General** On the Continental Divide among the Ten Peaks that surround Moraine Lake, near Lake Louise AB in Banff National Park.

**Specific** 82/N8 Lake Louise NAD83 5**566**40 6**832**63.
**Other pertinent maps** *Lake Louise & Yoho,* Gem Trek.
**Elevation** 2940 m (9700 ft).
**Elevation gain from Moraine Lake** 1067 m (3500 ft).
**Elevation gain from Marble Creek parking lot** 1463 m (4800 ft).
**Elevation gain from Fay Hut** 853 m (2800 ft).

## AMENITIES

**Heat** None, but well insulated.
**Cooking** Coleman stoves (guests supply own fuel); cookware and dishware provided.
**Lighting** Coleman lanterns.
**Sleeping** Two layers of bunks with foam pads.
**Capacity** 18 (16 in winter).

**COST** (as of Summer 2001)
Alpine Club Class B hut: $9 for

members; $13 for nonmembers; $11 for group members.

## ACCESS

***Summer from Moraine Lake via Perren Route (technical climbing involved)*** Follow the main trail along the shore of Moraine Lake and then cross the creek at the lake's western end. Angle your way up and left across scree and boulders to the base of the prominent buttress. Follow the trail as it hugs the base of this wall and then angles left through some ledges (an easy, well-cairned scramble) to a small snowfield. Keep to the left of the snow as you move up to the far left edge of the cliff where the climbing begins. A 25-m (80-ft) pitch of 5.6 rock (the route is well-marked and has bolts and chains) leads to a ledge; you may want to haul your packs up separately. Traverse right on this ledge for 25–30 m (80–100 ft) to the sling-laden rap anchor (note this for descending) and then angle up through ledges (5.4) to easy walking that leads to the glacier at approximately GR 573838. Head in a generally southern direction onto the glacier and then make your way to the obvious col between Mts Little and Bowlen.

***Time*** 5–8 hours, depending on snow presence and number of climbers in your party.

***Summer from Moraine Lake via Schiesser Ledges (a scramble, with rockfall hazard)*** Follow the main trail along the shore of Moraine Lake to a boardwalk section, and then carry on along the N shore of the creek before crossing near a swampy section toward the bottom of Peak 3. Make your

way along the left-hand side of the moraines as you aim for the long and prominent lateral moraine that curls up into the 3.5–4 couloir; there is a trail along its crest. Upon reaching the couloir (very dangerous—a shooting gallery at all times), look for an ugly red paint splotch on your left and then follow the red marks and cairns up through the ledges to the left of the couloir. Once reaching the glacier at the top, contour around Mt Bowlen to the hut at the Bowlen–Little col.

*Time* 5–7 hours

***Summer from Hwy 95 via Fay Hut (a walk with a glacier traverse)*** From Fay Hut, there are 2 routes to crest the ledges above the hut. One entails heading NW through the trees to some cliff-bands cut by a deep gorge; cross the creek at the outlet of the gorge and then take the trail that leads up through the ledges. The other route follows a trail alongside the little creek that is the hut's water supply; it also leads to the meadows atop the ledges. Once above the ledges, make your way across the flats onto the glacier directly ahead of you (or, if you prefer, first follow the lateral moraine and then access the glacier farther up). Head NE to the hut situated at the col between Mts Little and Bowlen (peaks 2 and 3 of the Ten Peaks).

*Time* 8–11 hours from parking lot; 4–6 hours from Fay Hut.

***Winter*** Although winter ascents of the Perren Route and Schiesser Ledges route have been done (the Perren route very infrequently), the more common approach is via Fay

hut. This route is essentially
the same as for summer, but
proceeding through the gorge
above Fay Hut provides the
easiest access to the open
plateau above. Attention to
avalanche conditions is needed.

## GUIDEBOOKS
*Selected Alpine Climbs in the
    Canadian Rockies,* Dougherty.
*Rocky Mountains of Canada–South,*
    Boles.

## INFORMATION & BOOKING
The Alpine Club of Canada
Box 8040
Canmore AB T1W 2T8
*Phone* (403) 678-3200
*Fax* (403) 678-3224
*E-mail* alpclub@telusplanet.net
*Website* www.alpineclubof
    canada.ca

# Castle Mountain Hut

The principal reason for coming here is rock-climbing on the walls right behind the hut, although some come up here just for the great views from this ledge high above the Bow Valley. Perched on the Goat Plateau halfway up the 1500 m (4900 ft) face of Castle Mountain, the small hut appears from Hwy 1 to be clinging to a miniscule ledge, but the plateau is actually quite broad. There is a wide array of climbing routes up to the top. The hut itself provides the minimum of amenities, although it is amply comfortable and secure.

## LOCATION
**General** On a plateau looking down on the Castle Junction intersection on Hwy 1, halfway between Banff and Lake Louise AB.

**Specific** 82O/5 Castle Mountain NAD83 743836 (Note that cabin site indicated is incorrect).

**Other pertinent maps** For a good orientation to the peaks visible from Castle Mountain, see Gem Trek's *Banff and Mt Assiniboine*.

**Elevation** 2390 m (7850 ft).

**Elevation gain** 914 m (3000 ft) for both routes.

## AMENITIES
**Heat** None, but hut is seldom used in very cold weather.

**Cooking** Coleman stove (guests supply own fuel); basic cookware and dishware provided.

**Lighting** Coleman lantern.

**Sleeping** Two layers of bunks with foam pads.

**Capacity** 6.

## COST (as of Summer 2001)
Alpine Club Class B hut: $9 for members; $13 for nonmembers; $11 for group members.

## ACCESS
General route descriptions are given below, but both routes involve some exposed climbing or scrambling; visitors may wish to consult the climbing guides listed for more precisely detailed route descriptions and photos.

### Summer via Fire Lookout Route

This standard route entails about 20 m 65 ft) of low 5th-class climbing, with some tricky route-finding. It begins at the signed parking lot (Castle Lookout Trail) on Hwy 1A about 4.8 km (3 mi) W of Castle Junction. Hike along the old fire road for 4 km (2.5 mi) to the lookout and then follow thin trails that angle right up to the lower cliffband which is the crux of this approach. Climb the diagonal break up and right (a belay is recommended) to more trails and ledges marked by cairns. Scramble up the final gully to the Goat Plateau. The hut is a few hundred meters E on a defined trail.

**Summer from the parking lot at the Rockbound Lake trailhead** A less technical scramble to the hut begins from the Rockbound Lake trailhead (on Hwy 1A, just E of Castle Junction). Follow the main trail toward Rockbound Lake for about 5 km (3 mi). Shortly after passing through a swampy section cut with many parallel trails, watch for a faint trail heading left and angling up toward the SE end of Castle Mtn. As you approach this end, you will have to scramble up to an obvious ledge that curls around the cliff-face to the highway side. Just around the corner, a slightly exposed section leads you up to the large gully accessing the Goat Plateau. (Remember to note landmarks for your return.) The best trail on to the hut is the one nearest the cliff-face on your right, but helmets are recommended here.

**Time** 3–4 hours for both routes.

**Winter** Same as for summer, but there is little reason to go here, except for those who like to brave avalanche slopes in order to rock climb in bitter cold.

### GUIDEBOOKS

*Selected Alpine Climbs in the Canadian Rockies,* Dougherty.
*Rocky Mountains of Canada–South,* Boles.

### INFORMATION & BOOKING

The Alpine Club of Canada
Box 8040
Canmore AB T1W 2T8
**Phone** (403) 678-3200
**Fax** (403) 678-3224
**E-mail** alpclub@telusplanet.net
**Website** www.alpineclubof canada.ca

# Lake O'Hara Lodge

If you want a luxurious end to a day's hiking or ski-touring in an alpine-postcard setting, this is the lodge. In the renowned Lake O'Hara region of Yoho National Park, this facility consists of a main lodge and several independent lakeside cabins. With 80 km (50 mi) of trails that lead to a variety of lakes and ridges, the environs here offer something for everyone, from the wildflower admirer to the mountaineer. Although accessed directly by bus in summer, visitors in winter must ski in along the 11 km (7 mi) fire road (a dog sled ride is also an option).

## LOCATION
*General* On the shore of Lake O'Hara in Yoho National Park BC.

*Specific* 82 N/8 Lake Louise NAD83 463894.

*Other pertinent maps* Lake Louise & Yoho, Gem Trek; *Lake O'Hara: The Adventure Map;* Map to local hiking trails available for free at the Parks Canada shelter near the lodge.

*Elevation* 2042 m (6700 ft).

*Elevation gain from parking lot* 418 m (1370 ft ).

## AMENITIES
*Heat* Propane.
*Cooking* All meals provided, including afternoon tea.
*Lighting* Electric.
*Sleeping* Private bedrooms; linen provided.
*Capacity* 55–60 in summer; 16 in winter.
*Features* Gourmet meals, spa-

cious lounge area, sauna (winter only), hot showers, winter guiding and safety equipment provided.

## COST (as of Summer 2001)
All prices below include meals, lodging, taxes, summer bus fare and winter guiding. All prices based on double occupancy (minimum 2-night stay).

**Summer Main Lodge room** (shared bathroom) $375/couple/night.
**Summer Lakeshore cabin** (private bathroom) $500/couple/night.
**Summer Panaview cabin** (private bathroom) $560/couple/night.
**Winter Main Lodge room** (shared bathroom) $205/person/night.

## ACCESS
See description for Elizabeth Parker Hut.

## GUIDEBOOKS
*The Canadian Rockies Trail Guide,*
    Patton and Robinson.
*Ski Trails in the Canadian Rockies,*
    Scott.
*Selected Alpine Climbs,* Dougherty.
*Lake O'Hara Trails,* Beers.

## INFORMATION & BOOKING
Lake O'Hara Lodge
Box 55
Lake Louise AB T0L 1E0
**In-season** (June 19–September 30;
    mid-January to mid-April).
**Phone** (250) 343-6418
**Off-season phone** (403) 678-4110
**Website** www.lakeohara.com

# Elizabeth Parker Hut

Due to its ease of access and spectacular location, this hut is extremely popular all year long. There are in fact 2 huts here: one is a large 2-room log cabin containing a kitchen and a separate dining/sleeping room; the other cabin functions purely as a dorm. The main building was refurbished in the late 1990s with a new roof, skylights, upholstered benches, big hardwood tables and propane appliances. There are numerous hiking trails in the Lake O'Hara area, all of which make you feel that you're walking through a postcard or a calendar photo. Mountaineers will also find many great climbs in the area, the best known being the Grassi Ridge route on Mt Wiwaxy. Skiers will find terrific tours and turns in the area.

## LOCATION

***General*** Near Lake O'Hara, about 13 km (8 mi) S of Hwy 1 close to the Alberta–BC border in Yoho National Park BC.

***Specific*** 82N/8 Lake Louise NAD83 457893.

***Other pertinent maps*** *Lake Louise & Yoho*, Gem Trek; *Lake O'Hara: The Adventure Map* (1:20,000); Map to local hiking trails available for free at the Parks Canada shelter near the lodge.

***Elevation*** 2040 m (6700 ft).

***Elevation gain from parking lot*** 396 m (1300 ft).

## AMENITIES

***Heat*** Efficient woodstoves in both cabins (wood provided).

***Cooking*** Propane stoves and oven; cookware and dishware provided.

*Lighting* Propane.

*Sleeping* In both cabins, there are two layers of bunks with foam pads.

*Capacity* 24 in total in summer, 20 in winter.

COST (as of Summer 2001) An Alpine Club Class A+ hut: $17.50 for members; $24 for nonmembers; $19.50 for group members.

ACCESS

*Summer* Get on the bus, ride in it, then get off. The hut is about 15 minutes along a well-defined trail. Be sure to get bus reservations when you book the hut. You can also walk up the fire road or take the slightly longer but well-marked Cataract Brook trail. Many people, however, find it preferable to take the bus so that they can spend the day hiking in the more spectacular alpine terrain.

*Time* 3–4 hours walking, 30 minutes by bus

*Winter* Follow the fire road, which is usually track-set.

GUIDEBOOKS

*The Canadian Rockies Trail Guide,* Patton and Robinson.

*The Wonder of Yoho,* Beers.

*Selected Alpine Climbs in the Canadian Rockies,* Dougherty.

*Ski Trails in the Canadian Rockies,* Scott.

*Rocky Mountains of Canada–South,* Boles.

*Scrambles in the Canadian Rockies,* Kane.

INFORMATION & BOOKING

The Alpine Club of Canada
Box 8040
Canmore AB T1W 2T8
*Phone* (403) 678-3200
*Fax* (403) 678-3224
*E-mail* alpclub@telusplanet.net
*Website* www.alpineclubof canada.ca

# Abbot Pass Hut

A Canadian classic, this stone structure was built by the CPR in 1922–23 as part of its attempt to attract adventurers to its mountain hotels. Now a National Historic Building, it is one of the ACC's most impressive huts and is set in a spectacular site at the narrow pass between Lakes O'Hara and Louise. It offers a warm and solid base from which to attempt climbs of Mts Lefroy and Victoria, although the views across to the peaks that ring Lake Louise make this hut a spectacular destination in itself. Note that the formerly straightforward route through the Death Trap has become much more severely crevassed in the last decade. The pass itself is named for Phillip Abbot, who fell during an 1896 climb of Lefroy and became the first mountaineering death in North America.

## LOCATION

**General** On the Continental Divide between Mts Victoria and Lefroy, about 10 km (6 mi) SW of Lake Louise AB in Banff National Park.

**Specific** 82N/8 Lake Louise NAD83 495903.

**Other pertinent maps** *Lake Louise & Yoho,* Gem Trek; *Lake O'Hara: The Adventure Map* (1:20,000).

**Elevation** 2926 m (9598 ft).

**Elevation gain from Lake O'Hara** 914 m (3000 ft).

## AMENITIES

**Heat** Woodstove (wood flown in, please use sparingly).

**Cooking** Propane stoves; cookware and dishware provided.

**Lighting** Propane.

**Sleeping** Foam pads in the loft above the main floor.
**Capacity** 24.

**COST** (as of Summer 2001) An Alpine Club Class A+ hut: $17.50 for members; $24 for nonmembers; $19.50 for group members.

## ACCESS

**From Lake O'Hara** This is the safer and recommended route. After getting off the bus at the lake (see description of Elizabeth Parker Hut), follow the well-marked trail to Lake Oesa and stay on the trail that angles up across the talus slope on the N side of the lake. Carry on through a small gully and then angle up across some ledges to the right; the route is well marked with big cairns and blue rectangles painted on the rocks. Above the ledges, take a thin but clear trail that soon curls left to the base of the long scree slope that leads to the pass. There will be remnants of several trails up through the ever-moving scree; pick out one and then plod upwards for over 330 m (1000 ft). Beware of rockfall from the left; helmets are recommended, as are ice axes and crampons in early season and after fresh snowfall (which could occur in any month).
**Time** 3–6 hours.
**From Lake Louise** This route involves significant objective hazards. Follow the broad trail along the lakeshore and on past the tea-house to the Plain of 6 Glaciers. Carry on into the obvious deep gorge between Mts Victoria and Lefroy—the Death Trap. Race through here as you hope for no serac-fall or avalanches from the glaciers overhanging above. Make your way through a maze of crevasses, but be prepared for a possibly impassable wall-to-wall 'schrund at the upper end. Clearly this is not an attractive route and should be attempted only by strong alpinists when there is deep snow cover on the glacier.
**Time** Highly variable depending on conditions.

## GUIDEBOOKS

*The Canadian Rockies Trail Guide,* Patton and Robinson.
*The Wonder of Yoho,* Beers.
*Selected Alpine Climbs in the Canadian Rockies,* Dougherty.
*Great Lodges of the Canadian Rockies,* Barnes.
*Rocky Mountains of Canada–South,* Boles.

## INFORMATION & BOOKING

The Alpine Club of Canada
Box 8040
Canmore AB T1W 2T8
**Phone** (403) 678-3200
**Fax** (403) 678-3224
**E-mail** alpclub@telusplanet.net
**Website** www.alpineclubof canada.ca

# Halfway/Ptarmigan Shelter

Not to be confused with the Halfway Lodge in the Assiniboine area (see the listing for Sundance and Halfway Lodges), this shelter is primarily used by those ski-touring in the Corral Creek valley or travelling on to Skoki Lodge. Officially, it is just a day-use shelter (and the wardens ensure it is not used overnight in the summer). However, in winter, hardy skiers sometimes use it for overnight shelter. Although solid and clean, this log cabin has literally nothing inside it. There are great opportunities for tele-turns on the nearby Purple and Hidden bowls, the Tylenols and Richardson Ridge. (If you use the shelter, be sure to leave it spotless, for if it were to become a garbage site, the wardens might choose to remove it.)

## LOCATION

*General* Near the headwaters of Corral Creek, about 8 linear km (5 mi) NE of the townsite of Lake Louise AB.

*Specific* 82 N/8 Lake Louise NAD83 5**626**23 7**029**07.

*Other pertinent maps* Lake Louise & Yoho, Gem Trek.

*Elevation* 2182 m (7180 ft).

*Elevation gain from ski hill parking lot* 527 m (1730 ft).

*From Temple day lodge* 176 m (580 ft).

## AMENITIES

*Heat* None.

*Cooking* None.

*Lighting* None.

*Sleeping* No beds.

*Capacity* 6–8.

COST (as of November 2000)
Free; no reservations (not recog-

nized as an overnight facility by Parks Canada).

## ACCESS

From Temple Day Lodge in the Lake Louise Ski Area, head uphill on the edge of the "Marmot" run for about 300 m (1000 ft) until you see the signpost identifying the start of the trail into the woods on your left. Follow the broad trail up the Corral Creek valley towards Boulder Pass. The shelter is not far from the base of the pass, about 4 km (2.5 mi) from the trailhead.

*Time* About 1 hour.

## GUIDEBOOKS

*Canadian Rockies Trail Guide,* Patton and Robinson.

*Ski Trails in the Canadian Rockies,* Scott.

# Skoki Lodge

Situated in a beautiful high alpine region of Banff National Park, this lodge is reached by an easy trail from the Lake Louise Ski Area. From the lodge, one can access high ridges and alpine lakes, or explore 5 different adjoining valleys. In winter, skiers of all abilities can find extensive terrain for touring and telemarking. The historic main lodge and 3 surrounding cabins provide rustic luxury: there is fresh-baked bread and afternoon tea, but no electricity or running water. Nonguest hikers or ski-tourers are welcome for afternoon tea.

### LOCATION
**General** Located in Skoki Valley about 11 km (7 mi) NNE of Lake Louise Ski Resort in Banff National Park AB.

**Specific** 82 N/8 Hector Lake NAD83 5**640**08 7**084**06.

**Other pertinent maps** 82 N/8 Lake Louise; *Lake Louise & Yoho,* Gem Trek.

**Elevation** 2165 m (7100 ft).

**Elevation gain from ski area parking lot** 770 m (2525 ft).

**From Temple Lodge** 465 m (1525).

### AMENITIES
**Heat** Wood and coal stove, propane heaters.

**Cooking** All meals provided.

**Lighting** Kerosene lamps.

**Sleeping** Private rooms with duvets and linen.

**Capacity** 22.

**Features** Sauna, large living room, well-appointed bedrooms.

### COST (as of Summer 2001)
**Cabin for 2** $147.45/person/night

**Cabin for 4** $136.75/person/night

**Lodge room** $131.40/person/night
(Reduced rates for kids 4–12)

**Note** Prices reduced by 10 percent for stays longer than 3 nights.

## ACCESS

Take the only turnoff from Hwy 1 into the Lake Louise area and head N toward the ski hill. Take the first right (marked "Fish Creek") and continue to the parking area at the end of the public road. Guests will be given a ride up along a road skirting the ski area to the trailhead near the Temple Day Lodge. From the lodge, head uphill on the edge of the "Marmot" run for about 300 m (1000 ft) until you see the signpost identifying the start of the trail into the woods on your left. Follow this broad trail up the Corral Creek valley towards Boulder Pass. (Alternatively, in winter you can ski down to this trail from the top of the ski lifts.) From Boulder Pass, walk around Ptarmigan Lake and follow the trail N over Deception Pass and then 3.5 km (2 mi) farther down to the lodge. In winter, the trail through open areas is plainly marked by stakes.

**Time** 4–5 hours.

## GUIDEBOOKS

*The Canadian Rockies Trail Guide,*
Patton and Robinson.

*Ski Trails in the Canadian Rockies,*
Scott.

*The Wonder of Lake Louise,* Beers.

## INFORMATION & BOOKING

Skoki Lodge
Box 5
Lake Louise AB T0L 1E0

**Phone** (403) 522-3555
**Fax** (403) 522-2095
**E-mail** skoki@skilouise.com
**Website** www.skilouise.com/skoki

# Scott Duncan Hut

Used almost exclusively by skiers or hikers doing the Wapta Traverse, this is the most southerly hut on Canada's Haute Route. Ascents of Mts Daly and Balfour can be done as day-trips from here. For those doing the traverse from the N (the most common direction), the hut is a vital facility: since it is located not far from the slopes leading down to Sherbrooke Lake (slopes which are prone to afternoon avalanches in late winter and spring), the hut affords a good base from which an early-morning descent can be undertaken. The building itself, the most recent one erected for the traverse, is well insulated and provides very secure shelter in this exposed spot on a ridge. Note that glacier gear and experience is needed.

## LOCATION
*General* on the NW ridge of Mt Daly about 19 km (12 mi) NW of Lake Louise AB in Banff National Park.

*Specific* 82N/9 Hector Lake NAD83 417084

*Other pertinent maps* 82 N/10 Blaeberry River (needed if carrying on N on the Wapta Traverse); *Touring the Wapta Icefield,* Toft; *Bow Lake & Saskatchewan Crossing,* Gem Trek.

*Elevation* 2773 m (9100 ft).

*Elevation change* From Balfour Hut 518 m (1700 ft) gain to Balfour High Col, then a 244 m (800 ft) loss to the hut.

*From West Louise Lodge parking lot* 1189 m (3900 ft) .

## AMENITIES
*Heat* None, but hut is well insulated.

**Cooking** Coleman stoves (guests supply own fuel); cookware and dishware provided.

**Lighting** Coleman lanterns.

**Sleeping** Two layers of bunks with foam pads.

**Capacity** 12 (but cramped quarters if full).

COST (as of Summer 2001)
An Alpine Club Class B hut: $9 for members; $13 for nonmembers; $11 for group members.

## ACCESS

**Summer from Balfour Hut** Ascend to the Balfour High Col, commonly regarded as the crux of the Wapta traverse. This route, although obvious from the hut, entails navigating around crevasses and past the base of a steep icefall. Be wary of proceeding in bad weather. From the col, a steady, gradual descent SE toward the NW ridge of Mt Daly leads to the hut located on the moraine shoulder.

**Time** 6–8 hours.

**From West Louise Lodge on Hwy 1** From the lodge (just W of the Alberta–BC border on Hwy 1), find the nearby trail that leads up Sherbrooke Creek to the Lake. Stay on the right (E) side around the lake and then take the trail along the W (not the N) fork of the creek. When you lose the trail, slog up through the thinning timber to meadows and finally to the SE ridge of Mt Niles. Carry on along the ridge (or on a bench lower

down) until you can cut across onto the Niles Glacier and then NE to the hut on the NW ridgeline of Daly, perched on a moraine above the glacier.

**Time** A full day, at least 7 hours.

**Winter** Same as in summer for both approaches, but if coming in from West Louise Lodge, beware of the avalanche hazard on the slopes from Niles Glacier to Sherbrooke Lake. In late winter or early spring, the slopes are especially dangerous in the afternoon. Note that an alternative descent is possible along the Bath Glacier in good conditions—see the route description in *Ski Trails* below.

## GUIDEBOOKS

*Summits and Icefields,* Scott.

*Ski Trails in the Canadian Rockies,* Scott.

*Rocky Mountains of Canada–South,* Boles.

## INFORMATION & BOOKING

The Alpine Club of Canada
Box 8040
Canmore AB T1W 2T8
**Phone** (403) 678-3200
**Fax** (403) 678-3224
**E-mail** alpclub@telusplanet.net
**Website** www.alpineclubof canada.ca

# Balfour Hut

This hut just east of the Continental Divide is used primarily by those doing the Wapta Traverse or climbing Mt Balfour (or both). Although less luxurious than Bow Hut, this facility at the approximate mid-point of the Wapta Traverse is a vital shelter, for the high winds commonly blowing through the flats at Balfour Pass make this quite forbidding terrain. The hut can be hard to locate in even partial whiteout conditions, so be wary of progressing past the Olive–Nicholas col in bad weather without a GPS. It can be reached from the Bow Lake parking lot in a day, although many people stop at Peyto or Bow hut on the way in. Note that the hut may be reached only by traversing glaciers.

## LOCATION

**General** In Banff National Park, about 28 km (17 mi) NW of Lake Louise AB on the moraine at the toe of the Vulture Glacier.

**Specific** 82N/9 Hector Lake NAD83 375157

**Other pertinent maps** 82N/10 Blaeberry River (for access to Bow and Peyto huts and the Wapta Icefield); *Touring the Wapta Icefield,* Toft; *Bow Lake & Saskatchewan Crossing,* Gem Trek.

**Elevation** 2470 m (8100 ft).

**Elevation change from Bow Hut** 580 m (1900 ft) gain to Olive–Nicholas Col, then a 457 m (1500 ft) loss to Balfour Hut.

## AMENITIES

**Heat** None provided, but hut is well insulated.

**Cooking** Coleman stoves (guests supply own fuel); cookware and dishware provided.
**Lighting** Coleman lanterns.
**Sleeping** Two layers of bunks with foam pads.
**Capacity** 18 in summer; 16 in winter.

## COST (as of Summer 2001)

An Alpine Club Class B hut: $9 for members; $13 for nonmembers; $11 for group members.

## ACCESS

From Bow Hut, ascend the center of the main slope to the W, and as it flattens out, pass along the W side of Mt St. Nicholas to the obvious col between it and Olive. From Peyto Hut, head SE up the glacier and across the long flats to this col. From the col, head down to the center of the glacier below you, keeping far from the crevasse field on your right. Once you're well away from the face of Olive, curl to your right and proceed directly to the flats ahead. See the description of Scott Duncan Hut for access from the S.

**Time** 3–4 hours from Bow Hut; 4–6 hours from Peyto Hut (possibly less in winter).

## GUIDEBOOKS

*Summits and Icefields,* Scott.
*Ski Trails in the Canadian Rockies,* Scott.
*Rocky Mountains of Canada–South,* Boles.

## INFORMATION & BOOKING

The Alpine Club of Canada
Box 8040
Canmore AB T1W 2T8
**Phone** (403) 678-3200
**Fax** (403) 678-3224
**E-mail** alpclub@telusplanet.net
**Website** www.alpineclubof canada.ca

# Bow Hut

Easily the most palatial and popular of the Wapta area huts, this multi-room facility is so pleasant that it's hard to bring yourself to leave on a blustery winter day. The main dining/lounging room features a wood-stove and is connected by a corridor to an unheated 3-room dorm area. This hut serves as the base for a wide array of ski tours and mountaineering ascents to half a dozen peaks fringing the Wapta Icefield. Travel on to Balfour Hut is easily done in a day, and some doing the Wapta Traverse make it from here to Scott Duncan Hut in a day in good weather. Reaching Stanley Mitchell Hut in a day is possible but only for the very fit travelling under ideal conditions. Note that travel beyond the hut requires glacier gear and experience.

## LOCATION

**General** Near the headwaters of the Bow River on the E edge of the Wapta Icefield, about 33 km (21 mi) NW of Lake Louise AB in Banff National Park.

**Specific** 82 N/9 Hector Lake NAD27 355203.

**Other pertinent maps** 82 N/10 Blaeberry River (for touring on the Wapta Icefield); *Touring the Wapta Icefield,* Toft; *Bow Lake & Saskatchewan Crossing,* Gem Trek.

**Elevation** 2350 m (7700 ft).

**Elevation gain from parking lot** 400 m (1310 ft).

## AMENITIES

**Heat** Woodstove (no heat in dorm area).

**Cooking** Propane stoves and oven; cookware and dishware provided.

**Lighting** Propane (none in dorm area).
**Sleeping** Two layers of bunks with foam pads.
**Capacity** 30 (3 rooms accommodating 10/room).

COST (as of Summer 2001)
An Alpine Club Class A+ hut: $17.50 for members; $24 for nonmembers; $19.50 for group members.

ACCESS
**Summer** From the main parking lot on the highway beside Bow Lake, follow the road past Num-Ti-Jah Lodge to the trail that hugs the N shore of the lake around to the main creek that feeds the lake. Ascend to the right of the canyon just upstream from the lake. Be alert for a junction to the left, which you follow across the canyon via a boulder-bridge. The trail stays on the E side of the creek for a few kilometers until it opens out near the treeline into a moraine-rubble basin. Follow any of the trails or cairns across until you get close to the massive headwall; cross the creek and follow any trail angling to the right up the steep slope of a few hundred meters.
**Time** 3–5 hours.
**Winter** The route is little different from the summer route, except that you cross the frozen lake and stay to the left of the creek as you follow a good trail that skirts the canyon just upstream from the lake. In about 700 m (2300 ft), the route drops down onto the creek-bed, which it follows through a gorge until the gorge becomes too rigorous and the slopes to the left are obviously easier going. Ascend here and then angle up through the trees, parallel to the canyon. When you reach the open basin and can see the hut high up on your right, aim for the right-hand corner of the huge headwall, staying left initially to avoid the worst of the moraine terrain. Angle to the right up one of the steep slopes; the hut is a few hundred meters from the top. Avalanche precautions must be taken.
**Time** 3–5 hours

GUIDEBOOKS
*Summits and Icefields,* Scott.
*Ski Trails in the Canadian Rockies,* Scott.
*Rocky Mountains of Canada–South,* Boles.

INFORMATION & BOOKING
The Alpine Club of Canada
Box 8040
Canmore AB T1W 2T8
**Phone** (403) 678-3200
**Fax** (403) 678-3224
**E-mail** alpclub@telusplanet.net
**Website** www.alpineclubof canada.ca

# Peter & Catharine Whyte (Peyto) Hut

Located on the northern end of the Wapta Icefield, this hut is typically the first day's destination for those doing the full Wapta Traverse. However, many people also use this snug building as a base for day-trips onto the mountains that ring the end of the Icefield. There are at least 2–3 days of good touring and half a dozen peaks and cols nearby for ski-mountaineers or for snow-and-ice scrambles in the summer. Just south of the hut are some great slopes for turns. Completely renovated and expanded in the summer of 2000, the hut itself is a surprisingly warm structure that now has propane cookstoves and lighting. Set on a bench well above the glacier, it affords spectacular views across to Mts Rhondda and Baker.

## LOCATION

*General* At the N end of the Wapta Icefield, about 38 km (24 mi) NW of Lake Louise AB in Banff National Park.

*Specific* 82 N/10 Blaeberry River NAD83 314237.

*Other pertinent maps* 82 N/9 Hector Lake (for any travel S on the Wapta Icefield); *Touring the Wapta Icefield,* Toft; *Bow Lake & Saskatchewan Crossing,* Gem Trek.

*Elevation* 2500 m (8200 ft).

*Elevation change from Bow Summit parking lot* 305 m (1000 ft) descent to lake, then 670 m (2200 ft) gain to hut.

## AMENITIES

*Heat* None, but hut is well insulated.

*Cooking* Propane stoves; cookware and dishware provided.

*Lighting* Propane lanterns.
*Sleeping* Two layers of bunks with foam pads.
*Capacity* 18 in summer, 16 in winter.

COST (as of Summer 2001) An Alpine Club Class B+ hut: $11.50 for members; $15.50 for nonmembers; $13.50 for group members.

## ACCESS

*Summer* From the Peyto Lake viewing platform near the parking lot at Bow Summit, follow the clear trail that drops down to the creek valley. The trail then makes its way across a bridge (approximately GR 327286) and then leads up along the sharp crest of a moraine on the N side of the creek. At the end of the moraine, ascend the rocky slope until it levels out somewhat and you can easily traverse left to the toe of the glacier. Go up the center of the glacier and describe a long arc around the open crevasses on the left. The hut is on the moraine below Mt Thompson.

*Time* 5–6 hours.

*Winter* From the parking lot about 1.5 km (1 mi) N of Bow Summit on Hwy 95, begin following the old road down to the lake, but watch for the trail that branches off to the left about 5 minutes from the parking lot. After reaching the frozen lake, head SW across it to the obvious

drainage (and take a compass bearing so that you can find the trailhead on your way out). Carry on W across the outwash rubble and, as the valley narrows, ascend either the crest of the moraine on your right (i.e., the summer route) or stay on the slopes on the left side of the creek. If taking this latter route (which can be 1–2 hours shorter than the right-hand side) note that you generally will have to cut through a cornice atop a short steep section and that this side is risky if avalanche conditions are considerable. Once you reach the toe of the glacier, proceed up the center and describe a long arc around the open crevasses on the left. The hut is on the moraine below Mt Thompson.

## GUIDEBOOKS

*Summits and Icefields,* Scott.
*Ski Trails in the Canadian Rockies,* Scott.
*Rocky Mountains of Canada–South,* Boles.

## INFORMATION & BOOKING

The Alpine Club of Canada
Box 8040
Canmore AB T1W 2T8
*Phone* (403) 678-3200
*Fax* (403) 678-3224
*E-mail* alpclub@telusplanet.net
*Website* www.alpineclubof canada.ca

# Stanley Mitchell Hut

If you want the quintessential Rocky Mountain experience, it's hard to beat this log structure rich in alpine history. Set on the edge of a meadow just below treeline, the hut serves as a great base for a broad array of alpine-meadow walks, peak scrambles or serious snow-and-ice climbs. It is also a great family destination. There are 7–8 striking peaks ringing this end of the Little Yoho valley, the most prominent being the President/Vice-President and Mt McArthur. The skiing near here can also be spectacular.

## LOCATION

**General** In the Little Yoho River Valley in Yoho National Park BC, about 11 km (7 mi) from the end of the Takakkaw Falls Road.

**Specific** 82N/10 Blaeberry River

NAD83 5**30**240 7**083**83.

**Other pertinent maps** 82 N/8 Lake Louise and 82 N/9 Hector Lake contain parts of the trail from the parking lot, but the route to the hut is so clearly sign-posted that maps aren't really necessary. Those climbing the President should note that this peak is on 82 N/7 Golden; *Touring the Wapta Icefields,* Toft; *Lake Louise & Yoho,* Gem Trek.

**Elevation** 2055 m (6742 ft).

**Elevation gain from Takakkaw Falls parking lot** 545 m (1788 ft).

## AMENITIES

**Heat** Woodstove.

**Cooking** Propane stoves/oven; cookware and dishware provided.

**Lighting** Propane (except in sleeping loft).

**Sleeping** One room with two layers of bunks with foam pads and a loft with foam pads.

**Capacity** 26 in summer, 22 in winter.

COST (as of Summer 2001) An Alpine Club Class A+ hut: $17.50 for members; $24 for nonmembers; $19.50 for group members.

## ACCESS

**Summer** Two very well defined and clearly signposted trails lead to the hut from the busy Takakkaw Falls area, which is reached by a 14 km (9 mi) paved road from near Field. The easiest route is to head upstream on the main trail from the most northerly parking lot. About 5 km (3 mi) in, at the Laughing Falls junction, head left and switchback up steeply for about 1 km (0.6 mi); the trail then levels out and follows the N bank of the Little Yoho River to the hut. Alternately, you can follow the Iceline Trail, which heads up steeply from the parking lot at the Whiskey Jack hostel (located just before the Falls parking lot). Once above treeline, follow the signs along very scenic trails down to the hut. Note that the trail can be difficult to follow in the early season and may require an ice axe.

**Time** 3–5 hours.

**Winter** The Laughing Falls route is the most practical. Since the road in from Hwy 1 is not plowed, you must ski 14 km (9 mi) that gain 275 m (900 ft) in elevation. Some skiers overnight at the Takakkaw Falls Campground picnic shelter, which has no amenities except a woodstove and picnic tables.

**Alternate approach** (used in winter by experienced ski-mountaineers) comes from the Icefields Parkway via Bow Hut, crossing the Wapta Icefield and Yoho and Des Poilus glaciers. Note that many fail to complete the traverse in one day and that the route entails travel up and down 3 very steep slopes that can pose avalanche hazards.

## GUIDEBOOKS

*The Canadian Rockies Trail Guide,* Patton and Robinson.

*Summits and Icefields,* Scott.

*Ski Trails in the Canadian Rockies,* Scott.

*The Wonder of Yoho,* Beers.

*Selected Alpine Climbs in the Canadian Rockies,* Dougherty.

*Rocky Mountains of Canada–South,* Boles.

## INFORMATION & BOOKING

The Alpine Club of Canada
Box 8040
Canmore AB T1W 2T8
**Phone** (403) 678-3200
**Fax** (403) 678-3224
**E-mail** alpclub@telusplanet.net
**Website** www.alpineclubof canada.ca

# Twin Falls Chalet

Located near the base of the dramatic Twin Falls in Yoho National Park, this popular log lodge is as renowned for its views as for its gourmet meals. In the immediate area are many hiking trails that lead into high alpine terrain fringed with glaciers. There are also many climbing and mountaineering opportunities nearby. The lodge, which has been attracting visitors from around the world for almost a century now, is very comfortable yet rustic, with outdoor privies and showers. It operates from July 1 to the first Monday in September only and should be booked well in advance. Day hikers can stop in for lunch.

## LOCATION

**General** At the base of Twin Falls near the headwaters of the Yoho River in Yoho Park, about 30 km (19 mi) N of Field BC.

**Specific** 82 N/10 Blaeberry River NAD83 5**323**86 7**105**14.

**Other pertinent maps** 82 N/8 Lake Louise; *Lake Louise & Yoho,* Gem Trek.

**Elevation** 1800 m (5905 ft).

**Elevation gain from parking lot** 290 m (950 ft).

## AMENITIES

**Heat** Woodstove.

**Cooking** All meals provided.

**Lighting** Gas lanterns; battery-powered lamps in bedrooms.

**Sleeping** 4 bedrooms; linen provided.

**Capacity** 14.

**Features** Outdoor privies with a view, outdoor shower.

**COST** (as of Summer 2001)
$140/night; 2 night minimum.

## ACCESS

From the turnoff to Takakkaw
Falls 3.7 km (2.3 mi) E of the
Field Information Centre on
Hwy 1, drive along the narrow
paved road 14 km (9 mi) to the
most northerly parking lot. Follow the broad, well-marked trail
along the Yoho River for 6.6 km
(4 mi) and then branch W for
1.5 km (1 mi) to Twin Falls. Note
that there are numerous alternate trails (all well signposted)
that can be taken for those wishing to rise above the valley floor.
Check the large map at the trailhead.

*Time* 2–3 hours.

## GUIDEBOOKS

*The Canadian Rockies Trail Guide,*
   Patton and Robinson.
*The Wonder of Yoho,* Beers.
*Rocky Mountain Retreats: Recom-*
   *mended Accommodation in the*
   *Canadian Rockies,* Schmaltz.

## INFORMATION & BOOKING

Twin Falls Chalet
Attention Fran Drummond
Suite 11, 230 21 Ave SW
Calgary AB T2S 0G6
*Phone* (403) 228-7079 after 6 pm
*Fax* (403) 228-7079

# Amiskwi Lodge

This spacious two-story log building is set at treeline and affords ready access to alpine hiking, ski touring and full-scale mountaineering. Set above Amiskwi Pass just outside Yoho Park, the lodge's sun-room offers spectacular views across to the glaciated peaks of the Mummery Range. Treks up onto the nearby ridges yield 360º panoramas of rugged mountains. With a full kitchen, BBQ, 4 bedrooms, sauna and equipment room, this lodge provides all that you could need for comfort after a day's outing. It can be accessed by foot or helicopter in summer and by helicopter only in winter. Winter visits are booked in week-long blocks (with the option of having a fully catered and fully guided visit).

## LOCATION

**General** Near Amiskwi Pass just outside the western boundary of Yoho National Park, NE of Golden BC.

**Specific** 82N/10 Blaeberry River NAD83 228187.

**Other pertinent maps** *Lake Louise & Yoho,* Gem Trek (for terrain to the E).

**Elevation** 2104 m (6900 ft).

**Elevation gain from Ensign Creek Road** (accessible summer only) 183 m (600 ft).

## AMENITIES

**Heat** Propane.

**Cooking** Propane stove, oven and BBQ; cookware and dishware provided in large kitchen.

**Lighting** Propane lanterns.

**Sleeping** Comfortable queen and twin beds in 4 bedrooms.

**Capacity** 16 maximum (ideal

group size in winter is 12).

**Features** Sun room, drying area and workshop, large windows, sauna, 250 cm (8 ft) snowpack.

COST (as of Summer 2001)
**Summer** $40/person/night (reduced rates for children).
**Winter** $600/person/week, including helicopter transport.
Fully catered and guided options available.

ACCESS
**Summer** A clear map will be sent you on registering. From Golden, you must drive 20 km (12.5 mi) NW on Hwy 1 and then turn N on the Blaeberry River Forest Service Road. A total of 70 km (44 mi) on this road and then the Ensign Creek Road leads to the staging area; a high-clearance vehicle is needed to make it all the way. A well-defined trail leads to the lodge. To see a topo map of the hike, follow the links on the website.

Much longer access through Yoho Park is also an option and can be combined with a stay at Stanley Mitchell Hut. See guidebooks and maps for descriptions of this long route.
**Time** About 30 minutes from parking lot.
**Winter** Heli-access only (20 minutes).

GUIDEBOOKS
*The Canadian Rockies Trail Guide,* Patton and Robinson.
*Ski Trails in the Canadian Rockies,* Scott.
*Rocky Mountain Retreats: Recommended Accommodation in the Canadian Rockies,* Schmaltz.

INFORMATION & BOOKING
Amiskwi Lodge
Attention Brenda Stanton
Box 8175
Canmore AB T1W 2T9
**Phone** (403) 678-1800
**Fax** (403) 678-4039
**E-mail** info@amiskwi.com
**Website** www.amiskwi.com

# Mistaya Lodge

Located in the upper basin of Wildcat Creek just outside Banff National Park, this remote post-and-beam lodge is surrounded by wildflower meadows, alpine lakes and rugged glaciers. In summer it serves as an ideal base for the casual hiker or the serious climber. In winter, a vast and varied terrain is available for tours and turns in the dry powder, ranging from glade skiing near the lodge to ski-mountaineering on the nearby peaks and glaciers. Full guiding is provided in the winter. With backcountry gourmet meals and duvet-covered beds, days begin and end in luxury.

## LOCATION

*General* Just W of the Continental Divide near the N end of the Wapta Icefield, about 60 km (38 mi) NE of Golden BC.

*Specific* 82 N/10 Blaeberry River NAD83 254274.

*Other pertinent maps* Gem Trek's *Bow Lake & Saskatchewan Crossing* map provides a good orientation to all that can be seen in Banff Park from the col on the Continental Divide just E of the lodge.

*Elevation* 2042 m (6700 ft).

*Elevation gain* N/a (heli-accessed).

## AMENITIES

*Heat* Woodstoves.

*Cooking* All meals are prepared, including afternoon tea.

*Lighting* Solar and hydro electric.

*Sleeping* Fully furnished bedrooms with duvets (2 to 4 persons/room).

*Capacity* 15.

*Features* Sauna/bath-house, big living room, equipment room, certified mountaineering

guides available, gourmet
meals, emergency radio.

**COST** (as of Summer 2001)

*Note* All costs below include heli-
access, all meals and linen, and
guiding in winter. All summer
guests receive a free half-day
of guided hiking; otherwise,
guides for mountaineering or
hiking cost extra. Hiking
guides can be hired on a daily
basis, but arrangements for a
mountaineering guide must be
established when registration
is being made.

*Summer* From $780/person for a
3-night stay (3–4/room) to
$1500/person for a 7-night
stay (private room).

*Winter* From $735/person for a 3-
night stay in low season
(3–4/room) to $1590/person
for a 7-night stay in high season (double room).

**ACCESS**

All guests are flown by helicopter to and from the hut. For
those who wish it (and if weather permits), a guided tour out
across the Wapta Icefield to the
Icefields Parkway is available.
Details are provided upon registration.

**GUIDEBOOKS**

*Summits and Icefields,* Scott.

**INFORMATION & BOOKING**

Mistaya Lodge Ltd.
Attention Tracy Amies
Box 809
Golden BC V0A 1H0
*Phone & Fax* (250) 344-6689
*E-mail* mistayalodge@redshift.
bc.ca
*Website* www.mistayalodge.com

*Feeding whiskey-jacks in Larch Valley*

*Ascending Mt Wilson*

# North Rockies

## PROVINCIAL & NATIONAL PARKS

*Map*
*Reference*

A ................Kakwa Provincial Park

B................Mount Robson Provincial Park

C ................Jasper NationalPark

D ................Cummins Lake Provincial Park

## HUTS & LODGES

*Map*                                              *Page*
*Reference*                                         *Number*

37................Campbell Icefield Chalet ............................102

38................Chatter Creek Lodge .....................................104

39................Lawrence Grassi (Mt Clemenceau) Hut........106

40................Lloyd MacKay (Mt Alberta) Hut ..................108

41................Fortress Lake Lodge.....................................110

42................Sydney Vallance (Fryatt) Hut.......................112

43................Wates–Gibson Hut .......................................114

44................Tonquin Valley Adventures Lodge ...............118

45................Tonquin Valley Backcountry Lodge .............120

46................Shangri-La Cabin .........................................122

47................Shovel Pass Lodge .......................................124

48................Mt Colin Centennial Hut .............................126

49................Dave Henry Lodge .......................................128

50................Swift Creek Cabins.......................................130

51................Ralph Forster Hut.........................................132

52................Berg Lake Shelter.........................................134

53................West Range Lodge ........................................136

54–55 .........Kakwa & Jarvis Lakes Cabins.......................138

56................North Rockies Ski Tours Lodge ....................140

# Campbell Icefield Chalet

A former Alpine Club hut, this building has been totally refurbished and airlifted to this new site alongside the Campbell Glacier NE of Golden. Accessed by helicopter or by ski-plane, this treeline lodge affords great access to ski-mountaineering on the nearby glaciers, and in bad weather there is lots of glade-skiing nearby. It currently is a winter-only facility, although it may soon be opened for summer mountaineering.

## LOCATION

*General* Near the head of Bluewater Creek, off the western edge of the Campbell Icefield in the Freshfield Range, about 60 linear km (36 mi) N of Golden BC.

*Specific* On the border of 82 N/11 Bluewater and 82 N/10 Blaeberry River NAD83 **499**55 7**275**33.

*Other pertinent maps* Mountaineering terrain around the lodge could involve 82 N/14 Rostrum Peak and 82 N/15 Mistaya Lake.

*Elevation* 2088 m (6850 ft).

*Elevation gain* N/a (air access only).

## AMENITIES

*Heat* Propane.

*Cooking* Propane stove.

*Lighting* Propane.

*Sleeping* Bunk beds with foam pads.

*Capacity* 12.

*Features* Large kitchen and dining area, sauna, outside storage room with covered porch.

## COST (as of Summer 2001)

*Summer* $35/person/night in self-guided and self-catered groups, with a minimum group charge of $2000/week.

*Winter* Same.

*Heli-flights* $235/person for the round trip; ski-plane flights with Alpenglow Aviation are considerably less, depending on numbers.

*Guided & catered trips* Available at extra cost; prices are determined by group size, duration of stay, heli or plane access and other such variables.

## ACCESS

All access is by helicopter or ski-plane, although multi-day overland access is not impossible.

## GUIDEBOOKS

*Rocky Mountains of Canada–North,* Bole.

## INFORMATION & BOOKING

*Phone* (403) 673-2198
*Fax* (403) 673-2652
*E-mail* lomas@telusplanet.net
*Website* www.skigolden.com

# Chatter Creek Lodge

L ocated in a sector of the Rockies that gets the deep snow-packs more often associated with the Selkirks, this new lodge caters to cat-skiers and snowmobilers. Currently, the lodge is given over to sledders from mid-November to mid-December and then from April to the end of the snow season. In between, the lodge caters to cat-skiers, who have access to 130 km² (50 mi²) of long glacier runs and excellent tree skiing suitable for all levels of ability, but catering especially to the high-end skiers. The skiing was featured in a recent issue of *Powder* magazine, and the movie

*Slednecks 3* will contain extensive footage of the area. The lodge is a handcrafted log-beam structure with an outdoor hot tub and indoor showers and toilets. This currently is a winter-only operation.

## LOCATION
**General** In the Chatter Creek valley about 75 linear km (47 mi) NW of Golden BC.
**Specific** 82 N/13 Sullivan River NAD83 approximately 580455.
**Elevation** 1670 m (5500 ft).
**Elevation gain** N/a (heli-accessed).

## AMENITIES
**Heat** Woodstove (possibly local-generated electric by Winter 2001).
**Cooking** All meals provided.
**Lighting** Electric.
**Sleeping** Semi-private rooms with bedding provided.
**Capacity** 12 cat-skiers; up to 18 sledders.
**Features** Hot tub, showers, toilets and large common area.

## COST (as of Summer 2001)
**Cat-skiing** $375/person/night for 3-, 4- or 7-day tours ($30 off for a second person sharing a double bed). Rates include lodging, 3 meals, guided cat-skiing and full use of the facilities.
**Snowmobiling** $120/person/night ($20 off for a second person sharing a double bed). Rates include lodging, 3 meals and

trail grooming. Guides available at $150/day/group. Check the website for lodge-availability dates.

*Heli-flight* $165/person return from Donald.

## ACCESS

Guests are helicoptered in from Donald BC (near the spot where Hwy 1 crosses the Columbia River N of Golden). Sledders follow an 88 km (53 mi) track to the lodge.

## INFORMATION & BOOKING

Chatter Creek Mountain Lodges
Attention Merle McKnight
Box 333
Golden BC V0A 1H0
*Phone* (250) 344-7199
*Fax* (250) 344-2229
*E-mail* info@catskiingbc.com
*Websites* www.catskiingbc.com
*and* www.bcsnowmobiling.com

# Lawrence Grassi (Mt Clemenceau) Hut

If you want to experience the sensation of being in a Yukon/Alaska Icefield, a flight in to this hut will provide you it at a fraction of the air travel cost. There are some huge peaks here (including one of only four 12,000-footers in the Canadian Rockies) and vast expanses of glacier. The site of numerous Alpine Club summer camps, this hut offers extensive opportunities for mountaineering, and in winter the access to tours and turns is spectacular. It would be easy to spend a week based in this hut and not come close to exhausting all the possible outings. Just sitting at the hut taking in the view would be a memorable way to spend a day. Access is almost exclusively by helicopter or ski-plane.

## LOCATION

*General* At the W edge of the Clemenceau Icefield, about 45 km (28 mi) by air due E of Mica Dam BC.

*Specific* 83C/4 Clemenceau Icefield NAD27 320813.

*Other pertinent maps* 83 C/4 (for travel on the Icefield); 83 D/1 Wood Arm (for views W of the hut).

*Elevation* 2100 m (6900 ft).

*Elevation gain* N/a (flight-accessed).

## AMENITIES

*Heat* Oil (guests supply own fuel-oil). Check for details when making reservations.

*Cooking* Coleman stoves (guests supply own fuel); cookware and dishware provided.

*Lighting* Coleman lanterns.

*Sleeping* Two layers of bunks with foam pads.

*Capacity* 18 in summer, 16 in winter.

COST (as of Summer 2001) An Alpine Club Class B hut: $9 for members; $13 for nonmembers; $11 for group members.

## ACCESS

*Summer* Because of the distance from the helicopter base, the cost can be considerable. If you can coordinate your flights with those for other groups leaving and arriving, you can reduce the costs substantially. Even planning your arrival/departure to overlap with that of a group visiting Fairy Meadow Hut can keep costs down. Another option is to contact the main CMH office in Banff to see if it is operating a helicopter in the area and would be willing to ferry people into the hut. Nonaviation access is possible, as is described briefly in the Dougherty guidebook, but only by tough, multi-day treks from the Icefields Parkway or from BC logging roads. Only very experienced mountaineers should consider such access.

*Winter* Same. Ski-plane access (in winter only) is less expensive, although planes can land no closer than 4 km (2.5 mi) from the hut. Contact Alpenglow Aviation at 1-888-244-7117 or visit their website (www. rockiesairtours.com) for more information about their flights to this hut. Some parties have used Alpenglow for access and then skied out via the Columbia Icefields—a long and challenging multi-day trip that would require significant planning by very experienced ski-mountaineers.

*Helicopter reservations* Canadian Helicopters
*Phone* (250) 344-5311 or Alpine Helicopters
*Phone* (250) 344-7444

## GUIDEBOOKS

*Selected Alpine Climbs in the Canadian Rockies,* Dougherty.
*Rocky Mountains of Canada–North,* Boles.
*Summits and Icefields,* Scott.

## INFORMATION & BOOKING

The Alpine Club of Canada
Box 8040
Canmore AB T1W 2T8
*Phone* (403) 678-3200
*Fax* (403) 678-3224
*E-mail* alpclub@telusplanet.net
*Websites* www.alpineclubof canada.ca *and* www.elp.gov.bc. ca/bcparks/explore/parkpgs/ cummins.htm

# Lloyd MacKay (Mt Alberta) Hut

Renovated in 2000, this hut may be small but it is very functional and certainly is beautiful in the eyes of those who have come to climb Mt Alberta, perhaps the hardest peak to summit in the Canadian Rockies. Nearby are several other peaks popular with climbers (such as Mt Woolley and the North Twin Tower). Because of the rigorous access, few nonclimbers stay at the hut, although those who make it at least as far as the Woolley Shoulder will be treated to outstanding views of the mammoth faces on Alberta and the Twins. The hut stays virtually empty for nine months of the year, although a few hardy skiers report good slopes nearby. Note that access to the hut may entail glacier travel.

## LOCATION

*General* In Jasper National Park AB, 2 km (1.2 mi) E of Mt Alberta, just NE of the Columbia Icefields.

*Specific* 83 C/6 Sunwapta Peak NAD27 702927.

*Other pertinent maps* *Exploring the Columbia Icefields,* Toft.

*Elevation* 2720 m (8900 ft)

*Elevation change* 1320 m (4330 ft) gain to Woolley Shoulder, then 220 m (720 ft) down to the hut.

## AMENITIES

*Heat* None, but the small hut warms easily.

*Cooking* Coleman stove (guests supply own fuel); cookware and dishware provided.

*Lighting* Coleman lantern.

*Sleeping* Bunks with foam pads.

*Capacity* 6.

**COST** (as of Summer 2001)
An Alpine Club Class B hut: $9
for members; $13 for nonmem-
bers; $11 for group members.

## ACCESS

*Summer* From an unmarked parking area about 13 km (8 mi) N
of the Icefields Information
Centre, wade across the frigid
Sunwapta River and when
your calves stop screaming,
find the good trail along the S
bank of Woolley Creek. Follow
the trail (watching for cairns)
along the creek until reaching
the sandy flats at the base of
Mt Woolley. You now must
turn S in order to scramble up
onto the moraine which leads
to a long scree slope. Plod
your way up through the scree
to the obvious pass (called the
Woolley Shoulder), the view
from which is legendary. The
hut (now visible) can be
reached by dropping directly
onto the glacier or (preferably)
contouring around the slopes
on the SW face of Woolley
and then gaining the glacier.
Once on the glacier, traverse
the slopes as you curl to your
left, aiming for the hut on a
ridge extending N from Little
Alberta. The hut may be
reached without crossing the
glacier by dropping down an
extra 100 m (325 ft) from
Woolley Shoulder and con-
touring around under the glacier. Note that while the topo
map shows the hut surrounded by glacier, such is no longer
the case.

*Time* 4–7 hours.
*Winter* Same, but the avalanche
hazard can be considerable.

## GUIDEBOOKS

*Selected Alpine Climbs in the
Canadian Rockies,* Dougherty.
*Rocky Mountains of Canada–North,*
Boles.

## INFORMATION & BOOKING

The Alpine Club of Canada
Box 8040
Canmore AB T1W 2T8
*Phone* (403) 678-3200
*Fax* (403) 678-3224
*E-mail* alpclub@telusplanet.net
*Website* www.alpineclubof
canada.ca

# Fortress Lake Lodge

L ocated on the south shore of Fortress Lake in Hamber Provincial Park, this remote lodge (the only structure in the park) affords access to a seldom visited corner of BC. It is primarily a fishing lodge, although guests can hike up through old growth forests to pristine alpine meadows, and mountaineers can carry on up across glaciers and onto high peaks. Boats are provided for those angling for trophy-size trout. The facility consists of wood-heated cabins, along with two other structures that serve as bath-house (hot and cold running water for showers) and toilet-center (with flush toilets). Refrigeration is provided by ice blocks cut from the lake in winter. It can be accessed by hiking trail or by float plane. Open from June 1–Oct 15.

## LOCATION

**General** On the shore of Fortress Lake BC in Hamber Provincial Park, about 29 km (18 mi) SW of Sunwapta Falls on Hwy 93.

**Specific** 83 C/5 Fortress Lake NAD83 473019.

**Other pertinent maps** 83 C/12 Athabasca Falls; 83 C/4 Clemenceau Icefield (for travel in the high country); *Jasper & Maligne Lake*, Gem Trek.

**Elevation** 1340 m (4396 ft).

**Elevation gain from Sunwapta Falls bridge** 60 m (197 ft).

## AMENITIES

**Heat** Woodstoves.

**Cooking** All meals provided.

**Lighting** Propane lanterns.

**Sleeping** Wood-heated cabins.

**Capacity** 12.

**Features** Hot and cold running

water, flush toilets and boats (motors and gas included).

**COST** (as of Summer 2001) $220/person/night (minimum 2 nights); reduced rates for stays over 5 nights; nonfishing guests receive a 15 percent lower rate, and children under 13 are half price); special rates for groups of 10 or more.
***Round-trip air fare*** $345/person.

## ACCESS

***Summer*** The easiest and most scenic access is by float plane which flies over the vast reaches of the Columbia and Clemenceau Icefields. The hike in starts at the Sunwapta Falls footbridge, a well-marked attraction 54 km (34 mi) S of Jasper townsite. From the far side of the bridge, follow the trail upstream along the Athabasca and then the Chaba Rivers for 25 km (15.5 mi) to Fortress Pass at the E end of Fortress Lake. Because the route on to the lodge on the S shore of the lake entails tough bushwacking, guests can arrange for boat transport from the E end of the lake.

## GUIDEBOOKS
*The Canadian Rockies Trail Guide,* Patton and Robinson.
*Jasper–Robson: A Taste of Heaven,* Beers.

## INFORMATION & BOOKING
Fortress Lake Lodge
Attention Mike Furfaro
Box 28
Field BC V0A 1G0
***Phone*** (250) 343-6386
***Fax*** (250) 343-6367
***Website*** bcrockies.com/adventure/ fishing/fortress.html *and* rockiesairtours.com/fortress. htm

# Sydney Vallance (Fryatt) Hut

Set in a lovely basin ringed by high peaks, this hut, like a well-kept secret, is visited far less frequently than its attractions warrant. In the past, the hut had been primarily used by alpinists intent on tackling Mt Fryatt and other big peaks nearby, but the valley offers much that would appeal to hikers and skiers as well. There is lots to explore on foot beyond the hut, and the slopes close by provide some good turns when the conditions are right. The hut was refurbished in the late 1990s, and now is a very comfortable and spacious cabin—a classic mountain hideaway.

## LOCATION

**General** In the Fryatt Creek Valley in Jasper National Park, approximately 40 km (25 mi) SSW of Jasper AB.

**Specific** 83C/12 Athabasca Falls NAD83 403174 (note that cabin site on map is incorrect).

**Other pertinent maps** 83C/5 Fortress Lake; *Jasper & Maligne Lake*, Gem Trek.

**Elevation** 1980 m (6495 ft).

**Elevation gain from parking lot** 765 m (2510 ft).

## AMENITIES

**Heat** Woodstove.

**Cooking** Coleman stoves (guests supply own fuel); cookware and dishware provided.

**Lighting** Coleman lanterns.

**Sleeping** 2-layer bunks with foam pads.

**Capacity** 12.

## COST (as of Summer 2001)

An Alpine Club Class A hut: $15 for members; $22 for nonmembers; $17 for group members.

## ACCESS

**Summer** From the Athabasca Falls turn-off located 31 km (19 mi) S of Jasper, take Hwy 93A for about 1 km (0.5 mi), turn left onto the Geraldine Fire Road, and follow it for 2 km (1.2 mi) to the well-marked Fryatt Valley parking lot. The first 11 km (7 mi) to the Lower Fryatt campground follows a fire road (which may be mountain-biked to save time). From here, follow the trail on the E side of the creek and, after 4.5 km (2.8 mi), the W side until reaching the Headwall campground. Take a break before grunting up the steep trail to the top of the headwall, after which the hut is only a short crawl away.

**Time** 6–9 hours (perhaps an hour less if the fire road is biked).

**Note** You can cut out 7 km (4.5 mi) of the fire road by boating across the Athabasca River. Fording the river on foot is not recommended, as the massive Athabasca Falls are only a short distance downstream.

**Winter** Same.

**Time** Allow a full day, but even this may not be enough if you have to trailbreak all the way. About 2 hours can be saved if the Athabasca River is sufficiently well frozen, usually by mid-December. Cross well upstream of the Falls, about 7.5 km (4.5 mi) S along the Parkway from the Athabasca Falls turn-off and then pick up the fire road. Be prudent: the ice on this turbulent river may be thin.

## GUIDEBOOKS

*The Canadian Rockies Trail Guide,* Patton and Robinson.

*Ski Trails in the Canadian Rockies,* Scott.

*Jasper–Robson: A Taste of Heaven,* Beers.

*Selected Alpine Climbs in the Canadian Rockies,* Dougherty.

*Rocky Mountains of Canada–North,* Boles.

## INFORMATION & BOOKING

The Alpine Club of Canada
 Box 8040
Canmore AB T1W 2T8
**Phone** (403) 678-3200
**Fax** (403) 678-3224
**E-mail** alpclub@telusplanet.net
**Website** www.alpineclubof canada.ca

# Wates–Gibson Hut

Another of the Alpine Club's old but nicely refurbished log cabins, this hut is situated on the shores of Outpost Lake and located not far from the post-card-perfect Tonquin Valley and Amethyst Lakes. The cabin, reached by a long trek, provides a snug base for climbing on the nearby Ramparts or for lovely day-hiking to various lakes and passes. Some hikers use the hut for an overnight stay on their traverse from Edith Cavell hostel to the Marmot Ski Hill area. Although a long slog in during winter (usually entailing an overnight stay at the Edith Cavell hostel), there are some good slopes for turns not far away, and the winter scenery is spectacular.

## LOCATION

***General*** About 27 km (17 mi) SW of the townsite of Jasper AB on Outpost Lake in the Tonquin Valley in Jasper National Park.

***Specific*** 83D/9 Amethyst Lakes NAD83 152353.

***Other pertinent maps*** 83 D/16 Jasper (for Maccarib Pass access); *Jasper & Maligne Lake,* Gem Trek.

***Elevation*** 1900 m (6235 ft).

***Elevation gain from Edith Cavell Hostel*** 168 m (550 ft).

***Elevation gain from Marmot Basin Road*** 732 m (2400 ft) to Maccarib Pass, down 396 m (1300 ft) to Chrome Lake and then 61 m (200 ft) up to the hut.

## AMENITIES

***Heat*** Woodstove.

***Cooking*** Coleman stoves (guests supply own fuel); cookware and dishware provided.

**Lighting** Coleman lanterns.
**Sleeping** Loft with foam pads above common area.
**Capacity** 30 in summer, 24 in winter.

COST (as of Summer 2001)
An Alpine Club Class A hut: $15 for members; $22 for nonmembers; $17 for group members.

## ACCESS

**Summer Option 1** The faster (although less scenic) trail leaves from the Edith Cavell Hostel at the end of the 12-km (7.5-mi) Edith Cavell Road that branches off Hwy 93A S of Jasper. Follow the trail along the Astoria River for just over 8 km (5 mi) to a well-marked junction where you take the left fork which crosses the river on a log bridge. It is another 10 km (6 mi) or so up to the hut on the N shore of Outpost Lake. In this latter section, the trail is well defined but tough going in wet weather.
**Time** 4.5–6 hours
**Summer Option 2** The other route, about 14 km (9 mi) longer, leaves from the Portal Creek parking lot, located 6.5 km (4 mi) up the Marmot Basin Ski Hill Road. Walk up the good trail for 12 km (7.5 mi) to Maccarib Pass and then descend to Amethyst Lake, with great views of the aptly named Ramparts. Carry on along the E side of the lake,

following the signs to Surprise Point campground and then on to Chrome Lake. Here you turn right, following Penstock Creek uphill to the hut on Outpost Lake.
**Time** 7–11 hours
**Summer Option 3** Those wishing a less travelled and more rigorous alpine access may follow a route past Buttress and Beryl lakes and on through 3 passes before dropping down into the Eremite Creek drainage that leads to the hut. The route begins by picking up the Verdant Pass trail about 4 km (2.5 mi) along the trail from the Cavell hostel, about 500 m (1600 ft) before the first crossing of the Astoria River). After about 3 km (2 mi), a faint trail leads off from Verdant Creek and heads SW, passing along the E side of Buttress Lake (some bushwacking involved) and then the W side of Beryl Lake before ascending to Campus Pass. To reach the Eremite Valley from here, you must map-navigate your way through cols at either GR 213309 or 220305 and then head generally W toward a col at GR 183315 (NAD27). From here the route down to Arrowhead Lake is obvious, and there is a thin trail along the E side of Eremite Creek to Chrome Lake, at which point the main trail to the hut can be picked up. The total distance from the Cavell parking

lot is about 24 km (15 mi), much of which is on rugged ground and requires good route-finding skills. This would be a very full day's challenge for a highly fit and experienced hiker.

**Note** The Park Information Office in Jasper townsite can provide more details about the route and a small map.

**Winter** Essentially the same, although if going along the Astoria Valley, you must ski up the 12 km (7.5 mi) road to the hostel, thus making a 2-day trip in almost mandatory. The locked hostel must be reserved. It contains the same amenities as the hut. Where the summer trail crosses the river, stay instead on the N-side trail or on the river itself up to Chrome Lake. The Maccarib Pass route is the same as in summer, but you can save time by cutting across Amethyst Lake to Surprise Point.

**Time** Allow 4–7 hours to the hostel, depending on track conditions, and another full day to the hut (but even very strong groups have had to bivy when the trail-breaking was rigorous).

**Winter via Maccarib Pass** A full day, but be prepared to bivy unless you know there is a good track in.

## GUIDEBOOKS

*The Canadian Rockies Trail Guide,* Patton and Robinson.

*Ski Trails in the Canadian Rockies,* Scott.

*Jasper–Robson: A Taste of Heaven,* Beers.

*Selected Alpine Climbs in the Canadian Rockies,* Dougherty.

*Rocky Mountains of Canada–North,* Boles.

## INFORMATION & BOOKING

The Alpine Club of Canada
Box 8040
Canmore AB T1W 2T8
*Phone* (403) 678-3200
*Fax* (403) 678-3224
*E-mail* alpclub@telusplanet.net
*Website* www.alpineclubof
   canada.ca
Edith Cavell Hostel Reservations
*Phone* 1-877-852-0781
*Fax* (780) 852-5560
*Website* www.hostellingintl.ca/
   Alberta/Hostels/EdithCavell.
   html

# Tonquin Valley Adventures Lodge

Appealing to hikers and skiers and even mountaineers, this historic lodge is set atop a knoll overlooking Amethyst Lakes and the towering Rampart Mountains. Having attracted the likes of Bing Crosby, Ansel Adams and the Group of Seven, this famous valley is one of the alpine highlights of Jasper National Park. Guests here can explore the terrain by foot, ski, horseback or boat—with an accredited guide, if desired. Guests enjoy private heated cabins and home-cooked meals in the central chalet. Boats for fishing are available free of charge.

## LOCATION

**General** In the Tonquin Valley of Jasper National Park, about 17 km (11 mi) SW of the townsite of Jasper AB.

**Specific** 83D/9 Amethyst Lakes NAD83 148391.

**Other pertinent maps** 83 D/16 Jasper (for Macarib Pass access); *Jasper & Maligne Lake,* Gem Trek.

**Elevation** 1980 m (6500 ft).

**Elevation gain from Mt Edith Cavell parking lot** 260 m (855 ft).

## AMENITIES

**Heat** Woodstoves and fireplaces.

**Cooking** All meals provided July–Sept; guests self-cater Oct–April.

**Lighting** Propane.

**Sleeping** Separate cabins with log beds and down duvets.

**Capacity** 20.

**Features** Hiking and fishing guides available (at extra cost), free use of boats, horse-packing of hikers/mountaineers' gear possible.

**COST** (as of Summer 2001)

**July–Sept** Catered, self-guided hiking trips start at $125/person/night.

**Oct–Apr** Self-catered trips are $35/person/night (minimum 4/cabin) or $50/person/night (minimum 2/cabin).

## ACCESS

**Summer** Check the access description for Wates–Gibson Hut for directions in via the two main routes. Note that when taking the Astoria River trail you stay on the N side of the river all the way into Amethyst Lake and the lodge.

**Time** 4–6 hours.

**Winter** Essentially the same as for summer, but because the 12 km (7.5 mi) road to the Edith Cavell hostel is not plowed, it must be skied. Most guests plan for a 2-day trip in, spending one night at the hostel, which must be booked in advance. Allow 3–5 hours to the hostel, depending on track conditions, and another full day to the lodge, although the trail in along the valley floor is often well packed by snowmobile and thus can make for efficient travel. The other route through Macarib Pass is 25 km (15 mi) long, and while it is 8 km (5 mi) shorter than the Astoria Valley route, it entails greater elevation gain and is recommended for skiers of at least intermediate ability and conditioning. On this route, plan on taking 6–8 hours, but possibly longer if travelling right after a heavy snowfall.

## GUIDEBOOKS

*The Canadian Rockies Trail Guide,* Patton and Robinson.

*Jasper–Robson: A Taste of Heaven,* Beers.

*Ski Trails in the Canadian Rockies,* Scott.

*Selected Alpine Climbs,* Dougherty.

## INFORMATION & BOOKING

Tonquin Valley Adventures
Attention Mike Day
Box 1795
Jasper AB T0E 1E0
**Phone** (780) 852-1188
**Fax** (780) 852-1155
**E-mail** info@tonquinadventures.com
**Website** www.tonquinadventures.com/lodge.html
**Mt Edith Cavell Hostel booking**
**Phone** (780) 439-3139
**Fax** (780) 433-7781

# Tonquin Valley Backcountry Lodge

Situated on the shores of Amethyst Lake in Jasper National Park, this remote lodge provides a lovely base from which to explore one of the most scenic sectors of the Rockies. Backed by the towering heights of the Ramparts, the Tonquin Valley has long been a destination for climbers, hikers and skiers. Guests stay in individual chalets and eat gourmet meals in the main lodge. Horseback travel into and around the lodge is available. Although a long ski in, there are great opportunities for day-touring based out of the lodge. Rock climbs on the Ramparts are some of the most popular in Jasper Park.

## LOCATION

**General** At the N end of Amethyst Lake in the Tonquin Valley of Jasper National Park, about 17 km (11 mi) SW of the townsite of Jasper AB.

**Specific** 83 D/9 Amethyst Lakes NAD83 130415.

**Other pertinent maps** *Jasper & Maligne Lake*, Gem Trek.

**Elevation** 1980 m (6500 ft).

**Elevation gain from Portal Creek parking lot** 731 m (2400 ft) to Macarib Pass, then 230 m (750 ft) descent to the lodge.

## AMENITIES

**Heat** Woodstoves.
**Cooking** All meals provided.
**Lighting** Oil lanterns.
**Sleeping** Individual chalets for 1–6 people; bedding provided.
**Capacity** 18.
**Features** Canoes and rowboats, great fishing in 2 lakes.

## COST (as of Summer 2001)

**Summer 5-day horse trip** $700/person.

**Summer hikers** $135/person/ night; includes guide, accommodation, meals, boat use and horse rides.

**Winter** $100/person/night.

## ACCESS

**Summer** Those coming in by horseback will be given full instructions upon registering. For those hiking in, see the description of the Macarib Pass route into Wates–Gibson Hut. It is 23 km (14.4 mi) from the trailhead to the lodge on the N end of Amethyst Lake.

**Time** 7–10 hours.

**Winter** Same.

## GUIDEBOOKS

*The Canadian Rockies Trail Guide,* Patton and Robinson.

*Jasper–Robson: A Taste of Heaven,* Beers

*Ski Trails in the Canadian Rockies,* Scott.

*Selected Alpine Climbs,* Dougherty.

## INFORMATION & BOOKING

Tonquin Valley Backcountry Lodge

Box 550

Jasper AB T0E 1E0

**Phone** (780) 852-3909

**Fax** (780) 852-3763

**E-mail** info@tonquinvalley.com

**Website** www.tonquinvalley.com

# Shangri-La Cabin

A beautiful cabin now operated by the Maligne Lake Ski Club, this winter-use-only facility lies close to the popular Skyline Trail. Located near the center of the Snowbowl Basin between Big and Little Shovel Passes, it provides a cozy base at treeline for ski tours into the nearby alpine meadows. Also, there are extensive opportunities for turns on the slopes that skirt the 7 km (4 mi) length of the basin. The cabin usually is available from early December to mid-April, but this can vary substantially depending on the conditions of the snowpack.

## LOCATION

**General** Just E of the Skyline Trail near the Snowbowl Campground site in Jasper National Park AB.

**Specific** 83 C/13 Medicine Lake NAD83 479448.

**Other pertinent maps** *Jasper & Maligne Lake*, Gem Trek; see *Summits & Icefields* for a small map of the Jeffrey Creek winter access route.

**Elevation** 2000 m (6550 ft).

**Elevation gain from Maligne Lake parking area** 320 m (1050 ft).

## AMENITIES

**Heat** Woodstove (wood provided) and propane heater.

**Cooking** Propane.

**Lighting** Coal-oil lanterns.

**Sleeping** Bunks with foam pads and blankets.

**Capacity** 6.

## COST (as of Summer 2001)

$180/night for the entire cabin (maximum stay of 3 nights).

## ACCESS

**Via Skyline Trail** From the Maligne Lake parking lot just beyond the bridge that crosses the outflow from the lake, find the well-marked start to the Skyline Trail. Follow this broad and clear trail to Little Shovel Pass and down the other side to the Snowbird campground. Proceed through the campground and follow the creek flowing NE. The cabin will appear on the edge of a meadow within 5–10 minutes.

**Via Jeffrey Creek** From Jasper, follow the paved road toward Maligne Lake. About 8 km (5 mi) beyond the SE end of Medicine Lake and just before a bridge crossing the Maligne River, park in the little lot on the left side of the road. Carry your skis across the bridge and then start heading downstream through the trees on a blaze-marked trail that soon angles up and then levels off. After a few kilometers, the trail becomes steep, goes through a shallow notch and then drops into the Jeffrey Creek drainage which it follows for 4–5 km (2.5–3 mi) before following a tributary S to the cabin. Note that the general route direction is fairly obvious although it may be easy to lose the trail at times. See the Scott guidebook below for detailed descriptions and a map.

## GUIDEBOOKS

*Summits & Icefields,* Scott.
*Ski Trails in the Canadian Rockies,* Scott.

## INFORMATION & BOOKING

Maligne Lake Ski Club
Attention Bette Weir
**Phone** (780) 852-3665
**Reservations** Start Nov 1 (Oct 1 for club members).

# Shovel Pass Lodge

Set in a treeline meadow near one of the passes on Jasper's busy Skyline Trail, these recently refurbished log chalets cater to both hikers and horse-riders who wish to explore the high country near the Endless Chain ridge. It's the flower-rich meadows and the easily accessed ridge walks that cause the Skyline Trail campsites to be booked solid months in advance. Shovel Pass features separate cabins for guests and a common lodge for meals and lounging. Hikers can have all their personal gear packed in by horses. The lodge is open in summer only.

## LOCATION

*General* NW of Big Shovel Pass on the Skyline Trail, about 18 km (11 mi) SE of the townsite of Jasper AB.

*Specific* 83 C/13 Medicine Lake NAD83 471488.

*Other pertinent maps* Jasper & Maligne Lake, Gem Trek.

*Elevation* 2250 m (7380 ft).

*Elevation gain from Icefields Parkway* 1150 m (3770 ft).

## AMENITIES

*Heat* Woodstove in dining lounge, propane furnaces in dorm cabins.

*Cooking* All meals provided.

*Lighting* Wall-mounted propane lights.

*Sleeping* Private and heated cabins; bedding provided.

*Capacity* 20.

*Features* Luxury accommodation, guides and multi-day wilderness trips (either on horseback or horse-assisted hiking) available.

**COST** (as of Summer 2001)

*Hikers* $130/person/night; includes freighting of packs, accommodation and 3 meals.

*Horseback Trips* 3-day $465/person; 4-day $595/person (includes horse, guide, accommodations and 3 meals daily).

*Freighting* Hikers of the Skyline Trail other than guests may have gear carried up by pack horse; rates available on request.

**ACCESS**

Full details and maps provided upon registration. Most guests ride horses up the drainage that flows W toward Wabasso Lake from Big Shovel Pass; hikers virtually never use this route (although it can be used as a "quick-out" in the event of bad weather up high). Most guests who choose to hike in follow the Skyline Trail starting at the Maligne Lake trailhead, a distance of 20.5 km (13 mi) that typically takes 6–7 hours.

**GUIDEBOOKS**

*Canadian Rockies Trail Guide,* Patton and Robinson.

**INFORMATION & BOOKING**

*Summer*

Skyline Trail Rides

Box 207

Jasper AB T0E 1E0

*Winter*

Skyline Trail Rides

Box 26

Brule AB T0E 0C0

*Phone* 1-888-852-7787

*Fax* (780) 852-4215

*E-mail* skyline@agt.net

*Website* www.skylinetrail.com

# Mt Colin Centennial Hut

*Specific* 83C/13 Medicine Lake NAD83 334723.

*Other pertinent maps* 83 D/16 Jasper (for much of the approach); 83 E/1 Snaring River (if starting at the N end of Overlander Trail); *Jasper & Maligne Lake,* Gem Trek.

*Elevation* 2000 m (6560 ft).

*Elevation gain from 6th Bridge picnic area* 985 m (3230 ft).

## AMENITIES

*Heat* None, but the hut is seldom used in cold weather.

*Cooking* Coleman stove (guests supply own fuel); cookware and dishware provided.

*Lighting* Coleman lantern.

*Sleeping* Two layers of bunks with foam pads.

*Capacity* 6.

## COST (as of Summer 2001)

An Alpine Club Class B hut: $9 for members; $13 for nonmembers; $11 for group members.

## ACCESS

*Summer* From the 6th Bridge picnic area, 7 km (4.5 mi) N of Jasper off the Maligne Lake Road, take the Overlander Historic Trail to Garonne Flats, but check with park wardens to see if this 6 km (3.8 mi) section may still be biked. Take any of several thin trails to the obvious gorge whose creek drains into the flats, and then scramble up high onto the

Constructed primarily to facilitate climbs on the popular Mts Colin and CR6, this small hut would also appeal to hikers and scramblers wishing to spend a full day exploring the valley. It has been recently refurbished and comfortably sleeps 6 people. Note that the limited skiing or ice-climbing options in the valley mean that very few people travel to the hut in winter.

## LOCATION

*General* On the SW side of Mount Colin, 14 km (9 mi) NNE of the townsite of Jasper AB in Jasper National Park.

steep slopes on the N side of the creek. Side-hill gouge your way parallel to the gorge across several small drainages until you can easily drop down to the creek-side, from where a fairly well-cairned trail leads to the hut.

*Time* 4.5–6 hours.

*Note* A longer and more rigorous route follows the Overlander Historic Trail from much farther N. Also, the Garonne Flats can be accessed with a bit of bushwacking by those who boat across the Athabasca River near the local airfield.

*Winter* Same, but the hut is seldom visited in this season.

### GUIDEBOOKS

*Selected Alpine Climbs in the Canadian Rockies,* Dougherty.

*Rocky Mountains of Canada–North,* Boles.

### INFORMATION & BOOKING

The Alpine Club of Canada
Box 8040
Canmore AB T1W 2T8
*Phone* (403) 678-3200
*Fax* (403) 678-3224
*E-mail* alpclub@telusplanet.net
*Website* www.alpineclubof canada.ca

# Dave Henry Lodge

Set among subalpine meadows and lakes near the border of Mt Robson Park, this comfortable log lodge serves as a great base for hiking, riding, ski-touring or fishing. With striking views of the nearby peaks (including Mt Robson) and lots of trails through the wildflower-rich meadows, this is a true alpine experience. The skiing opportunities are extensive, with a wide variety of terrain for all levels of skiers. The lodge is fully appointed, and you have the option of being entirely self-reliant throughout your trip or taking advantage of various options for catering and access. Another option is the 15 km (9 mi) trek over to the Swift Creek cabins.

## LOCATION

*General* Near Dave Henry Lake on the Mt Robson Park border, about 20 km (12 mi) due E of Valemount BC.

*Specific* 83 D/15 Lucerne NAD83 686588.

*Other pertinent maps* 83 D/14 Valemount (for travel to Swift Creek Cabins).

*Elevation* 1829 m (5925 ft).

*Elevation gain from Kinbasket Lake* 1158 m (3800 ft).

## AMENITIES

*Heat* Woodstove.

*Cooking* Propane stove/oven; cookware and dishware provided.

*Lighting* Propane (on main floor only).

*Sleeping* On the upper level is a large semi-divided room with 2 double beds on one side and a sleeping platform and futon on the other; guests supply own sleeping bags.

**Capacity** 10.

**Features** Sauna, large windows, big dining/common area, emergency radio.

## COST (as of Summer 2001)

**Self-catered & self-guided hikers** $41/person/night (in groups of at least 6).

**Other prices for hikers** From $125/person/night for a catered, unguided stay with no heli-flights to $930/person for a fully guided and catered 6-day hut-to-hut package that includes a heli-flight in.

**Guided & catered horseback trips to Dave Henry Lodge** From $620/person for a 4-day stay to $880/person for a 6-day stay.

**Ski trips** From $41/person/night (not including heli costs) for uncatered and unguided groups to $1260/person for a fully guided and catered week-long package that includes return heli fare.

## ACCESS

**Summer** Follow the East Canoe Forest Service Road due S from Valemount for 24 km (15 mi) to the trailhead. A high-clear-ance 4x4 may be needed, but the lodge owners may be able to shuttle you to the trailhead in theirs. The hike in is about 14 km (8 mi) and takes about 4 hours. Clear directions are provided upon registration. Alternatively, a 12-minute heli-flight from Valemount is possible at extra cost.

**Winter** Most guests helicopter in. Guests may then choose to reduce costs by skiing out along a route out which involves a 22 km (15 mi) trek down to the Forest Service road and then a further 14 km (8 mi) along the road to Valemount.

## GUIDEBOOKS

*Summits & Icefields,* Scott.

## INFORMATION & BOOKING

Headwaters Outfitting
Attention Liz Norwell or Brian McKirdy
Box 818
Valemount BC V0E 2Z0
**Phone & Fax** (250) 566-4718
**E-mail** headwaters@davehenry.com
**Website** www.davehenry.com

# Swift Creek Cabins

Bordering Mt Robson Park, these cabins in a treed basin provide easy access to high ridges whose panoramic views include Mt Robson, the highest peak in the Canadian Rockies. For the ambitious, a stay here can be combined with a 15 km (9 mi) ski or hike to Dave Henry Lodge. The skiing on the upper slopes is superb, although more challenging than at the Dave Henry Creek area. The 2 cabins (one for cooking/dining, the other a dorm) are steel-sided frame structures heated by woodstoves.

## LOCATION

*General* Near the headwaters of Swift Creek close to the border of Mt Robson Park, about 15 km (9 mi) NE of Valemount BC.

*Specific* 83 D/14 Valemount NAD27 608638.

*Other pertinent maps* 83 D/15 Lucerne (for travel to Dave Henry Lodge).

*Elevation* 1920 m (6300 ft).

## AMENITIES

*Heat* Woodstove.

*Cooking* Propane stove; cookware and dishware provided.

*Lighting* Propane in cooking cabin; solar in dorm cabin.

*Sleeping* Bunks with foam pads (guests supply own sleeping bags).

*Capacity* 8.

## COST (as of Summer 2001)

*Self-catered & self-guided hikers* $41/person/night (in groups of at least 6).

*Other prices for hikers* A fully guided and catered 6-day hut-to-hut package that includes a heli-flight in costs $930/person. Custom catered packages can be arranged.

*Ski trips* From $41/person/night (not counting heli costs) for uncatered and unguided groups to $1075/person for a fully guided and catered week-long package that includes return heli fare.

## ACCESS
Access from Valemount is by helicopter only. The overland trip from Dave Henry Lodge usually involves a 7-plus-hour ski or hike.

## GUIDEBOOKS
*Summits & Icefields,* Scott.

## INFORMATION & BOOKING
Headwaters Outfitting
Attention Liz Norwell or Brian
    McKirdy
Box 818
Valemount BC V0E 2Z0
*Phone & Fax* (250) 566-4718
*E-mail* headwaters@davehenry.
    com
*Website* www.davehenry.com

# Ralph Forster Hut

Used almost exclusively by those climbing Mt Robson from the south, this durable little hut is set on a ledge below the promontory known as Little Robson. Of course, any non-climbers wanting to slog up a vertical mile will be rewarded with great views. The trail is steep and entails some scrambling on rock and up carved-log ladders, but the glacier travel does not begin until above the hut. The open-air toilet nearby affords a grand seat from which to view the world. Be prepared for high winds and the notorious Robson bad weather.

## LOCATION
**General** On a ridge about 1460 m (4800 ft) below the summit of Mt Robson and 1520 m (5000 ft) above Kinney Lake in Mt Robson Provincial Park BC.

**Specific** 83 E/3 Mt Robson NAD27 559846.

**Other pertinent maps** *Mt Robson Provincial Park Map;* the Dougherty book provides a very detailed map of the route from Kinney Lake to the hut.

**Elevation** 2522 m (8300 ft).

**Elevation gain from parking lot** About 1670 m (5500 ft).

## AMENITIES
**Heat** None.

**Cooking** Coleman stove; no cookware or dishware provided.

**Lighting** Coleman lantern.

**Sleeping** Two layers of bunks with foam pads.

**Capacity** 8.

## COST (as of Summer 2001)
Free; no reservations.

## ACCESS
**Summer** Turn N off Hwy 16 at the confluence of the Robson and Fraser Rivers in Mt Robson Provincial Park and drive about 2 km (1.2 mi) to the parking lot (all well signposted). From there, follow the broad, well-marked trail over the Robson River and on to Kinney Lake. The trail to the

hut branches to the right here. Since most users of this hut will be carrying on to climb Robson and will no doubt have a climbing guidebook that details the route from Kinney Lake, no attempt will be made to reproduce it here.

*Time* 10–14 hours, perhaps longer in bad weather.

*Winter* Same, but because of the steepness of the access, this hut is seldom visited in winter.

## GUIDEBOOKS
*Selected Alpine Climbs,* Dougherty.

## INFORMATION & BOOKING
No reservations accepted; for information and map contact:
Park Visitor Centre
Box 579
Valemount BC V0E 1Z0
*Phone* (250) 566-4325
*Fax* (250) 566-9777
*Website* www.elp.gov.bc.ca/
bcparks/explore/parkpgs/mtro
bson.htm

# Berg Lake Shelter

This is a winter shelter only (in summer you must tent in a reserved spot at the nearby campground). Not designed for overnight use, this cabin contains only picnic tables and a woodstove, although it is a welcome refuge for those few who ski into here, usually on their way around to the east side of Mt Robson or to Mt Resplendent.

## LOCATION
**General** On the shore of Berg Lake in Mt Robson Provincial Park BC.
**Specific** 83E/3 Mount Robson NAD83 5**59**5**85 891**6**66.
**Other pertinent maps** *Mount Robson Provincial Park Map.*
**Elevation** 1640 m (5380 ft).
**Elevation gain from parking lot** 786 m (2580 ft).

## AMENITIES
**Heat** Woodstove.
**Cooking** Woodstove.
**Lighting** None.
**Sleeping** Picnic tables.
**Capacity** 6+.

## COST (as of Summer 2001)
Free; no reservations.

## ACCESS
Turn N off Hwy 16 at the confluence of the Robson and Fraser Rivers in Mt Robson Provincial Park and drive about 2 km (1.2 mi) to the parking lot (all well signposted). From there, follow the broad, well-marked trail over the Robson River and on past Kinney Lake to a campground at about the 7.5-km (4.5-mi) mark, after which the trail turns quite steeply uphill for the 610 m (2000 ft) climb to Berg Lake; this

hike through the Valley of 1000 Falls is perhaps the most spectacular walk in the Rockies. The shelter is at the NW corner of the lake, a total of about 17 km (11 mi) from the parking lot. In summer, a fit hiker can do the trip in a day. In winter, deep snow could make it impossible to reach the shelter in a day.

## GUIDEBOOKS

*Canadian Rockies Trail Guide,* Patton and Robinson.
*Selected Alpine Climbs,* Dougherty.
*Summits & Icefields,* Scott.
*Jasper–Robson: A Taste of Heaven,* Beers.

*Ski Trails in the Canadian Rockies,* Scott.

## INFORMATION

Park Visitor Centre
Box 579
Valemount BC V0E 1Z0
*Phone* (250) 566-4325
*Fax* (250) 566-9777
*Website* www.elp.gov.bc.ca/
bcparks/explore/parkpgs/
mtrobson.htm

# West Range Lodge

This lodge is located in the new Rock Lake Solomon Creek Wildland Provincial Park, which borders Jasper National Park. It's open to guided groups of hikers, skiers or horseback riders following a 30 km (19 mi) traverse through rolling, subalpine terrain on the Mountain Shadow Trail. This trail is ideal for the novice backcountry enthusiast. In the summer, there is the opportunity for hiking up onto the high ridges or for pursuing on horseback a herd of free-range cattle. In winter, the ski traverse on gentle terrain is well suited for beginning to intermediate skiers. The lodge features a central chalet and separate heated cabins, as well as all meals and gear transport.

## LOCATION
***General*** In the Solomon Creek Valley E of Jasper National Park, about 28 km NW of Hinton AB.
***Specific*** 83 E/8 Rock Lake NAD83 107266.
***Elevation*** 1380 m (4526 ft).
***Elevation gain from northern trail terminus*** 53 m (176 ft).

## AMENITIES
***Heat*** Propane.
***Cooking*** All meals provided.
***Lighting*** Propane.
***Sleeping*** Private heated cabins; linen provided.
***Capacity*** 12.
***Features*** Good fishing nearby.

## COST (as of Summer 2001)
***Horseback trips*** From $125–$140/person/day (trips from 1–5 days long).
***Guided 4-day trip hiking trips*** $460/person for a group of 2 (reduced rates for larger groups).
***Guided 4-day ski trips*** $512/person.

## ACCESS

**Summer** Directions by road to the Black Cat Guest Ranch outside Hinton are provided upon registration. All transportation from there to the trailhead is provided.

**Winter** Same.

## GUIDEBOOKS

*Trail Riding in Rocky Mountain Country,* Llewellyn.

## INFORMATION & BOOKING

Horseback Adventures

Attention Shawn Vinson

**Phone** (780) 865-4777

**Fax** (780) 865-5433

**E-mail** horsebac@telusplanet.net

**Website** www.horseback adventuresltd.com

# Kakwa & Jarvis Lakes Cabins

These cabins are the summer headquarters for the Kakwa Park wardens but are open to the public in winter. This remote park straddles the Continental Divide and has lots of alpine terrain that is popular with snowmobilers and, to a lesser extent, ski-tourers. There are few developed trails in the area, but experienced backcountry travelers will enjoy the high meadows with their proximity to glaciated peaks such as Mt Sir Alexander. The road in to the cabins is not plowed in winter, so a long snowmobile trip is required. The cabins themselves are rustic but comfortable. Note that the wardens have year-round priority and may require anyone staying in the cabins to vacate them. Also, since no booking is possible, visitors should be prepared to camp out if the cabins are full.

## LOCATION

**General** In Kakwa Provincial Park, about 180 linear km (113 mi) E of Prince George BC.

**Specific** 93 H/16 Mt Sir Alexander NAD27 approximately 852868 (for Kakwa Lake Cabins).

**Other pertinent maps** 93 I/1 Jarvis Lakes (for Jarvis Lakes Cabin).

**Elevation at Kakwa Lake** 1483 m (4880 ft).

**Elevation gain from Buchanan Creek trailhead** 500 m (1650 ft) to McGregor Pass, then 50 m (170 ft) descent to Kakwa Lake.

## AMENITIES

**Heat** Woodstoves in all cabins.

**Cooking** No facilities other than woodstove.

**Lighting** None.

**Sleeping** Bunks, no foam pads provided.

**Capacity at Kakwa Lake** Two dorm cabins accommodating 4 and 6 (plus room for 3–4 on floor of cooking cabin).

**Capacity at Jarvis Lake** One cabin with room for 10–12.

**COST** (as of November 2000) Free; no reservations.

### ACCESS

Turn off Hwy 16 onto the Walker Creek Forest Road about 70 km (44 mi) W of McBride, between the towns of Dome Creek and Crescent Spur. The route in follows the road and then the broad trail through McGregor Pass to Kakwa Lake. The total distance is about 103 km (64 mi), although the first 6 km may be plowed.

### INFORMATION

Prince George District Parks Office
Box 2045
Prince George BC V2N 2J6
**Phone** (250) 565-6759
**Fax** (250) 565-6940
**Website** www.elp.gov.bc.ca/bcparks/explore/pgdis.htm

# North Rockies Ski Tours Lodge

Located in an alpine bowl in the Dezaiko Range, this remote lodge affords access to alpine terrain in a region of the Rockies that is seldom visited. With 60 km² (23 mi²) of bowls, ridges and gladed slopes nearby, there is ample opportunity for tours and turns in winter, as well as high-alpine hiking in summer. Accessible only by helicopter, the lodge offers various packages, all inclusive of guiding and meals. The operators plan to offer summer hiking packages starting in the summer of 2001—contact them for details.

## LOCATION

**General** In the Dezaiko Range 100 km (62 mi) E of Prince George BC.

**Specific** 93 I/3 Gleason Creek NAD27 approximately 210080.

**Elevation** 1500 m (4900 ft).
**Elevation gain** N/a (heli-accessed).

## AMENITIES

**Heat** Woodstove.
**Cooking** All meals provided.
**Lighting** Propane.
**Sleeping** Open loft of the lodge; foam pads and sleeping bags provided.
**Capacity** 8–10.
**Features** Sauna, lots of wildlife nearby.

## COST (as of Summer 2001)

5 days $800/person; 7 days $975/person.

## ACCESS

All transportation from Prince George (including ground transport and heli-flight) is included in the package cost.

## GUIDEBOOKS

*Summits & Icefields*, Scott.

## INFORMATION & BOOKING

North Rockies Ski Tours
Attention Craig Evanoff
***Phone & Fax*** (250) 962-5272
***E-mail*** northrockies@north
    rockies.bc.ca
***Website*** www.northrockies.bc.ca

*Nearing Big Shovel Pass on the Skyline Trail*

*Approaching the Notch on the Skyline Trail*

# South Columbias

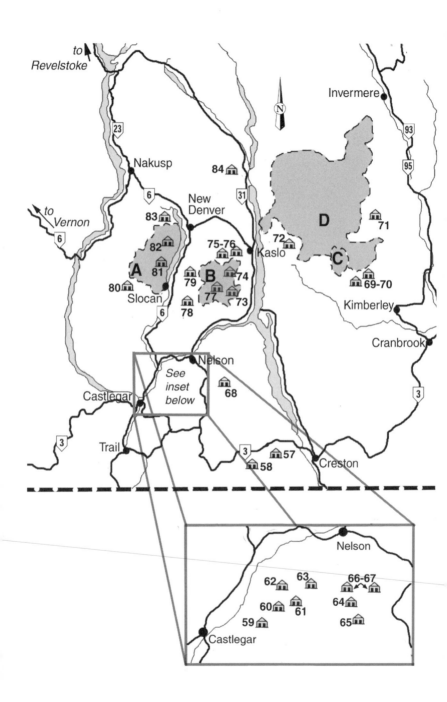

## PROVINCIAL PARKS

*Map*
*Reference*

A ................Valhalla Provincial Park

B................Kokanee Glacier Provincial Park

C ................St Mary's Alpine Provincial Park

D ................Purcell Wilderness Conservancy Park

## HUTS & LODGES

| *Map Reference* | | *Page Number* |
|---|---|---|
| 57 | Char Creek Cabin | 146 |
| 58 | Ripple Ridge Cabin | 148 |

### The Bonnington Traverse

| 59 | Grassy Hut | 150 |
|---|---|---|
| 60 | Steed/Marble Hut | 152 |
| 61 | Snowwater Hilton Hut | 154 |
| 62 | Snowwater Lodge | 156 |
| 63 | Copper Hut | 158 |
| 64 | Barrett Lake Cabin | 160 |
| 65 | Huckleberry Hut | 162 |
| 66–67 | Bonnington Yurts | 164 |

| 68 | Ymir Yurts | 166 |
|---|---|---|
| 69–70 | Boulder & Ptarmigan Lodges | 168 |
| 71 | Doctor Creek Cabin | 170 |
| 72 | Powder Creek Lodge | 172 |
| 73 | Woodbury Cabin | 174 |
| 74 | Silver Spray Cabin | 176 |
| 75–76 | Flint Lake Lodge & Mt Carlyle Hut | 178 |
| 77 | Slocan Chief Cabin | 180 |
| 78 | Crusader Creek Cabin | 182 |
| 79 | Enterprise Creek Cabin | 184 |
| 80 | Valhalla Lodge | 186 |
| 81 | Evans Lake Cabin | 188 |
| 82 | Wee Sandy Creek (Jules Holt) Cabin | 190 |
| 83 | Ruby Creek Lodge | 192 |
| 84 | Meadow Mountain Lodge | 194 |

# Char Creek Cabin

This two-story cabin, primarily used in winter by snowmobilers, is jointly managed by the British Columbia Forest Service and the Creston Snowmobile Club, although it may be used by skiers who wish to tour in the valley. There are also some good runs nearby down the logged-off slopes. Located in a small subalpine site near the confluence of two creeks, the cabin is not overly attractive, but it is roomy and comfortable. Nonclub members should contact the British Columbia Forest Service office in Nelson before using it. Note: there is another cabin in the nearby Echo Basin (along the Maryland Creek Road), but it is in such a state of disrepair that it is seldom used as anything other than a stopover point for day-tripping snowmobilers in this basin.

## LOCATION

*General* About 30 linear km (19 mi) W of Creston BC, near Kootenay Pass Summit.

*Specific* 82 F/2 Creston NAD27 5**020**98 4**346**40.

*Other pertinent maps* A trail access map can be found by following the links at the forest district website: www.for.gov.bc.ca/nelson/district/kootenay.

*Elevation* 1550 m (5100 ft).

*Elevation gain from Hwy 3* 245 m (800 ft).

## AMENITIES

*Heat* Woodstove.

*Cooking* No gas stove, cookware or dishware provided.

*Lighting* None.

*Sleeping* Two carpeted loft areas, no foam pads.

*Capacity* 24.

**Cost** (as of Summer 2001)
Free; no reservations.

**Access**

*Summer* Drive W on Hwy 3 for 34 km (21 mi) from the Hwy 3/3A junction in Creston. Turn left onto the gravel road signed "Char Creek" and after crossing Summit Creek in 500 m (1600 ft), turn left again and follow this road for another 500 m (1600 ft) before branching right onto the road that swings S along the W side of Char Creek. The cabin is located just beyond the first bridge, a total of about 4.5 km (3 mi) from Hwy 3. The road is suited for high-clearance vehicles only.

*Winter* Same, but the road is usually not plowed.

**Information**

Kootenay Lake Forest District Office
1907 Ridgewood Rd
RR 1 S-22 C-27
Nelson BC V1L 5P4
*Phone* (250) 825-1101
*Website* www.for.gov.bc.ca/nelson/district/kootenay

# Ripple Ridge Cabin

Located above Telemark Basin, this easily accessed cabin is mainly used in winter by those looking for tours or good glade-skiing in the deep snowpack of this region of the Selkirks. It also makes for a lovely spot to spend the night in summer, as it's located on the end of a promontory that faces south across a deep valley and on towards the mountains of Idaho. There are several ridge-walks that can be done from the cabin, the most striking being the trail that leads to the summit of Mt Ripple. This new cabin built by the British Columbia Forest Service—very clean and nicely finished—has replaced an older cabin that, in the summer of 2000, became firewood for the new one.

## LOCATION

***General*** Just S of the Kootenay Pass Summit on Hwy 3 W of Creston BC.

***Specific*** 82 F/3 Salmo NAD27 **497**624 4**317**90.

***Other pertinent maps*** For a ski trail map contact Alex Nielsen of the Creston Valley Ski Club at (250) 428-3232 or 428-4960; a trail access map can be found by following the links at www. for.gov.bc.ca/nelson/district/kootenay.

***Elevation*** 1950 m (6400 ft).

***Elevation gain from Hwy 3*** 182 m (600 ft).

## AMENITIES

***Heat*** Woodstove (wood provided).

***Cooking*** No cookstove or dishware; limited cookware.

***Lighting*** None.

***Sleeping*** Loft area, no foam pads.

*Capacity* 6–8.

COST (as of Summer 2001)
Free; no reservations.

ACCESS
From the Bridal Lake rest area at the Kootenay Pass summit about 43 km (27 mi) W of Creston, cross the highway and follow the gravel road to the right of the Highways Yard that heads S up to the ridge. Once the road levels off, do not take the trail marked "Ripple Ridge Trail." Instead, carry on along the road for about 400 m (1300 ft) to an old road that branches right and leads to the cabin in about 200 m (650 ft). The total distance is about 3 km (2 mi) and can be covered by high-clearance vehicles in summer, although this whole area is closed to motorized vehicles in winter.
*Time* 1 hour.

GUIDEBOOKS
*Summits and Icefields,* Scott.

INFORMATION
Kootenay Lake Forest District
   Office
1907 Ridgewood Rd
RR 1 S-22 C-27
Nelson BC V1L 5P4
*Phone* (250) 825-1101
*Website* www.for.gov.bc.ca/
   nelson/district/kootenay

# Grassy Hut

This cozy, well-maintained cabin high in the Grassy Creek drainage provides a good base for hikers wishing to wander through the meadows of Grassy Mountain, but it is most commonly used in winter by ski tourers. Located at the western end of the 5-hut Bonnington Traverse (a spectacular ski trip), the cabin also makes for a good destination in itself since it affords access to some great touring and turning opportunities. The hut is free and may not be booked, so be prepared to camp out. Note that in summer the access entails some unpleasant bushwacking through overgrown logging slash.

## LOCATION

*General* In the Bonnington Range S of Nelson BC.

*Specific* 82 F/6 Nelson NAD83 **4642**20 **4598**79.

*Other pertinent maps* 82 F/5 Castlegar (for western portion of access); *The Bonnington Traverse* (1:20,000), contact Patric Maloney at the Snowwater Lodge; *Backroad Mapbook* for logging road access.

*Elevation* 1840 m (6035 ft).

*Elevation gain from Bombi summit* 520 m (1700 ft).

## AMENITIES

*Heat* Woodstove (no wood provided).

*Cooking* No cookstove, cookware or dishware provided.

*Lighting* None

*Sleeping* Bunks, no foam pads.

*Capacity* 4–6

**COST** (as of Summer 2001)
Free; no reservations.

**ACCESS**
From the Bombi Summit 17 km
(10.5 mi) E of Castlegar on Hwy
3, turn N into and through the
gravel pit and then drive or ski
along the good gravel road that
follows the power lines. Note 2
forks: turn left at 2.5 km (1.5 mi)
and right at 3.8 km (2.4 mi).
Stop near some orange tape at
7.1 km (4.4 mi, approximately
GPS **4628**00 **4591**00, NAD83).
Hike or ski E through tough
bush up to the col; there are no
trails or markers. Once at the
col, look for a profusion of
orange tape that leads directly to
the cabin about 400 m (1300 ft)
away; the tape begins at GPS
**4634**00 **4597**64, just N of the
col's low point. The total hiking
distance from the powerline is
about 3 km (2 mi).
*Time* 1–2 hours from the power
line.

**GUIDEBOOKS**
*Hiking in the West Kootenays,*
Carter

**INFORMATION**
Arrow Forest District Office
845 Columbia Ave
Castlegar BC V1N 1H3
*Phone* (250) 365-8600
*Fax* (250) 365-8568
*Website* www.for.gov.bc.ca/
nelson/district/arrow

# Steed/Marble Hut

Although a summer road passes within 1.5 km (1 mi) of it, this hut is used mainly in winter by ski tourers doing a traverse from Grassy to Copper huts. Some snowmobilers are in the area from late January to April. The hut is located above Marble Lake just S of Siwash Mtn, with lots of telemarking opportunities nearby. It is not far from Snowwater Lodge for those who wish to have a night of relative luxury during the traverse. The route from Grassy Hut is unmarked and requires good map-navigating skills. The hut may not be booked, so be prepared to camp out.

## LOCATION
**General** In the Bonnington Range S of Nelson BC.
**Specific** 82 F/6 Nelson NAD83 approximately 675661.

**Other pertinent maps** *The Bonnington Traverse* (1:20,000), contact Patric Maloney at the Snowwater Lodge; *Backroad Mapbook* for logging road access.
**Elevation** 2090 m (6855 ft).
**Elevation gain from Grassy Hut** 250 m (820).

## AMENITIES
**Heat** Woodstove.
**Cooking** No cookstove, cookware or dishware provided.
**Lighting** None.
**Sleeping** Bunks, no foam pads.
**Capacity** 4–6.

## COST (as of Summer 2001)
Free; no reservations.

## ACCESS
**Summer** See the directions for access to Grassy Hut. Instead

of stopping at the 7.1-km (4.3-mi) mark, carry on along the good gravel road. When the road enters the Glade Creek drainage, you will have to use topo map-navigation skills to identify the closest point of approach to the cabin—which is only about 1.5 km (1 mi) of bushwhacking from the road.

**Winter** Again, good map-navigational skills are needed to get from either Grassy or Copper huts to this cabin. The hut is on the slope below a sub-peak of Siwash Mountain, about 600 (2000 ft) NNW of Marble Lake.

## GUIDEBOOKS

*Hiking in the West Kootenays,* Carter.

## INFORMATION

Arrow Forest District Office
845 Columbia Ave
Castlegar BC V1N 1H3
**Phone** (250) 365-8600
**Fax** (250) 365-8568
**Website** www.for.gov.bc.ca/nelson/district/arrow

# Snowwater Hilton Hut

This was an old miner's cabin named by someone with a wry sense of humor, for it was very rustic and not terribly clean. However, during the winter of 2001, it became a pile of ashes. Plans are afoot, however, for it to be rebuilt in the summer of 2001. Contact Patric Maloney at the nearby Snowwater Lodge for an update on the status of this project. Once it's completed, it will serve the same purpose as its predecessor. It can be a stopover for skiers between Steed and Copper huts, and it does provide shelter for anyone wishing to stay in the flats near the headwaters of Snowwater Creek, from where there is quick access to some good bowl skiing. Other than a woodstove, its amenities are unknown at this time.

## LOCATION

*General* Near the headwaters of Snowwater Creek SW of Nelson BC in the Bonnington Range.

*Specific* 82 F/6 Nelson NAD83; approximately 685680.

*Other pertinent maps* The Bonnington Traverse (1:20,000), contact Patric Maloney at the Snowwater Lodge; Backroad Mapbook for logging road access.

*Elevation* 1900 m (6250 ft).

*Elevation gain from Kootenay River* 1300 m (4270 ft).

## AMENITIES

*Heat* Woodstove.

*Cooking* No cookstove, cookware or dishware provided.

*Lighting* None.

*Sleeping* Unknown.

*Capacity* Unknown.

**COST** (as of Summer 2001)
Free; no reservations.

## ACCESS

From the S side of the Kootenay River near the Bonnington and Corra Linn dams, follow the Rover Creek Forest Service Road that goes up Rover and then Snowwater Creeks for about 12 km (7.5 mi). When the road starts to curl up onto the ridge that angles down N from Mt Snowwater, stay on the valley floor until it flattens out near the headwaters of the creek.

## GUIDEBOOKS

*Hiking in the West Kootenays,*
    Carter.
*Summits and Icefields,* Scott.

## INFORMATION

Arrow Forest District Office
845 Columbia Ave
Castlegar BC V1N 1H3
***Phone*** (250) 365-8600
***Fax*** (250) 365-8568
***Website*** www.for.gov.bc.ca/
    nelson/district/arrow

# Snowwater Lodge

Set amid the alpine bowls and old-growth glades of the Bonnington Range, this lodge enables skiers and sledders to take advantage of the huge snowpack that has been featured in *Snowboard Life, Blue* and *Powder* magazines and major skiing films. Runs range from 300–1100 vertical meters (975–3575 ft) and include part of the terrain accessed by the Bonnington Traverse. The lovely timber-frame lodge is usually reached by a 10-minute heli-flight from Castlegar or by snowcat along a summer road from the north. While all meals are catered, guests can be fully independent for their day's activities, or they can take advantage of a broad range of options, such as guided ski-touring, heli-skiing and guided sledding—or even a mix of all three throughout their stay.

## LOCATION

*General* N of Mt Snowwater approximately 15 linear km (9 mi) SW of Nelson BC.

*Specific* 82 F/6 Nelson 468307 468538.

*Other pertinent maps* The Bonnington Traverse (1:20,000), contact Patric Maloney below.

*Elevation* 1900 m (6250 ft).

*Elevation gain from Kootenay River* 1350 m (4410 ft).

## AMENITIES

*Heat* Wood and electric.

*Cooking* All meals provided.

*Lighting* Electric (creek-generated).

*Sleeping* Private and semi-private bedrooms with duvets and bedding.

*Capacity* 12.

*Features* Full bathrooms, hot tub, sauna and laundry facilities.

**COST** (as of Summer 2001)
From $125/person (including meals) for self-guided guests to $600/person/day for heli-skiing in groups of 4. Other options include guided ski-touring, snowmobile rentals, heli-skiing and snowmobile-assisted touring.

*Heli-flight* $125 one way (guests commonly ski out).

*Snowcat transport* $75/person in deluxe 12-person snowcat.

**ACCESS**

Guests are met in either Nelson or Castlegar (and groups can be picked up in Spokane) and then transported by helicopter or snowcat to the lodge. Guests may also ski in to the lodge to reduce the net cost of the visit.

**GUIDEBOOKS**

*Hiking in the West Kootenays,* Carter.

*Summits and Icefields,* Scott.

**INFORMATION & BOOKING**

Snowwater Lodge
Attention Patric Maloney
Box 1340
Rossland BC V0G 1Y0
*Phone* (250) 354-8238
*Fax* (250) 365-2752
*E-mail* snowwaterlodge@yahoo. com
*Website* www.snowwater.com/ index.htm

# Copper Hut

This remote log cabin in the center of the Bonnington Range is used mainly in winter by ski tourers. It is commonly accessed as part of the Bonnington traverse, although the hut is not easy to locate. A very rough road comes to within 1 km (0.6 mi) of it, but high-clearance 4WD vehicles are needed to reach the trailhead. Winter access is easier if logging operations result in plowed roads. This hut is located high up in a bowl near the headwaters of Erie Creek, just SW of a fire lookout on top of Copper Mtn. Good glade skiing and ridge traverses are possible from here. The hut is free and may not be booked, so be prepared to camp out, since it can accommodate at most 6 people.

## LOCATION

**General** In the Bonnington Range S of Nelson BC.

**Specific** 82 F/6 Nelson NAD83 723705.

**Other pertinent maps** *The Bonnington Traverse* (1:20,000), contact Patric Maloney at the Snowwater Lodge; *Backroad Mapbook* for logging road access.

**Elevation** 1970 m (6461 ft).

**Elevation gain from parking area** Varies depending on access used.

## AMENITIES

**Heat** Woodstove.

**Cooking** No cookstove, cookware or dishware provided.

**Lighting** None.

**Sleeping** Bunks, no foam pads.

**Capacity** 4–6.

**COST** (as of Summer 2001)
Free; no reservations.

## ACCESS

**Summer** Check with the local
British Columbia Forest Service office for road conditions.
The most direct route is to follow the Blewett Road W of
Nelson to the Copper Mountain Forest Service Road which
heads SE up (steeply, at times)
Fortynine Creek. The very
rough road (which may be
impassable even by 4x4s)
heads straight for the summit
of Red Mtn for about 9 km
(5.5 mi) and then swings SW
for another 4 km (2.5 mi)
before ending just below the
summit of Copper Mtn. The
hut is less than 3 km (2 mi)
SW of the road-end (down
into the upper Erie Creek
drainage). You should, however, check with the British
Columbia Forest Service office
in Nelson in order to deter-
mine if other roads (particular-
ly the roads up Rover, Giveout
or Barrett Creeks) are in better
condition.

**Time** Varies depending on how
much of the road can be driven.

**Winter** The summer route is possible by snowmobile, although
skiers typically include this
hut in the traverse from
Grassy to Huckleberry or Barrett Lake huts. Good map-
reading skills are needed.

## GUIDEBOOKS
*Hiking in the West Kootenays,*
Carter.

## INFORMATION
Arrow Forest District Office
845 Columbia Ave
Castlegar BC V1N 1H3
**Phone** (250) 365-8600
**Fax** (250) 365-8568
**Website** www.for.gov.bc.ca/
nelson/district/arrow

# Barrett Lake Hut

This lakeside cabin is a great destination in both summer and winter. Nestled in the cirque of two mountains (and below a hillside thick with huckleberry bushes), the cabin serves as a base for playing on the snow slopes that ring the hut or for traversing on to Copper or Huckleberry huts. In summer, there is some very scenic ridge-walking along the Dominion–Commonwealth chain. However, although it's in a lovely setting, the cabin is a bit dark and in need of some repair and cleaning. In summer, camping in the nearby meadows may be preferable.

## LOCATION

*General* In the Bonnington Range S of Nelson BC.

*Specific* 82 F/6 Nelson NAD83 474502 465891.

*Other pertinent maps* The Bonnington Traverse (1:20,000), contact Patric Maloney at the Snowwater Lodge; *Backroad Mapbook* for logging road access.

*Elevation* 1840 m (6035 ft).

*Elevation gain from Hwy 6* 1040 m (3410 ft).

## AMENITIES

*Heat* Woodstove (no wood provided).

*Cooking* No cookstove, cookware or dishware provided.

*Lighting* None.

*Sleeping* Loft area, no foam pads.

*Capacity* 5–6.

## COST (as of Summer 2001)

Free; no reservations.

## ACCESS

From the town of Salmo, head N on Hwy 6 for 18.3 km (11.5 mi) and, after crossing to the N side of Barrett Creek, turn W onto Porto Rico Road. From here, hike/ski/drive/sled (depending on road conditions and type of vehicle you drive) up the road along the N side of the creek to the cabin located on the N shore of the lake; the total distance is about 9 km (5.5 mi). In summer, the last 4–5 km (2.5–3 mi) are accessible only by ATV. Note that the route to Huckleberry Hut turns left over a bridge at about the 6-km (3.6-mi) mark. The cabin can also be accessed from Copper Hut to the N (as part of the Bonnington traverse) or from Huckleberry Hut via a loop around Dominion Mtn.

**Time** Variable, depending on amount of road that can be driven.

## GUIDEBOOKS
*Hiking in the West Kootenays,* Carter.
*Summits and Icefields,* Scott.

## INFORMATION
Arrow Forest District Office
845 Columbia Ave
Castlegar BC V1N 1H3
**Phone** (250) 365-8600
**Fax** (250) 365-8568
**Website** www.for.gov.bc.ca/
nelson/district/arrow

# Huckleberry Hut

This lovely small log cabin affords access to good skiing and ridge-walking. Skiers will want to ascend the ridge west of the hut (between Cabin and Midday peaks), for it opens out into some open bowls with long runs. An ascent on foot or ski of the southern ridge of Dominion Peak, followed by a traverse around onto the slopes of Empire or Commonwealth mountains, makes for a classic circle tour. The cabin is in very good shape and would make a great mountain hideaway for 2–3 people in any season.

## LOCATION

*General* In the Bonnington Range S of Nelson BC.

*Specific* 82 F/6 Nelson NAD83 4**768**78 4**636**97.

*Other pertinent maps* The Bon-nington Traverse (1:20,000), contact Patric Maloney at the Snowwater Lodge; *Backroad Mapbook* for logging road access.

*Elevation* 1560 m (5132 ft).

*Elevation gain from Hwy 6* 760 m (2500 ft), some of which may be covered by vehicle.

## AMENITIES

*Heat* Woodstove (no wood provided).

*Cooking* No cookstove, cookware or dishware provided.

*Lighting* None.

*Sleeping* Bunks, no foam pads.

*Capacity* 4.

## COST

Free; no reservations.

## ACCESS

From the town of Salmo, head N

on Hwy 6 for 18.3 km (11.5 mi) and, after crossing to the N side of Barrett Creek, turn W onto Porto Rico Road. From here, hike/ski/drive/sled (depending on road conditions and type of vehicle you drive) up the road along the N side of the creek for about 7 km (4.2 mi). About 700 m (2300 ft) after the first switchback (at GPS 4**774**39 4**649**35, NAD83), follow a road that branches left and then carry on over a bridge across Barrett Creek. (Note that trail leading left at the first switchback also reaches this bridge, but this trail is very overgrown.) Once over the bridge, the road (driveable in summer only by ATVs) starts climbing and crosses two small avalanche slopes, arriving at the

cabin in about 2 km (1.2 mi). The cabin is on the left hand side of the road. From the cabin the trail continues up to the Cabin–Midday Ridge.

*Time* Variable, depending on amount of road that can be driven.

## GUIDEBOOKS
*Hiking in the West Kootenays*, Carter.
*Summits and Icefields*, Scott.

## INFORMATION
Arrow Forest District Office
845 Columbia Ave
Castlegar BC V1N 1H3
*Phone* (250) 365-8600
*Fax* (250) 365-8568
*Website* www.for.gov.bc.ca/ nelson/district/arrow

# Bonnington Yurts
## (Colony Lakes & Commonwealth Ridge)

Not yet finished as this book went to press (but to be ready for the 2001–2002 winter season), these two yurts are being built to accommodate those wanting access to the beautiful high country of the Bonnington Range. They can be destinations in themselves or can be linked up with Snowwater Lodge in an east–west traverse through the Bonningtons. Some skiers doing the public hut traverse (Grassy–Huckleberry) may wish to plan on a few nights of greater luxury by staying at the yurts or the lodge. There are extensive opportunities for tours and turns in the nearby bowls, and summer hikers will find numerous meadows, lakes and ridges to visit. Very solid and warm, these structures will pro-vide a sturdy shelter and all the comfort one could need at the end of a day in the backcountry. (For more information on yurts, visit www.yurts.com).

**General** In the Bonnington Range S of Nelson BC.

**Specific** 82 F/6 Nelson NAD 83 Site 1: 4**745**79 4**664**23; Site 2: 4**794**28 4**682**56.

**Other pertinent maps** *The Bonnington Traverse* (1:20,000), contact Patric Maloney.

**Elevation** Site 1: 2040 m (6710 ft). Site 2: 1640 m (5340 ft).

**Elevation gain from Hwy 6** Site 1: 1240 m (4080 ft). Site 2: 840 m (2760 ft).

### AMENITIES
**Heat** Propane.
**Cooking** All meals provided.

*Lighting* Propane and solar.
*Sleeping* Common sleeping room.
*Capacity* 8.
*Features* Propane toilet, sauna.

COST (as of Summer 2001)
From $75/person/night with self-propelled access to $650/person for five nights including heli-access.

ACCESS
Guests can ski in or be flown in. Arrangements are made upon registering.

GUIDEBOOKS
*Hiking in the West Kootenays,* Carter.
*Summits and Icefields,* Scott.

INFORMATION & BOOKING
Snowwater Lodge
Attention Patric Maloney
Box 1340
Rossland BC V0G 1Y0
*Phone* (250) 354-8238
*Fax* (250) 365-2752
*E-mail* snowwaterlodge@yahoo. com
*Website* www.snowwater.com/ index.htm

# Ymir Yurts
## (Seeman Creek & Qua Lake)

These new yurts, just finished in the summer of 2000, are the first of several planned for this region of the southern Selkirks renowned for its powder. Reached by helicopter or by ski-touring from the top of the lifts at the Whitewater Ski Area south of Nelson, both facilities provide access to a good mix of tree skiing and open bowls, with lots of north-facing powder on terrain that varies from gentle slopes to steep chutes. The skiing requires solid intermediate telemark or alpine touring skill in variable backcountry terrain. Skiers should also be of at least intermediate fitness. Ski packages include all meals and guiding. Guests need pack in only their clothing and personal items. The yurts operate in winter only.

## LOCATION
*General* Near Mt Ymir, about 15 km (9 mi) SE of Nelson BC.

*Specific* 82 F/6 Nelson NAD83 Seeman Creek 948745; Qua Lake 914712.

*Elevation* Seeman Creek: 1855 m (6100 ft); Qua Lake: 1720 m (5600 ft).

*Elevation change from Whitewater Ski Area* Access routes to both yurts leave from the top of ski lifts and entail several elevation gains and losses.

## AMENITIES
*Heat* Woodstoves in kitchen and dorm yurts.

*Cooking* All meals provided.

*Lighting* Propane.

*Sleeping* Bunk beds in the dorm yurt; bedding provided.

*Capacity* 8.

**COST** (as of Summer 2001)

***Catered, no guiding once at hut*** 3 nights: $445/person; 4 nights: $645/person; 7 nights: $995/person.

***Catered, full guiding*** 3 nights: $445/person; 4 nights: $795/person; 7 nights: $1295/person.

***Option*** Packages involving no catering or guiding can be arranged.

**ACCESS**

Complete access descriptions are given on the website. Note that moderate physical condition is needed to reach the yurts. Guests are driven from Nelson to Whitewater Ski Hill and then guided in to the yurts from the top of one of the lifts. All routes usually take about 4–6 hours, although strong parties may choose to take longer in order to get in some extra runs.

**INFORMATION & BOOKING**

The Kootenay Experience
306 Victoria St
Nelson BC V1L 4K4
***Phone*** 1-888-488-4327
***E-mail*** yurts@kootenayexperience. com
***Website*** www.kootenayexperience. com

# Boulder & Ptarmigan Lodges

These two log chalets in the Purcells west of Kimberley serve as the base for week-long ski tours, including a 10 km (6 mi) hut-to-hut traverse. The extremely varied terrain provides exciting areas for skiers of all ability levels to practice their telemarking or randonnée skills, whether they prefer rolling alplands, glade skiing or long cirque runs near some of the big peaks in the area. The trips are fully catered and guided, with heli-access from Kimberley. The two lodges are quite spacious with large dining and lounging areas. Open in winter only.

Location

**General** In the southern Purcells, 20 km (12 mi) W of Kimberley BC.

**Specific** 82 F/16 Dewar Creek NAD27 Boulder 543103; Ptarmigan 543150.

**Other pertinent maps** 82 F/9 St Mary Lake; 82 F/16 Dewar Creek.

**Elevation** Boulder: 1980 m (6500 ft); Ptarmigan: 1525 m (5000 ft).

**Elevation gain** N/a (heli-accessed).

## AMENITIES

**Heat** Woodstove.

**Cooking** All meals provided.

**Lighting** Local hydro-generated electric light.

**Sleeping** Bunks with foam pads; sleeping bags and liners provided.

**Capacity** 12.

**Features** Shower house and Canada's highest backcountry hot tub at Boulder; sauna available at Ptarmigan.

**COST** (as of Summer 2001)
$1195/person/week, including
return heli-flight, all meals and
guiding.

**ACCESS**
Heli-access only.

**GUIDEBOOKS**
*Summits and Icefields,* Scott.

**INFORMATION & BOOKING**
Ptarmigan Tours
Box 7
Ta Ta Creek BC V0B 2H0
***Phone*** (250) 422-3270
***Fax*** (250) 422-3596
***E-mail*** ptarmigan@cyberlink. bc.ca
***Website*** www.cyberlink.bc.ca/~
ptarmigan

# Doctor Creek Cabin

This small log cabin near an abandoned mine provides great shelter for anyone skiing, snowmobiling or hiking in the upper reaches of the Doctor Creek drainage. Located near treeline and easily accessed in summer, it serves as a wonderful base for day-hikes onto ridges or into a nearby lake—an ideal locale for novice hikers or a weekend outing. The skiing here is reputed to be very good. A BC Forest Service cabin, it now is maintained by (and used mainly as a day shelter by) the Windermere Valley Snowmobile Club. Most vehicles can get within 2–3 km (1.5–2 mi) of the cabin in summer, but in winter the only practical means of access is snowmobile. The cabin itself is well finished and has been carefully maintained. There is

another cabin between this one and the lake, and while it is rather dilapidated, it could be used for shelter if the main cabin is full.

## LOCATION

**General** In the Purcell Mountains, about 42 km (26 mi) by road SW of Canal Flats BC.

**Specific** 82 K/1 Findlay Creek NAD27 5**59**492 5**405**42 (Note: the other cabin is at 5**59**292 5**402**83).

**Other pertinent maps** 82 J/4 Canal Flats (for eastern portion of road access); *Backroad Mapbook* or *British Columbia Forest Service Map* of Forest Service road access to trailhead.

**Elevation** 2280 m (7500 ft).

**Elevation gain from end of road** About 150 m (500 ft).

## AMENITIES

**Heat** Woodstove (no wood provided).

**Cooking** Coleman stove; limited cookware, no dishware.

**Lighting** Coleman lantern.

**Sleeping** Bunks, no foam pads.

**Capacity** 4–6.

## COST (as of Summer 2001)

Free; no reservations.

## ACCESS

**Summer** From the town of Canal Flats, head NW on Hwy 93/95 for about 5 km (3 mi) and then turn left onto the gravel road that heads SW toward Findlay Creek. After another 5 km, the road forks, with one branch crossing the creek. Take the right branch to stay on the N side of the creek. Follow alongside the creek ignoring all right forks to the 20.5-km (13-mi) mark and then take a left fork that crosses the bridge and continues SW to enter the Doctor Creek drainage. Stay left at all the following junctions on what is plainly the main road as it carries on up the valley to the parking area at 39.2 km (24.5 mi). A very rugged vehicle could carry on a bit farther up the road. From the parking area, follow the old road for 2–3 km (1.2–2 mi) to the cabin which is plainly visible from the road.

**Winter** Same, but the road may not be plowed, depending on logging activity in the area. Plan on using a snowmobile to reach the cabin.

## GUIDEBOOKS

*Mountain Footsteps: Selected Hikes in the East Kootenays,* Strong.

## INFORMATION & BOOKING

As this book goes to press, the cabin is free and available on a first-come basis. For the winter of 2001–2002, it has been proposed that the cabin be available for reservation through the Windermere Valley Snowmobile Club. For details, contact:

Al Bergen, President
**Phone** (250) 345-4598 or contact:
Invermere Forest District Office
Box 189
625 4 St
Invermere BC V0A 1K0
**Phone** (250) 342-4200
To obtain the British Columbia Forest Service road map, contact the Invermere Forest District Office.

# Powder Creek Lodge

Located high in a remote basin overlooking Lise Nicola Lake, this heli-accessed ski lodge offers spectacular views of the surrounding alpine scenery. With an average annual snowpack of over 3 m (10 ft), this area offers a wide variety of treed and open terrain and great skiing for all ability levels. The four alpine basins that surround the lodge contain everything from gentle treed and gladed slopes to wide open 900-m (3000-ft) runs. The lodge is a roomy two and one-half story building that has been richly finished with hardwood floors and exposed beams, and it provides a host of creature comforts such as inside toilets and spacious bathing facilities. The facility is open from mid-December to mid-April. Guests can choose to be fully self-sufficient or use catering and guiding services.

## LOCATION
*General* In the Southern Purcell Mountains, 18 km (11 mi) E of the town of Kaslo BC.
*Specific* 82 F/15 Kaslo NAD27 5**234**50 5**278**50.
*Other pertinent maps* For a topographic map of the area, see "Terrain" page of the website.
*Elevation* 2164 m (7100 ft).
*Elevation gain* N/a (heli-accessed).

## AMENITIES
*Heat* Wood and propane.
*Cooking* Propane stove/oven and BBQ; spacious, well-appointed kitchen.
*Lighting*: Electric lights and power from local mini hydro system.
*Sleeping* Six 2–3 person private, carpeted bedrooms with duvets and bedding.
*Capacity* 12+
*Features* Large living and dining areas; bathhouse and sauna; inside liquids toilets; private bedrooms; electric lights and power; experienced guiding services and gourmet catering services available; no heli-skiing in the area.

**COST** (as of Summer 2001)
All stays are for 7 nights, Sunday–Sunday; prices include return helicopter transport.

*Self-guided & self-catered* $950/person/week.

*Guided & catered* $1600/person/week.

*Discounts* For groups of 12.

*Minimum group size* 6 (smaller groups will be accepted if space permits). Groups wishing exclusive use must make reservations for 11.

**ACCESS**
Heli-access only via an 11-minute flight from Kaslo BC.

**INFORMATION & BOOKING**
Powder Creek Lodge
(Operated by Tamarack Alpine Adventures Inc)
Attention Gus Diks or Heather Smith
Box 832
Nelson BC V1L 5S9
*Phone* (250) 226-7186
*Fax* (250) 226-7373
*E-mail* powder@netidea.com
*Website* www.netidea.com/powder

# Woodbury Cabin

Uniquely designed to deflect avalanches, this cabin is a popular destination for hikers and mountaineers wishing to access the rugged mountains of Kokanee Glacier Park or just to spend time in a postcard alpine setting. The nicely finished cabin provides a marvelous overlook of Woodbury Glacier and the Wolf Cascade. From here it is possible to do a traverse on to Slocan Chief Cabin or to return to the parking lot via a high-level traverse to Silver Spray Cabin. Because of the avalanche hazard (the cabin itself has been hit twice in recent years), the cabin is officially closed in winter.

## LOCATION

*General* In Kokanee Glacier Park NE of Nelson and SW of Kaslo BC.

*Specific* 82 F/14 Slocan NAD27 490946 516311.

*Other pertinent maps* 82 F/11 Kokanee Peak (for travel into southern parts of the park); *Kokanee Glacier Provincial Park Map* (available at trailhead).

*Elevation* 2070 m (6790 ft).

*Elevation gain from parking lot* 762 m (2500 ft).

## AMENITIES

*Heat* Woodstove (wood provided).

*Cooking* Propane stove; no cookware or dishware provided.

*Lighting* Propane.

*Sleeping* Loft area, no foam pads.

*Capacity* 8–10.

COST (as of Summer 2001) $15/person/night; $30/family /night (honor pay system). No reservations.

## ACCESS

From the marked turnoff 23 km (14 mi) N of Balfour on Hwy 31, follow the gravel road along Woodbury Creek for 13.2 km (8 mi) to the trailhead, the last 2 km (1.2 mi) of which requires a high-clearance vehicle. The clear, well-maintained trail follows the creek for 9 km (5.5 mi) to the cabin above the Wolf Cascade. Note that when the trail forks after 2.5 km (1.5 mi), you head left (W)—the right fork leads to Silver Spray cabin.
*Time* 4 hours.

## GUIDEBOOKS

*Don't Waste Your Time in the West Kootenays*, Copeland and Copeland.

*A Climber's Guide to the Interior Ranges of BC–South*, Krusyna and Putnam.
*Summits and Icefields*, Scott.

## INFORMATION

British Columbia Parks
West Kootenay Office
*Phone* (250) 825-3500
*Fax* (250) 825-9509
*Websites* www.elp.gov.bc.ca/ bcparks/explore/kootney.htm *and* www.bcadventure.com/ adventure/explore/kootenays/ trails/kohaneep.htm (a good summary of trails within the park)

# Silver Spray Cabin

Originally used by those working in a nearby silver mine, this cabin was replaced in the mid-1990s with a spacious and beautifully finished post-and-beam building. It offers very comfortable shelter for those hiking or climbing in the rugged alpine terrain in the NE corner of Kokanee Glacier Park. A high-level traverse to the Woodbury and Slocan Chief cabins is possible. The danger of avalanches, most notably the one which claimed 6 lives not far from here in the mid-90s, has led to the official closure of this cabin in winter.

## LOCATION

*General* In Kokanee Glacier Park NE of Nelson and SW of Kaslo BC.

*Specific* 82 F/14 Slocan NAD27 **498**41**8 518**70**6.

*Other pertinent maps* 82 F/11 Kokanee Peak (for travel into southern parts of the park); *Kokanee Glacier Provincial Park Map* (available at trailhead).

*Elevation* 2340 m (7670 ft).

*Elevation gain from parking lot* 1016 m (3330 ft).

## AMENITIES

*Heat* Propane heater and woodstove (wood provided).

*Cooking* Propane stove; no cookware and dishware provided.

*Lighting* Propane.

*Sleeping* Loft area with foam pads.

*Capacity* 11.

## COST (as of Summer 2001)

$15/person/night; $30/family/night (honor pay system) No reservations.

## ACCESS

From the marked turnoff 23 km (14 mi) N of Balfour on Hwy 31, follow the gravel road along Woodbury Creek for 13.2 km (8 mi) to the trailhead, the last 2 km (1.2 mi) of which requires a high-clearance vehicle. The trail follows the creek for a short distance before it forks near the confluence with Silver Spray Creek. Follow the right (N) fork and steadily gain elevation along the clear trail for the next 6 km (3.7 mi) until you reach the cabin in Clover Basin. Total distance is about 8 km (5 mi). Note the substantial vertical gain involved in reaching the cabin.

*Time* 4–5 hours.

## GUIDEBOOKS

*Don't Waste Your Time in the West Kootenays,* Copeland and Copeland.

*A Climber's Guide to the Interior Ranges of BC–South,* Krusyna and Putnam.

*Summits and Icefields,* Scott.

## INFORMATION

British Columbia Parks
West Kootenay Office
*Phone* (250) 825-3500
*Fax* (250) 825-9509
*Websites* www.elp.gov.bc.ca/ bcparks/explore/kootney.htm *and* www.bcadventure.com/ adventure/explore/kootenays/ trails/kohaneep.htm (a good summary of trails within the park)

# Flint Lakes Lodge & Mt Carlyle Hut

Located just north of the well-known Kokanee Glacier Park, these winter-use-only facilities provide access to 10 different alpine basins that get an average of 180 cm (6 ft) of powder/year. The opportunities for long open runs and exceptional tree skiing are endless. The extent of trackless snow available to guests has been expanded substantially with the opening of the new Mt Carlyle Hut. Guests now fly in to the Flint Lakes cabin and, for part of the week, traverse south for a few nights at this remote cabin close to great skiing. Both cabins offer all the comforts that one needs in the backcountry, including saunas.

## LOCATION

*General* In the Kokanee Range, about 50 km (31 mi) N of Nelson BC and about 9 km NE of where Keen Creek Road enters Kokanee Park.

*Specific* 82 F/14 Slocan NAD27 926307 Flint Lake.

*Other pertinent maps* For a topo map of nearby terrain, follow links on the website.

*Elevation* Flint Lake Cabin: 1950 m (6390 ft); Mt Carlyle Hut: 2133 m (7000 ft).

*Elevation gain* N/a (heli-accessed).

## AMENITIES

*Heat* Woodstove and propane.
*Cooking* Propane stove/oven; limited cookware.
*Lighting* Propane.
*Sleeping* 2 bunk-rooms.
*Capacity* 8.
*Features* Sauna.

## COST (as of Summer 2001)

*Fully guided & catered* $1400/person/week; $880/person/4-day stay (Sat–Wed). Maximum group of 6. Prices inclusive of return heli-flight.

*Self-guided & self-catered* $800/person/week (high season); $750/person/week (low season). Minimum group of 6. Prices inclusive of return heli-flight.

## ACCESS
Heli-flight from Kaslo.

## GUIDEBOOKS
*A Climber's Guide to the Interior Ranges of BC–South,* Krusyna and Putnam.

## INFORMATION & BOOKING
Kootenay Mountain Huts
Attention Jeff Gfroerer
Box 1167
Kaslo BC V0G 1M0
*Phone* (250) 353-7179
*E-mail* info@mountainhuts.com

# Slocan Chief Cabin

Built in 1896, this log cabin at the heart of Kokanee Park provides a great base for an array of hikes, climbs and ski-tours. The alpine meadows are thick with flowers in summer, and mountaineers have a choice of almost a dozen peaks that can be climbed . in a day. The skiing is so popular that bookings are made by lottery draw. The hut is quite spacious, with a sleeping loft. To commemorate the life of Michel Trudeau, a new cabin is to be constructed.

## LOCATION

*General* In Kokanee Glacier Park, NE of Nelson BC.

*Specific* 82 F/14 Slocan NAD27 873128.

*Other pertinent maps* 82 F/11 Kokanee Peak (for some tours or climbs); *Kokanee Glacier Provincial Park Map.*

*Elevation* 2010 m (6600 ft).
*Elevation gain from Gibson Lake parking lot* 490 m (1610 ft).

## AMENITIES

*Heat* Propane and woodstove.
*Cooking* Propane cookstove; cookware and dishware provided.
*Lighting* Propane.
*Sleeping* Loft with foam pads.
*Capacity* 12.
*Features* Heated outdoor toilet.

COST (as of Summer 2001)
*Summer* $15/person/night; $30/ family/night (no reservations accepted).
*Winter* $35/person/night ($2,940/ week for a group of 12).
*Heli-flight* $200/person (one way), based on a group of 12; cost higher for smaller groups or extra gear.

## ACCESS

**Summer** The 3 principal access trails and several less common routes are all well marked on the provincial park map.

**From Gibson Lake** At the marked turnoff from Hwy 3A 19 km (12 mi) NE of Nelson, follow the road 15 km (9.5 mi) to Gibson Lake parking lot. The trail heads up steeply and then becomes gentler as it passes Kokanee Lake and reaches Kokanee Pass. From here, it passes several lakes (with good fishing) before reaching the cabin.

**Time** 4 hours.

**From Keen Creek** From Hwy 31A about 7 km (4.5 mi) W of Kaslo, follow the Keen Creek Road S for about 18 km (11 mi) to its end near a recent washout about 7.5 km (4.6 mi) before the Joker Millsite. Follow the road in to the Millsite and then carry on up the well-marked but steep trail to Helen Deane Lake, where the trail levels out. The cabin is about 15 minutes farther along the trail. Closed from mid-August until October, when grizzlies feed on the huckleberry crop. Even when the trail is open, be wary.

**Time** 3 hours.

**From Enterprise Creek** About 1.5 km (1 mi) N of the Enterprise Creek bridge on Hwy 6, 14.4 km (9 mi) N of Slocan City, turn E onto the road that follows the creek for 16 km (10 mi). From the parking area, follow the well-marked trail to Tanal Lake and Enterprise Pass, and then down to the cabin.

**Time** 5 hours.

**Winter** Same, although most people heli in because no access roads are plowed. Snowmobiles are allowed up to the park boundary. Groups usually ski out via Gibson Lake and the main access road. There is an enclosed shelter with no amenities at Gibson Lake, if needed.

## GUIDEBOOKS

*Don't Waste Your Time in the West Kootenays,* Copeland and Copeland.

*A Climber's Guide to the Interior Ranges of BC–South,* Krusyna and Putnam.

*Summits and Icefields,* Scott.

## INFORMATION & BOOKING

British Columbia Parks
West Kootenay Office
**Phone** (250) 825-3500
**Fax** (250) 825-9509
**Websites** www.elp.gov.bc.ca/bc parks/explore/kootney.htm *and* www.bcadventure.com/ adventure/explore/kootenays/ trails/kohaneep.htm (a good summary of trails within the park).

**Winter Lottery Draw**
**Phone** (250) 354-4092
**E-mail** kevin@kokanee-glacier.com
**Website** www.kokanee-glacier.com
**Heli-flight** Kokanee Helicopters
**Phone** (250) 354-8485
**Fax** (250) 825-4425

# Crusader Creek Cabin

This spacious new cabin just west of of Kokanee Glacier Park is very well finished and appointed—it even has a barbecue, propane stove and real mattresses. Jointly maintained by the British Columbia Forest Service and the Nelson Sno-goers Snowmobile Club, it is mainly used by snowmobilers in winter, although there is ample opportunity for ski-touring and turns in the nearby high basins. In summer it makes a lovely and even luxurious destination; experienced hikers could make their way onto the high ridges that ring the cabin and provide views east into the park.

## LOCATION

**General** At the head of Crusader Creek, W of Kokanee Glacier Park BC.

**Specific** 82 F/14 Slocan NAD27 4**762**07 5**129**19.

**Elevation** 1730 m (5700 ft).

**Elevation gain from Hwy 6** 1190 m (3940 ft).

## AMENITIES

**Heat** Woodstove (replace firewood used).

**Cooking** Propane stove/oven; cookware and dishware provided.

**Lighting** Diesel-generated electricity (winter only).

**Sleeping** Loft with real mattresses.

**Capacity** 8 mattresses

**COST** (as of Summer 2001) Free; no reservations.

## ACCESS

About 6 km (3.7 mi) S of Slocan City, turn at the prominent signs identifying the Lemon Creek access to Kokanee Glacier Park. Follow this good gravel road for 16 km (10 mi) to the park trailhead, at which point the road carries on N and is renamed Crusader Creek Road. Watch for the yellow roadside kilometer markers. Stay on this road until the 5-km sign and then take the right fork, which is passable only by very rugged vehicles. (You may have to park at the open area where the main road crosses the creek 100 m (325 ft) beyond this fork.) After about 3 km (2 mi) along this rough road, it curls left over the creek and, in a further 600 m (2000 ft), there is the unmarked turnoff to the cabin—watch for this trail on your right. The cabin is only a few hundred meters along the trail.

## INFORMATION

Arrow Forest District Office
845 Columbia Ave
Castlegar BC V1N 1H3
**Phone** (250) 365-8600
**Fax** (250) 365-8568
**Website** www.for.gov.bc.ca/
 nelson/district/arrow

# Enterprise Creek Cabin

Formerly used as part of a small mining operation in the 1920s, this 2-room frame building was refurbished in the 1980s by the Valhalla Wilderness Society. The cabin now makes for a bright and spacious shelter and affords a good base for those touring on into the high country on the western edge of Kokanee Glacier Park. This building now has no official caretakers, so visitors are urged to treat it with care. Be prepared for few amenities.

## LOCATION

*General* At an abandoned mining site about 7 km up Enterprise Creek in the Slocan River Valley BC.

*Specific* 82 F/14 Slocan NAD27 4**766**07 5**189**72.

*Other pertinent maps* A Visitor's *Guide to the Valhalla Provincial Park,* Valhalla Society.

*Elevation* 1220 m (4000 ft).

*Elevation gain from Hwy 6* 683 m (2240 ft).

*Elevation gain from Enterprise Creek* 35 m (100 ft).

## AMENITIES

*Heat* Woodstove (but in need of repair as of Summer 2001).

*Cooking* No cookware or dishware provided.

*Lighting* None.

*Sleeping* Separate room, carpeted floor.

*Capacity* 6–8.

## COST (as of Summer 2001)
Free; no reservations.

## ACCESS
About 15 km (10 mi) N of Slocan City on Hwy 6, turn E at the

"Kokanee Glacier Park" sign. Follow the good road along the creek for 7.8 km (5 mi) and turn right at the fork (where the "Kok. Glac. Park" sign points left). This road ends in 200 m (650 ft) at the former bridge crossing. Ford the creek (it may be frozen in winter) and carry on past some derelict buildings and up through 2 switchbacks to the cabin. Total distance from the creek is about 800 m (2600 ft). The road may be snowmobiled in winter.

*Time* 15 minutes from the creek.

### INFORMATION

For the *Visitor's Guide Map*, contact:
The Valhalla Society
Box 329
New Denver BC V0G 1S0
*Phone* (250) 358-2333
*Fax* (250) 358-7950
*E-mail* vws@vws.org
*Website* www.rmec.org/valhalla

# Valhalla Lodge

Just outside the southwest boundary of Valhalla Park, this lodge provides access to the scenery and mountain experiences that the Valhalla alpine—Canada's Shangri-la—is renowned for. Ten different basins are easily accessed for ski tours and turns or for meadow and ridge hiking amid numerous alpine lakes. The clean granite peaks nearby draw climbers from around the world. The lodge on the shores of McKean Lake offers all the comforts that one could want in the backcountry, including a sauna.

## LOCATION
**General** About 50 km (31 mi) NW of Nelson BC in the Southern Valhalla Range.
**Specific** 82 F/13 Burton NAD27 412184.

**Other pertinent maps** For topo map of nearby terrain, follow links on the website.
**Elevation** 2130 m (6980 ft).
**Elevation gain from trailhead** 760 m (2500 ft).

## AMENITIES
**Heat** Woodstove.
**Cooking** Propane stove/oven; cookware and dishware provided.
**Lighting** Propane.
**Sleeping** 3 double and 1 quad bedroom; linen provided.
**Capacity** 10.
**Features** Sauna, swimming in summer.

## COST (as of Summer 2001)
**Summer catered** $100/person/ night (minimum group of 4; guide for day-hikes available on request).

**Winter guided & catered** $1400/
person/week.

**Winter self-guided & self-catered**
$820/person/week (high sea-
son); $770/person/week (low
season). Only week-long packages are available in winter.

## ACCESS

**Summer** Three hour guided hike
from trailhead. Guests are met
near the town of Passmore
and then driven along logging
roads to the trailhead. The
trail is well-defined but steep,
gaining about 760 m (2500 ft)
over 4 km.

**Winter** Heli-flight from Burton, S
of Nakusp.

## GUIDEBOOKS

*A Climber's Guide to the Interior
Ranges of BC–South,* Krusyna
and Putnam.
*Summits and Icefields,* Scott.

## INFORMATION & BOOKING

Kootenay Mountain Huts
Attention Jeff Gfroerer
Box 1167
Kaslo BC V0G 1M0
**Phone** (250) 353-7179
**E-mail** info@mountainhuts.com
**Website** www.mountainhuts.com

# Evans Lake Cabin

tacular high country is possible for tough, experienced hikers prepared to find their own route. There is a yellow cedar ecological reserve at the west end of the lake.

## LOCATION

**General** In the center of Valhalla Provincial Park, about 18 km (11 mi) NW of Slocan BC.

**Specific** 82 F/13 Burton NAD27 approximately 549227.

**Other pertinent maps** 82 F/14 Slocan (for the E part of the park); *Valhalla Provincial Park Map*.

**Elevation** 1555 m (5100 ft).

**Elevation gain from Slocan Lake** 1015 m (3340 ft).

## AMENITIES

**Heat** Woodstove.

**Cooking** Wood cookstove; no cookware or dishware provided.

**Lighting** None.

**Sleeping** Bunks with foam pads.

**Capacity** 5.

## COST (as of Summer 2001)

Free; no reservations.

This old log building in Valhalla Park was originally built as a fly-in fishing base, and while float plane access is clearly the easiest, a long day of very rigorous hiking and bushwacking can get you there. The fishing in this seldom visited lake is great, and access to some spec-

## ACCESS

**Summer** From Slocan city, hike the 8-km (5-mi) trail along the W side of Slocan Lake to Evans Creek (or, if possible, boat to here). Direct access up Evans Creek is next to impossible. Instead, the trail from the lakeshore starts on the N side of the creek and goes over a steep ridge into the Beatrice Creek drainage, which it then follows past two smaller lakes before reaching a campground on Beatrice Lake (a popular destination for fishers). From here, bushwhack and slog through talus up to the ridge S of the lake, traverse SE along the ridge and then descend when in a direct line with the midpoint between the two small lakes just downstream from Evans Lake clearly visible below you. Once on the Evans Creek valley floor, bushwhack up to the lake. The cabin is on the SE corner of the lake.

**Time** 12–15 hours from Slocan Lake (6 hours to Beatrice Lake; 6+ hours to cabin).

**Winter** Access by skis would be extremely rigorous and dangerous.

## GUIDEBOOKS

*Don't Waste Your Time in the West Kootenays,* Copeland and Copeland.

*A Climber's Guide to the Interior Ranges of BC–South,* Krusyna and Putnam.

*A Visitor's Guide to Valhalla Provincial Park,* a Valhalla Wilderness Society brochure and map.

## INFORMATION

British Columbia Parks
West Kootenay Office
**Phone** (250) 825-3500
**Fax** (250) 825-9509

**Website** www.elp.gov.bc.ca/
  bcparks/explore/kootney.htm
For the *Visitor's Guide Map,*
contact:
The Valhalla Society
Box 329
New Denver BC V0G 1S0
**Phone** (250) 358-2333
**Fax** (250) 358-7950
**E-mail** vws@vws.org
**Website** www.rmec.org/valhalla

# Wee Sandy Creek (Jules Holt) Cabin

This lovely new log cabin is set in an old-growth cedar grove at the confluence of Wee Sandy and Iron Creeks. It is primarily used by those heading on to Wee Sandy Lake (where the fishing is great and there's a free boat to use) or to the high alpine country near Iron Mountain and the New Denver Glacier. Longer traverses to points farther south in the park have been done, but there are no trails beyond Wee Sandy Lake or up the Iron Creek valley. The cabin is small but very nicely finished; a skylight keeps it bright inside. Note that the trailhead can be accessed only by boat from the town of New Denver, but water-taxi service is available.

## LOCATION

*General* Near the N boundary of Valhalla Provincial Park, about 15 km (9 mi) due W of New Denver BC.

*Specific* 82 F/13 Burton NAD27 462837 538071.

*Other pertinent maps* 82 F/14 Slocan (for first half of hike); *Valhalla Provincial Park Map; A Visitor's Guide to Valhalla Provincial Park,* a Valhalla Wilderness Society brochure and map.

*Elevation* 1490 m (4900 ft).

*Elevation gain from Slocan Lake* 957 m (3140 ft).

## AMENITIES

*Heat* Woodstove (wood provided).

*Cooking* Coleman stove (guests supply own fuel).

*Lighting* None.

*Sleeping* 1 2-person bunk layer and floor beneath, no foam pads.

*Capacity* Maximum 4 (2 is ideal)

**COST** (as of Summer 2001)
Free; no reservations.

**ACCESS**

*Summer* After boating across Slocan Lake to the outlet of Wee Sandy Creek (see below for water-taxi information), pick up the trailhead on the S side of creek. The trail follows the creek valley and is generally clear and well-maintained, although it does get a bit overgrown where it crosses slide paths. There are 2 creek crossings involving logs (with wire-mesh foot-grips) and cable hand-rails. The total distance is about 10.5 km (6.6 mi). It is not recommended for novice hikers.

*Time* 4–6 hours.

*Winter* The hut register does show that a few people have trudged up here through late-Spring snow, but the avalanche hazard would make for dangerous winter access. Note that the high-level traverse described in *Summits and Icefields* crosses Wee Sandy Lake, but does not come near the cabin.

**GUIDEBOOKS**

*Don't Waste Your Time in the West Kootenays,* Copeland and Copeland.
*Summits and Icefields,* Scott.

**INFORMATION & BOOKING**

British Columbia Parks
West Kootenay Office
*Phone* (250) 825-3500
*Fax* (250) 825-9509
*Website* www.elp.gov.bc.ca/
    bcparks/explore/kootney.htm
*Water-taxi service* Kingfisher
    Water Taxi
*Phone* (250) 358-2334
For the *Visitor's Guide Map,*
contact:
The Valhalla Society
Box 329
New Denver BC V0G 1S0
*Phone* (250) 358-2333
*Fax* (250) 358-7950
*E-mail* vws@vws.org
*Website* www.rmec.org/valhalla

# Ruby Creek Lodge

Located just north of Valhalla Provincial Park, this timber-frame lodge is located amid the alpine scenery and terrain for which the Valhallas are renowned. Deep powder in winter and extensive wildflower meadows in summer make this a backcountry paradise. The varied terrain provides alpine opportunities for people of all skill levels, and there are mountain bike loop-trails as well. The two-story lodge contains a large sitting room and dining room, and a fully equipped, spacious kitchen. Accessible by car in summer, the lodge is reached by snowcats in winter.

## LOCATION
*General* Just N of Valhalla Park, NW of New Denver BC.
*Specific* 82 K/4 Nakusp NAD27 579488.

*Elevation* 1768 m (5760 ft).
*Elevation gain from Hwy 6* 1211 m (3973 ft).

## AMENITIES
*Heat* Woodstove (wood provided).
*Cooking* Propane stove/oven and BBQ; cookware and dishware provided.
*Lighting* Electric.
*Sleeping* 6 bedrooms (guests provide own bedding).
*Capacity* 12.
*Features* Shower, sauna, guides available.

COST (as of Summer 2001)
*Summer self-guided & self-catered* $400/group/night (minimum group of 12).
*Guiding* $30/person/day (minimum group of 10).
*Catering* $50/person/day (minimum group of 10).

***Winter self-guided & self-catered***
$825/person/week (minimum
group of 12).
***Winter fully guided & catered***
$1200/person/week.
(Winter prices include return
snowcat transportation.)

## ACCESS

***Summer*** From New Denver, drive
13 km (8 mi) N to Hills and
then turn W at the Bonanza
Creek Road sign. Follow this
road for 4 km (2.5 mi) and
then follow the Shannon
Creek Road for a further 9 km
(5.5 mi). The lodge is 200 m
(650 ft) from the parking lot.

***Winter*** Guests are transported up
the Shannon Creek Road by
snowcat.

## INFORMATION & BOOKING

Valhalla Mountain Touring
Attention Dale Caton
RR 1
New Denver BC V0G 1S0
***Phone*** (250) 358-7905
***E-mail*** vmt@netidea.com
***Websites*** www.vMt.ca *and* www.
for.gov.bc.ca/nelson/district/
invermer

# Meadow Mountain Lodge

This spacious lodge north of Kootenay Lake caters both summer and winter to those looking for a luxurious hideaway in a beautiful, remote region of the Selkirks. Accessible by car in summer, it can be reached only by snowcat in winter. Guests have the option of guided or self-guided hiking from late June to September, whereas winter stays consist of week-long guided snowcat-skiing packages, in which guests normally ski 3700–5000 vertical m (12,000–16,000 ft)/day in trackless powder. The lodge offers all you could need at the end of a day in the mountains, including luxurious food, a hot tub, games room and library. It also provides full catering and amenities for conventions.

## LOCATION

*General* In the Goat Range of the Southern Selkirks, about 40 km (25 mi) N of Kaslo BC.

*Other pertinent maps* Unguided hikers may need 82 K/3 Rosebery and 82 K/6 Poplar Creek.

*Elevation* 1280 m (4210 ft).

## AMENITIES

*Heat* Hydro-generated electricity (with back-up diesel generator).

*Cooking* All meals provided.

*Lighting* Electric.

*Sleeping* Double and single rooms; bedding provided.

*Capacity* 24.

*Features* Gourmet meals, late-afternoon hors d'oeuvres, sauna, hot tub, pool table, shuffleboard, great vistas of Macbeth Icefield.

## COST (as of Summer 2001)

**Summer** From $129/person/night for unguided visits to $885/person for 6-night guided hiking packages (inclusive of all meals and access to amenities).

**Winter** From a low-season rate of $2280 to a high-season rate of $2990. (All packages are for 6 nights and 5 days of guided snowcat skiing, including meals, instruction and return snowcat transport to the lodge.)

## ACCESS

**Summer** Vehicle accessed (call ahead for road conditions).
**Winter** Snowcat accessed.

## GUIDEBOOKS

*Don't Waste Your Time in the West Kootenays*, Copeland and Copeland.

## INFORMATION & BOOKING

Meadow Mountain Adventures
Attention Bronwyn C. Murray
921 Observation St
Nelson BC V1L 4Z6
**Phone** 1-888-354-4571
**E-mail** info@meadow-mountain.com
**Website** www.meadow-mountain.com

For information on the snowcat ski packages, contact:
Selkirk Wilderness Skiing
1 Meadow Creek Road
Meadow Creek BC V0G 1N0
**Phone** 1-800-799-3499
**Fax** (250) 366-4419
**E-mail** info@selkirkwilderness.com
**Website** www.selkirkwilderness.com

*Enjoying the world-renowned Selkirk powder*

*An outhouse with a view of Woodbury Glacier*

# Central Columbias

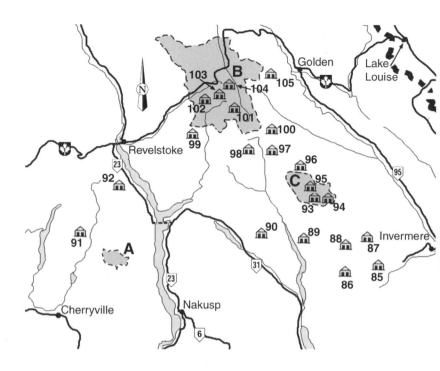

## NATIONAL & PROVINCIAL PARKS

*Map*
*Reference*

A ................Monashee Provincial Park
B................Glacier National Park
C ................Bugaboo Provincial Park

## HUTS & LODGES

*Map*                                                      *Page*
*Reference*                                                *Number*

85................Sultana Creek Cabin ....................200
86................Jumbo Pass Cabin .......................202
87................Forster Creek Cabin ....................204
88................Olive Hut.........................................206
89................Dunn Creek Cabin.......................208
90................Galena Lodge ...............................210
91................Monashee Powder Lodge...............212
92................Blanket Glacier Chalet.................214
93................Bugaboo Lodge.............................216
94................Conrad Kain Hut .........................218
95................Malloy Igloo..................................220
96................Bobbie Burns Lodge ....................222
97................International Basin Hut................224
98................Battle Abbey Lodge .....................226
99................Selkirk Lodge................................228
100..............McMurdo Creek Cabin ................230
101..............Glacier Circle Hut ........................232
102..............Sapphire Col Shelter ....................234
103..............Asulkan Cabin...............................236
104..............A.O. Wheeler Hut .........................238
105..............Purcell Lodge................................240

# Sultana Creek Cabin

Part of an old townsite, this cabin was once used by the operators of the defunct Thunderbird Mine. While the hike to the cabin makes for a great day-trip into wildflower meadows with spectacular views, the cabin is also used for overnight shelter, mainly by skiers and those attempting the tough scramble to the summit of Sultana Peak. The slopes near the cabin provide good long ski runs, but the area should not be approached if avalanche conditions are considerable (the access trail crosses several large avalanche paths). The cabin has no official caretakers, so users are requested to leave it clean and orderly. Note that the cabin has few amenities and is showing its age; also, the stove was not operational as of the summer of 2001.

## LOCATION

**General** In the Purcell Mountains, about 10 linear km (6 mi) W of Invermere BC.

**Specific** 82 K/8 Toby Creek NAD27 5**44**15 2 5**876**86.

**Other pertinent maps** *Backroad Mapbook* or *British Columbia Forest Service Map* of Forest Service road access to trailhead; see small map in *Hikes Around Invermere*.

**Elevation** 2225 m (7300 ft).

**Elevation gain from Delphine Creek** 820 m (2700 ft).

## AMENITIES

**Heat** Woodstove (possibly not operational).

**Cooking** None.

**Lighting** None.

**Sleeping** Wooden platforms, no foam pads.

**Capacity** 6–8.

**COST** (as of Summer 2001)
Free; no reservations.

**ACCESS**

*Summer* From Invermere, follow the paved road to the Panorama Ski Hill and then carry on past it along the Toby Creek Road. After 8 km (5 mi) on the gravel road, turn right onto the well-marked Delphine Creek Road, which may be driven by any vehicle if the gate is unlocked. Follow this road for 3.0 km (1.8 mi) to a small parking area at the trailhead which is marked with tape (no sign; GPS 5**462**83 5**851**73). Hike, ski or bike up the old skid road until reaching the 4th switchback (GPS 5**454**86 5**856**98), at which point you pick up the old mule trail that carries on into the Sultana Creek valley. This trail ascends through 6 switchbacks and then angles NW

across 4 slide-paths. The cabin is on the right of the trail about 400 m (1300 ft) beyond the last slide-path.

*Time* 3 hours.

*Winter* Same, except Delphine Creek Road and possibly Toby Creek Road may not be plowed. Note the avalanche hazard along the trail.

**GUIDEBOOKS**

*Hikes Around Invermere,* Cameron and Gunn.

**INFORMATION**

To obtain the British Columbia Forest Service road map, contact:
Invermere Forest District Office
Box 189
625 4 St
Invermere BC
V0A 1K0
*Phone* (250) 342-4200
*Website* www.for.gov.bc.ca/ nelson/district/invermer

# Jumbo Pass Cabin

This hut built in 1997 sits on a ridge along the Purcell divide, about 500 meters north of the actual pass. Because of its easy access and impressive setting, it is quite popular in summer with hikers. There are superb views (especially from the outhouse picture window) across to the Karnak and Jumbo Mountains, and the Cauldron/Horseshoe glaciers. The nearby meadows and ridges make for great walks, and several of the peaks (such as Bastille Mtn) can be scrambled. Although not easily accessed in winter except by snowmobile, extensive ski touring can be had in the high alpine around the cabin.

## LOCATION
***General*** On the Purcell Divide, about 55 km (34 mi) by road W of Invermere BC.

***Specific*** 82 K/7 Duncan Lake NAD27 5**267**32 5**788**80.
***Other pertinent maps*** *Backroad Mapbook* or *British Columbia Forest Service Map* of Forest Service road access to trailhead; see small map in *Hikes Around Invermere.*
***Elevation*** 2350 m (7710 ft).
***Elevation gain from end of summer road*** 670 m (2200 ft).

## AMENITIES
***Heat*** Woodstove (not to be used between June 1–Sept 15).
***Cooking*** Coleman or propane stove; cookware and dishware provided.
***Lighting*** Coleman lantern.
***Sleeping*** Bunks with foam pads.
***Capacity*** 8+.

## COST (as of Summer 2001)
***Summer*** $10/person/night or $40

for groups of less than 4 who do not wish to share; groups of 6 or more will not have to share.

*Winter* Same.

## ACCESS

*Summer from the east* From Invermere, drive up the Toby Creek Road. About 18 km (11.5 mi) beyond the Panorama ski area, turn N onto the Jumbo Creek Road. Travel for 15.8 km (9.8 mi) and park just before a bridge where an old skid road heads W (GR 290789). Note that in wet weather the Jumbo Creek Road may be impassable after the 7-km (4.2-mi) mark. Walk along the skid road for about 500 m (1600 ft) to the well-flagged trailhead of the 3-km (2-mi) trail up to Jumbo Pass. From the pass, the trail leading NNW to the hut is indistinct, but the hiking along the open, grassy ridgeline is very easy and the hut soon becomes visible.

*Time* 2–3 hours.

*Summer from the west* From the SE corner of Duncan Lake, follow the Glacier Creek Forest Service Road to the trailhead at the 27-km (17-mi) mark. The trail to the pass is well defined. Note that in Summer 2001, this road was closed. It may re-open once logging activity ceases.

*Winter* Most skiers snowmobile to the trailhead from the parking lot at the end of the (gen-erally plowed) Toby Creek Road. Otherwise, it takes most of a day to ski the 21.5 km (13 mi) to the cabin.

## GUIDEBOOKS

*A Climber's Guide to the Interior Ranges of BC–South*, Krusyna and Putnam.

*Mountain Footsteps: Selected Hikes in the East Kootenays,* Strong.

*Don't Waste Your Time in the West Kootenays,* Copeland and Copeland.

*Hikes Around Invermere,* Cameron and Gunn.

## INFORMATION & BOOKING

Columbia Valley Hut Society
Box 322
Invermere BC V0A 1K0
*Phone* (250) 342-5005
*Website* Follow links at www.for.gov.bc.ca/nelson/district/invermer/recreation
*Maximum advance booking* 2 months for nonmembers; 2.5 months for members; memberships cost $25/year.
*Maximum stay* 2 nights.
To obtain the British Columbia Forest Service road map, contact:
Invermere Forest District Office
Box 189
625 4 St
Invermere BC V0A 1K0
*Phone* (250) 342-4200
*Website* www.for.gov.bc.ca/nelson/district/invermer

# Forster Creek Cabin

This new cabin (now open for bookings for the winter of 2001) is a winter-use-only facility built by the Windermere Valley Snowmobile Club in conjunction with the BC Forest Service. It is designed to accommodate snowmobilers and skiers taking advantage of the deep snow in the upper reaches of the Forster Creek drainage. Skiers may wish to carry on up to Olive Hut, an area that is closed to snowmobiles, but whose access entails glacier travel. Note: this new cabin is not far from the site of a recently removed cabin known as the General Store. The Columbia Valley Hut Society also plans to build another cabin in the no-snowmobile zone on the north side of the valley. Check with the society for details.

## LOCATION

**General** Near the headwaters of Forster Creek, about 40 linear km (25 mi) NW of Invermere BC.

**Specific** 82 K/10 Howser Creek NAD27 5**338**32 6**114**85.

**Other pertinent maps** *Backroad Mapbook* or *British Columbia Forest Service Map* of Forest Service road access to trailhead; see small map in *Hikes Around Invermere.*

**Elevation** 1885 m (6200 ft).

**Elevation gain from end of summer road** 130 m (500 ft).

## AMENITIES

**Heat** Woodstove.

**Cooking** Coleman stove; no cookware or dishware provided.

**Lighting** Coleman lantern.

**Sleeping** Bunks, no foam pads.

**Capacity** 4 on bunks (room for 2 on floor).

**Cost** (as of Summer 2001)
Undetermined as yet; contact
Windermere Valley Snowmobile
Club.

## ACCESS
From the 4-way stop in Radium
Hot Springs, drive W on the
Horsethief Forest Service Road to
km 13.5. Turn right onto the
well-marked Forster Creek Forest
Service Road and drive as far up
it as is plowed. Carry on via ski
or snowmobile to the end of the
summer road at km 42. Cross the
narrow bridge and carry on up
the rather overgrown roadbed
for about 2 km (1.2 mi). The
cabin appears on your left shortly after the trail flattens out.

## GUIDEBOOKS
*Summits and Icefields,* Scott (for
   Catamount Glacier descrip-
   tion).
*A Climber's Guide to the Interior
   Ranges of BC–South,* Krusyna
   and Putnam.
*Hikes Around Invermere,* Cameron
   and Gunn.

## INFORMATION
Windermere Valley
Snowmobile Club
Attention Al Bergen, President
**Phone** (250) 345-4598
To obtain the British Columbia
Forest Service road map, contact:
Invermere Forest District Office
Box 189
625 4 St
Invermere BC V0A 1K0
**Phone** (250) 342-4200

**Website** www.for.gov.bc.ca/
   nelson/district/invermer

# Olive Hut

This lovely stone hut built in 1991 serves as a high elevation base for climbing various peaks of the Starbird Ridge complex, for traverses of the Catamount and North Star glaciers, and for ski mountaineering. It sits on a granite rib on the east edge of Catamount Glacier and provides a panoramic view of nearby peaks. Only mountaineers and hikers with glacier travel experience should use the area. Note that the cabin can accommodate only 6, but tenting nearby is possible.

## LOCATION

**General** Near the Catamount Glacier, about 60 linear km (36 mi) NW of Invermere BC.

**Specific** 82 K/10 Howser Creek NAD27 5**31**2**93 6108**777.

**Other pertinent maps** *Backroad Mapbook* or *British Columbia Forest Service Map* of forest service road access to trailhead; see small map in *Hikes Around Invermere*.

**Elevation** 2850 m (8700 ft).

**Elevation gain from end of summer road** 910 m (3000 ft).

## AMENITIES

**Heat** Woodstove (no stove use between July 1–Sept 1).

**Cooking** Propane stove (propane provided); cookware and dishware provided.

**Lighting** Coleman lantern.

**Sleeping** Bunks with foam pads.

**Capacity** 6.

## COST (as of Summer 2001)

**Summer** $10/person/night or $40 for groups of less than 4 who do not wish to share.

**Winter** Same.

## ACCESS

**Summer** From the 4-way stop in Radium Hot Springs, drive W on the Horsethief Forest Service Road to km 13.5. Turn right onto the well-marked Forster Creek Forest Service Road and park at the road's end trailhead at km 42. Follow the old road up the creek for about 3 km (2 mi), past North Star Creek and through the meadows until you reach a big headwall on your left. The outlet stream from Catamount Glacier runs down the center of it. Make your way through a boulder field to a thin trail that heads up a moraine crest on the E side of the creek (do not cross the creek). Carry on straight up (the route-finding is somewhat obvious with several possibilities) until reaching the glacier. Proceed up the glacier (fairly flat, with minimal crevasse problems) for 3 km (2 mi), aiming for a prominent buttress that cuts into the glacier. The hut can be reached either by ascending the buttress from the N or (less steeply) by curling around it and ascending from the S. The total hike is about 7.5 km (5 mi).

**Time** Variable.

**Winter** Unless helicoptering in, most skiers snowmobile to the trailhead from the staging area at the 18.5-km (11-mi) mark on Forster Road. Snowmobiles are prohibited above and S of the point where the trail hits treeline, including Catamount–North Star glaciers. The ascent to Catamount Glacier can pose a serious avalanche risk. Note also that in winter it usually is easiest to ascend the headwall on the W (right-hand) side of the cascade.

## GUIDEBOOKS

*Summits and Icefields,* Scott.

*A Climber's Guide to the Interior Ranges of BC–South,* Krusyna and Putnam.

*Hikes Around Invermere,* Cameron and Gunn.

## INFORMATION & BOOKING

Columbia Valley Hut Society
Box 322
Invermere BC V0A 1K0
**Phone** (250) 342-5005
**Website** Follow links at www.for.gov.bc.ca/nelson/district/invermer/recreation
**Maximum advance booking** 2 months for members; 2.5 months for nonmembers; memberships cost $25/year.
**Maximum stay** 5 nights
To obtain the British Columbia Forest Service road map, contact:
Invermere Forest District Office
Box 189
625 4 St
Invermere BC V0A 1K0
**Phone** (250) 342-4200
**Website** www.for.gov.bc.ca/nelson/district/invermer

# Dunn Creek Cabin

This cabin's sole function was to serve as a base for mountaineers approaching the huge Four Squatters Icefield via the Dunn Creek trail. However, a new logging road farther south seems to have made this approach—and the cabin—redundant. The trail has plainly seen little use and no maintenance in at least the last 10 years; as a result, it has become overgrown and very indistinct. The first kilometer or so of the trail is fairly well marked with tags of orange tape, but these soon become widely spaced and easily lost. And at best they identify the route, for there soon becomes no real trail. In effect, those heading up the valley to the cabin will have to do their own route-finding up through 1400 vertical meters (4300 ft) of heavy bush.

**Note** I could not make it in to the cabin and thus cannot report on its present condition. If anyone can provide with any current information, photos, GPS readings, trail descriptions, etc., that would be much appreciated.

## ACCESS

The trailhead is located along the Duncan River Forest Service Road, which begins at the N end of Kootenay Lake. At the 46-km (27.6-mi) marker, the road crosses Dunn Creek, and the trailhead is a further 500 m (1600 ft) beyond the bridge. However, in the Summer of 2001, the signpost had rotted through and fallen down. I repositioned it upright, but it may not not last long. For those with a high-clearance vehicle, there is a preferable route (which involves a bit more horizontal but far less vertical) to the Four Squatters. Take the logging road signed as "Omo Creek" shortly before the 41-km (25-mi) roadside marker. This road gains about 1000 vertical meters (3300 ft) and ends a little below treeline. From here, you will have to map-navigate your way to the ridge-line that crosses above the cabin and on to the Icefield.

# Galena Lodge

This lodge located in the remote Badshot Range of the Selkirks currently serves solely as a heli-skiing operation. Three major valleys converge nearby, offering a wide variety of skiable terrain both above and below treeline, although the skiing here is recommended for strong, aggressive skiers only. The 180 cm (6 ft) average snowpack is one of the deepest that CMH accesses. As with all CMH lodges, this one provides all the amenities of a first-class hotel, including a hot tub, sauna, bar, gourmet meals and large common room.

## LOCATION

**General** In the Selkirk Mountains, about 80 km (50 mi) SE of Revelstoke BC.

**Specific** 82 K/11 Trout Lake NAD83 **0472**260 6**1253**5.

**Elevation** 1050 m (3440 ft).

**Elevation gain** N/a (heli-accessed).

## AMENITIES

**Heat** Hot water radiant, thermostat controlled.

**Cooking** All meals provided.

**Lighting** Electric.

**Sleeping** Bedrooms with duvets and private baths.

**Capacity** 14 single rooms, 16 double/twin rooms.

**Features** Sauna, hot tub, massage, laundry room, bar, ski shop, exercise room, games room.

## COST (as of Summer 2001)

**Winter heli-skiing** From $4409–$7495/person/week, depending on time of season and single or double occupancy. Rate includes guides and a guarantee of 30,500 vertical m (100,000 ft).

## ACCESS
All transport from Banff is provided. Details provided upon registration.

## INFORMATION & BOOKING
Canadian Mountain Holidays
Box 1660
Banff AB T0L 0C0
**Phone** 1-800-661-0252
**Fax** (403) 762-5879
**Websites** www.cmhhike.com *and*
   www.cmhmountaineering.com
   *and* www.cmhski.com

# Monashee Powder Lodge

This new (1999) facility is one of the few remote lodges that provide access to the deep snow and striking peaks NW of Monashee Provincial Park (between the Selkirks and the Okanagan). With 1500 vertical m (4800 ft) of snowcat-accessed runs both above treeline and in glades, the skiing is superb, and the 18 m (60 ft) snowfall assures you of fresh powder all season long. With creek-generated electricity and hot-water radiant heating, the lodge offers all the comforts that one could want after a full day's skiing. This currently is a winter-only operation.

## LOCATION

*General* On Tsuius Mountain, about 70 km (43 mi) N of Cherryville BC.

*Specific* 82 L/9 Gates Creek NAD27 4**130**14 5**866**36.

*Elevation* 1616 m (5300 ft).

*Elevation gain from valley floor to lodge* 730 m (2400 ft).

## AMENITIES

*Heat* Wood-fueled boiler (hot-water radiant heat in rooms); airtight stove.

*Cooking* All meals provided in winter.

*Lighting* Creek-generated electricity (diesel generator backup).

*Sleeping* Private double bedrooms; bedding provided.

*Capacity* 24.

*Features* Hot tub, large dining and lounging areas, large picture windows for fabulous views.

## COST (as of Summer 2001)

*Winter* From $400–$450/person/day depending on time of ski season. Prices include snowcat skiing, all meals, guiding and transportation to lodge on snowmobile.

## ACCESS

Guests meet in Cherryville (E of Vernon), enjoy dinner and then drive up the Sugar Lake Road to the snowmobile staging area. Guests then drive themselves (with guide) up to the lodge— about one hour.

## INFORMATION & BOOKING

Monashee Powder Adventures

Attention Nick and Ali Holmes-
Smith

RR 2, Comp 11

Chase BC V0E 1M0

*Phone* 1-888-353-8877

*Fax* (250) 679-2999

*E-mail* monasheepowder@idmail.
com

*Website* www.monasheepowder.
com

# Blanket Glacier Chalet

This lovely A-frame chalet near treeline provides easy access to the meadows and glaciers in the Blanket Mountain area. Like most of the Monashees, this region is blanketed in a snowpack as deep as 8 m (26 ft) that makes for excellent skiing for skiers/boarders of all levels, with long runs both above and below treeline, including the 1000 m (3300 ft) descent from Blanket summit. Groups can be fully independent or can choose to have guiding and catering provided, including ski and snowboard instruction courses. The 3-story chalet accommodates 20 people on the upper

two levels, while the main level contains a large kitchen and lounge area. There is a separate sauna-and-shower building. The chalet can be booked for summer use, although the snow-free period may be less than a month.

## LOCATION
*General* S of Revelstoke BC, W of Blanket Creek Provincial Park.
*Specific* 82 L/16 Revelstoke NAD27 122277.
*Elevation* 1782 m (5800 ft).
*Elevation gain from Hwy 23* N/a (heli-accessed).

## AMENITIES
*Heat* Woodstove and propane furnace.
*Cooking* Propane stove/oven; cookware and dishware provided.
*Lighting* Propane; solar for reading and kitchen.
*Sleeping* Various rooms that accommodate 2–6/room; (guests provide own sleeping bags).
*Capacity* 20.
*Features* Sauna with shower, spectacular views from big windows.

## COST (as of Summer 2001)
*Summer* The chalet is available for group bookings in July and August, although the deep snowpack may not be gone from the meadows until mid-

July. Phone for availability and costs.

**Winter** $600/person/week, including return heli-flight (minimum booking of 14 in a group).

**Note** Some weeks are set aside for ski and snowboard instruction camps.

## ACCESS

**Summer** While most guests fly in, there is a rigorous and thin trail that leads to the chalet. A detailed description of the land access will be provided to those guests who register for a summer group booking and who wish to consider hiking in.

**Winter** Heli-accessed only.

## GUIDEBOOKS
*Summits and Icefields,* Scott.

## INFORMATION & BOOKING
Nordic Ski Institute
Box 8150
Canmore AB T1W 2T9
**Phone & Fax** (403) 678-4102
**E-mail** aschaffe@telusplanet.net
**Website** Under construction.

# Bugaboo Lodge

The site of the first heli-skiing operation in Canada, this lodge near the base of the dramatic granite spires of the Bugaboos remains a spectacular destination in itself. The skiing is superb, and the mountaineering opportunities are world-renowned. A lodge-to-lodge traverse is a hiking option. As with all the CMH lodges, this one provides all the amenities of a first-class hotel, including a hot tub, sauna, bar, gourmet meals and large common room. Guides for all activities are provided.

## LOCATION
**General** In the Purcell Mountains, inside Bugaboo Provincial Park, about 65 linear km (40 mi) S of Golden BC.
**Specific** 82 K/15 Bugaboo Creek NAD83 5**20**7**98** 6**225**29.

**Elevation** 1490 m (4890 ft).
**Elevation gain** N/a (heli-accessed).

## AMENITIES
**Heat** Hot water radiant, thermostat controlled.
**Cooking** All meals provided.
**Lighting** Electric.
**Sleeping** Bedrooms with duvets and private baths.
**Capacity** 4 single rooms, 20 double/twin rooms.
**Features** Sauna, hot tub, large stone fireplace, bar, climbing wall, exercise room, games room.

## COST (as of Summer 2001)
**Summer guided hiking** $1382–$1626/person for 3 nights; $2597–$3055/person for 6 nights lodge to lodge
**Guided mountaineering** $1822–$2144/person for 3 nights;

$3462-$4073 for 6 nights lodge to lodge. Rates based on double occupancy (reduced rates for children under 15). Rates include transport from Banff, heli-flights, guides and use of all necessary equipment.

*Winter heli-skiing* From $4409–$7068/person/week, depending on time of season and single or double occupancy. Rate includes guides and a guarantee of 30,500 vertical m (100,000 ft).

### ACCESS

All transport from Banff is provided. Details provided upon registration.

### INFORMATION & BOOKING

Canadian Mountain Holidays
Box 1660
Banff AB T0L 0C0
*Phone* 1-800-661-0252
*Fax* (403) 762-5879
*Websites* www.cmhhike.com *and* www.cmhmountaineering.com *and* www.cmhski.com

# Conrad Kain Hut

Set in perhaps the most spectacular section of the Purcell Mountains, this hut is heavily used by mountaineers who are drawn to the mammoth granite spires and vast icefields of the Bugaboos. Although full glacier-travel and climbing gear is needed to access most of the park, a nontechnical circle hike that includes the hut and Cobalt Lake is an option. The hut is very well maintained, and the views it affords of the towering jagged spires make it an attractive destination in itself. A traverse across several glaciers to the Malloy Igloo hut is also an option. Note that because of receding glaciers in recent years, the once-easy ascent to the Bugaboo-Snow-patch col has become very difficult and may be dangerous except under heavy snow cover.

## LOCATION

**General** Near the southern boundary of Bugaboo Provincial Park in the Purcell Mountains SW of Golden BC.

**Specific** 82 K/10 Howser Creek NAD27 166204.

**Other pertinent maps** 82 K/15 Bugaboo Creek (for the N of the park); *Backroad Mapbook* or *British Columbia Forest Service Map* of Forest Service road access to trailhead; *Bugaboo Provincial Park Map;* see small map in *Hikes Around Invermere.*

**Elevation** 2195 m (7200 ft).

**Elevation gain from parking lot** 700 m (2300 ft).

## AMENITIES

**Heat** Hydro electric (summer only).

**Cooking** Propane; cookware and dishware provided.

**Lighting** Propane in kitchen/

common area in winter; hydro in summer.

*Sleeping* common loft area with foam pads.

*Capacity* 40.

COST (as of November 2000)
*Reservation* $18/person/night.
*Pay at the hut* $15/person/night.

## ACCESS

*Summer* From the town of Brisco N of Radium Hot Springs on Hwy 95, follow the clearly marked signs to Bugaboo Park. The 45-km (27-mi) road is in good condition but is used by logging trucks. From the parking lot at the end of the road, a 5-km (3-mi) trail leads to the hut. Although clearly defined, this trail is quite steep and strenuous in places. Ladders and steel cables must be used to get through some steep and exposed sections of the trail. Try to avoid getting too distracted by the spectacular vistas.

*Time* 2–3 hours.

*Winter* The hut is closed in winter because of danger from avalanches, but it can be booked by ski-tourers from mid-March to May.

## GUIDEBOOKS

*Bugaboo Rock: A Climber's Guide,* Green and Benson.
*Summits & Icefields,* Scott.
*Hikes Around Invermere,* Cameron and Gunn.

## INFORMATION & BOOKING

The Alpine Club of Canada
Box 8040
Canmore AB T1W 2T8
*Phone* (403) 678-3200
*Fax* (403) 678-3224
*E-mail* alpclub@telusplanet.net
*Website* www.alpineclubof canada.ca

For a map and other park information, contact:
Kootenay District Parks Office
Box 118
Wasa BC V0B 2K0
*Phone* (250) 422-4200
*Fax* (250) 422-3326
*Website* www.elp.gov.bc.ca/ bcparks/explore/kootney.htm

# Malloy Igloo

As its name suggests, this shelter is a white dome made of fiberglass. Although small, drafty and without amenities, it provides much-appreciated shelter for climbers attempting peaks in the Vowell and Conrad groups, where climbing opportunities are both extensive and very impressive. Set on a small outcropping of rock, this hut should be a destination only for experienced mountaineers. It can be reached by a traverse from Conrad Kain Hut farther south; note, however, that because of receding glaciers in recent years, the once-easy ascent from Kain Hut to the Bugaboo–Snowpatch col is very dangerous except under heavy snow-cover. The much longer route around the south of Snowpatch Spire may be required.

## LOCATION

*General* On the edge of the Malloy Glacier in Bugaboo Provincial Park, 60 km S of Golden BC.

*Specific* 82 K/15 Bugaboo Creek NAD27 104262.

*Other pertinent maps* Backroad Mapbook or *British Columbia Forest Service Map* of Forest Service road access to trailhead; *Bugaboo Provincial Park Map;* 82 K/10 Howser Creek (for southern portion of park and access from Kain Hut); 82 K/16 Spillimacheen (may be needed for navigation along logging roads to northern access point).

*Elevation* 2680 m (8800 ft).

*Net elevation gain from Conrad Kain Hut* 488 m (1600 ft).

## AMENITIES

*Heat* None.

*Cooking* None.

*Lighting* None.

*Sleeping* Platform; no foam pads.

*Capacity* 6.

## COST (as of Summer 2001)

Free; no reservations.

## ACCESS

*Summer from Conrad Kain Hut* If the snow is sufficiently thick all the way to the Bugaboo-Snowpatch col, climb to this point and then bear generally NW across the Vowell Glacier. Alternately, loop around Snowpatch Spire to attain this Glacier. Pass to the W of Wallace Peak and carry on NW across the Malloy Glacier to the hut. Good map-reading skills and glacier-travelling experience are needed. Net distance about 13 km (8 mi).

**Time** Allow a full day.

**Summer from logging roads to the north** From Spillimacheen on Hwy 93, cross the Columbia River and follow a series of logging roads up Bobbie Burns Creek and then Vowell Creek to its confluence with Malloy Creek. A current Forestry Service road map is indispensable, and it is advised that you check with the Invermere British Columbia Forest Service office to find out which roads may have recently become impassable. Hike up along the E side of Malloy Creek (no defined trail) and get on the crest of the moraine as soon as possible. The headwall below the hut may require roped climbing in late summer when all snow has melted.

**Time** Allow a full day.

**Winter** The hut is unlocked but there is no easy ground access. The southerly approach via Kain Hut poses high avalanche risk until late in the season, although heli access to Kain Hut or to the Vowell-Malloy Glaciers is possible. Ground access from the N is rare, unless logging activity in the area has resulted in the roads being plowed.

**GUIDEBOOKS**

*Summits and Icefields,* Scott.

*A Climber's Guide to the Interior Ranges of BC–South,* Krusyna and Putnam.

**INFORMATION**

Kootenay District Parks Office
Box 118
Wasa BC V0B 2K0
**Phone** (250) 422-4200
**Fax** (250) 422-3326
**Website** www.elp.gov.bc.ca/
  bcparks/explore/kootney.htm
To obtain the British Columbia Forest Service road map, contact:
Invermere Forest District Office
Box 189
625 4 St
Invermere BC V0A 1K0
**Phone** (250) 342-4200
**Website** www.for.gov.bc.ca/
  nelson/district/invermer

# Bobbie Burns Lodge

This luxury, heli-accessed lodge located just north of Bugaboo Provincial Park affords access to 1600 km² (615 mi²) of remote and spectacular regions of both the Selkirk and Purcell Ranges. The typical 150 cm (4.8 ft) snowpack makes for superb skiing, and in summer the alpine meadows and high ridges provide dramatic hiking. There are many nearby peaks to challenge mountaineers, especially those in the celebrated Bugaboos. A lodge-to-lodge traverse is an option. As with all the CMH lodges, this one provides all the amenities of a first-class hotel, including a hot tub, sauna, bar, gourmet meals and large common room. Guides for all activities are provided.

## LOCATION

**General** In the Purcell Mountains, N of Bugaboo Provincial Park BC.

**Specific** 82 K/15 Bugaboo Creek NAD83 5**049**77 6**427**29.

**Elevation** 1370 m (4490 ft).

**Elevation gain** N/a (heli-accessed).

## AMENITIES

**Heat** Hot water radiant, thermostat controlled.

**Cooking** All meals provided.

**Lighting** Electric.

**Sleeping** Bedrooms with duvets and private baths.

**Capacity** 9 single rooms, 13 double/twin rooms.

**Features** Sauna, hot tub, ski shop, massage, laundry room, bar, exercise room, games room.

**COST** (as of Summer 2001)

**Summer guided hiking** $1382–$1626/person for 3 nights;

$2597–$3055/person for 6 nights lodge to lodge.

**Guided mountaineering** $1822–$2144/person for 3 nights; $3462–$4073 for 6 nights lodge to lodge. Rates based on double occupancy (reduced rates for children under 15). Rates include transport from Banff, heli-flights, guides, use of all necessary equipment.

**Winter heli-skiing** From $4748–$8038/person/week, depending on time of season and single or double occupancy. Rate includes guides and a guarantee of 30,500 vertical m (100,000 ft).

## ACCESS

All transport from Banff is provided. Details provided upon registration.

## INFORMATION & BOOKING

Canadian Mountain Holidays
Box 1660
Banff AB T0L 0C0
**Phone** 1-800-661-0252
**Fax** (403) 762-5879
**Websites** www.cmhhike.com *and* www.cmhmountaineering.com *and* www.cmhski.com

# International Basin Hut

A remote cabin in very rugged country, this new hut (built in 1999) was erected by the Columbia Valley Hut Society to provide serious climbers, hikers and skiers with a secure shelter. It also is a welcome sight for skiers doing the long Bugaboo–Rogers Pass traverse. Much of the terrain and many of the peaks in this area are very seldom visited; you are generally on your own for route-finding. Note that access from the McMurdo Creek area entails glacier travel.

## LOCATION

**General** Near the headwaters of Bobbie Burns Creek in International Basin, about 40 linear km (25 mi) SW of Golden BC.

**Specific** 82 K/14 Westfall River NAD27 **489**590 6**443**72.

**Other pertinent maps** *Backroad Mapbook* or *British Columbia Forest Service Map* of Forest Service road access to trailhead; see small map in *Hikes Around Invermere*.

**Elevation** 2185 m (7170 ft).

**Elevation gain from end of summer road** 840 m (2755 ft).

## AMENITIES

**Heat** Woodstove (not to be used between June 1–Sept 15).

**Cooking** Coleman or propane stove; cookware and dishware provided.

**Lighting** Coleman lantern.

**Sleeping** Bunks with foam pads.

**Capacity** 6.

## COST (as of Summer 2001)

**Summer** $10/person/night or $40 for groups of less than 4 who do not wish to share; groups of 4 or more will not have to share.

*Winter* Same.

## ACCESS
*Summer* See the directions for access to McMurdo Creek Cabin. From the cabin, continue S along an old mine road until it reaches the base of the old mine site and then ascend SSE across glaciated bedrock and a small pocket glacier to reach the shoulder at 2540 m (8335 ft). Carry on up the W ridge and traverse the edge of the Spillimacheen Glacier. Continue to traverse southerly while losing 355+ m (1000 ft) to an open forested meadow and the cabin site. See the Cameron and Gunn text for very detailed descriptions of the route into and throughout International Basin (although the first edition of this book pre-dates the existence of the hut).

*Time* 5–7 hours from McMurdo Creek Cabin.
*Winter* Same.

## GUIDEBOOKS
*Summits and Icefields,* Scott.
*A Climber's Guide to the Interior Ranges of BC–South,* Krusyna and Putnam.

## INFORMATION & BOOKING
Columbia Valley Hut Society
Box 322
Invermere BC V0A 1K0
*Phone* (250) 342-5005
*Website* Follow links at www.for. gov.bc.ca/nelson/district/ invermer/recreation
*Maximum advance booking* 2 months for nonmembers; 2.5 months for members; memberships cost $25/year.
*Maximum stay* 5 nights.

# Battle Abbey Lodge

This marvelous stone chalet is set deep in the Battle Range of the Purcells and provides access to some very remote and spectacular terrain in the "Herman Melville" group (near Mts Moby Dick, Ahab and Omoo). There are great slopes for turns in the Schooner Pass area south of the lodge, and farther up the Butters Creek valley are long runs down the slopes of Mts Pequod and Typee. The lodge itself is a very comfortable two-story chalet built by Hans Gmoser, and it features hot running water and local-generated electricity. The facility is currently not available for summer use.

### LOCATION

*General* About 32 km (20 mi) S of Roger's Pass BC.

*Specific* 82 K/14 Westfall River NAD27 **475**9**3**6 6**476**85.

*Elevation* Approximately 2100 m (6900 ft).

*Elevation gain* N/a (heli-accessed).

### AMENITIES

*Heat* Woodstove.

*Cooking* Woodstove and oven; cookware and dishware provided.

*Lighting* Solar and wind-generated electric.

*Sleeping* Foam mattresses in 4 semi-private rooms in loft area.

*Capacity* 12.

*Features* Hot and cold running water.

### COST (as of summer 2001)

Costs for week-long summer and winter packages are being adjusted as this book goes to press.

Contact the owners directly for
updates.

## ACCESS
Heli-access only.

## GUIDEBOOKS
*Summits and Icefields*, Scott.

## INFORMATION & BOOKING
Robson Gmoser
*Phone* (250) 344-0594
*E-mail* mail@alpineroutes.com
Roger Laurilla
*Phone* (250) 344-5292
*E-mail* rwlvam@rockies.net

# Selkirk Lodge

**LOCATION**
*General* Near the SW corner of Glacier National Park, 35 linear km (22 mi) E of Revelstoke BC.
*Specific* 82 N/4 Illecillewaet NAD27 490548.
*Elevation* 2200 m (7218 ft).
*Elevation gain* N/a (heli-accessed).

**AMENITIES**
*Heat* Woodstoves.
*Cooking* All meals provided.
*Lighting* Solar.
*Sleeping* 4 bedrooms; bedding provided (including goose down duvets).
*Capacity* 12.
*Features* Shower, sauna, indoor plumbing, accredited guides, radio phone, propane-powered incinerating toilet.

L ocated alongside the Albert Icefield, this lodge provides access to the huge snowpack of over 15 m (50 ft) on the west side of the Selkirks. The lodge is close to glaciers and gladed slopes and provides opportunities for long tours or for as much vertical as your legs can take in a day; many runs exceed 900 vertical m (3000 ft). Summer opportunities range from alpine meadow-walking to high-end mountaineering. The lodge provides all the amenities (including showers) needed for a comfortable stay in remote terrain, as well as meals with a "West Coast/fusion twist."

**COST** (as of Summer 2001)
*Summer* Guided or unguided trips of 3, 4 and 7 days can be booked. The prices vary depending on length of stay, the level of service expected and the number of guides needed.
*Winter* Fully catered and guided $1290/person/week (including GST and return heli-flights).

**ACCESS**
Heli-access only.

**GUIDEBOOKS**
*Summits and Icefields,* Scott.
*Columbia Mountains of Canada–Central,* Fox.

## INFORMATION & BOOKING

Selkirk Lodge Ltd.
Box 130
Revelstoke BC V0E 2S0
**Phone** 1-800-663-7080 *or*
    (250) 837-5378
**Fax** (250) 837-5766
**E-mail** selkirk@rockies.net
**Website** Under construction

# McMurdo Creek Cabin

L ocated in a meadow near the headwaters of McMurdo Creek, this cabin at a former mine site is used by both hikers/skiers and snowmobilers. A ski zone (no motorized access) has been established for all areas south of the cabin, including Spillimacheen Glacier. Great hikes and ski tours are possible into the basins south of the cabin, and the nearby Silent Pass is renowned for its summer flowers and winter skiing. The cabin is fairly easily accessed from the end of a long drive on logging roads.

## LOCATION

**General** In the Spillamacheen Range, just E of the Purcell Divide, about 30 km (19 mi) SW of Golden BC.

**Specific** 82N/3 Mt Wheeler NAD27 **4896**34 **6554**35.

**Other pertinent maps** *Backroad Mapbook* or *British Columbia Forest Service Map* of Forest Service road access to trailhead; see small map in *Hikes Around Invermere.*

**Elevation** 1760 m (5775 ft).

**Elevation gain from end of summer road** 80 m (260 ft).

## AMENITIES

**Heat** Woodstove (not to be used between June 1–Sept 15).

**Cooking** Coleman and propane stoves (no fuel provided); cookware and dishware provided.

**Lighting** Coleman lantern.

**Sleeping** Bunks with foam pads.

**Capacity** 5–7 (a bit crowded with 7).

## COST (as of Summer 2001)

**Summer** $10/person/night or $40 for groups of less than 4 who do not wish to share; groups of 5 or more will not have to share.

*Winter* Same.

## ACCESS

*Summer* From Parson on Hwy 95, drive W along the Spillimacheen–North Fork Road and turn onto the clearly marked McMurdo Creek Road at km 45.8. Drive up this road, ignoring a left fork that leads over a bridge at km 55.2. At the 57-km (34.2-mi) mark is a well-marked junction; the right fork leads up to the Silent Pass trailhead, and the left fork (negotiable only by 4x4s, and risky when wet) carries on for about 1 km (0.6 mi) to the trailhead. The cabin is an easy 600 m (2000 ft) walk along the old roadbed.

*Time* Under 15 minutes from the trailhead.

*Winter* The Spillimacheen Road is usually plowed to the McMurdo Road until mid-December, after which snowmobile staging/parking is either at km 27 or 21 for the duration of the winter. Ski access over the 30 km (18 mi) of unplowed road is possible but rigorous. Heli-access is also possible.

## GUIDEBOOKS

*Summits and Icefields,* Scott.

*A Climber's Guide to the Interior Ranges of BC–South,* Krusyna and Putnam.

*Hikes Around Invermere,* Cameron and Gunn.

## INFORMATION & BOOKING

Columbia Valley Hut Society
Box 322
Invermere BC V0A 1K0
*Phone* (250) 342-5005
*Website* Follow links at www.for. gov.bc.ca/nelson/district/ invermer/recreation
*Maximum advance booking* 2 months for members; 2.5 months for nonmembers; memberships cost $25/year.
*Maximum stay* 3 nights
To obtain the British Columbia Forest Service road map, contact:
Invermere Forest District Office
Box 189
625 4 St
Invermere BC V0A 1K0
*Phone* (250) 342-4200

# Glacier Circle Hut

This 80-year-old log cabin is set in a spectacular cirque and affords access to a wide array of mountaineering options—which is why it was heavily used by the early Swiss guides leading parties up any of the 7 or 8 nearby peaks. A welcome sight for anyone doing the Bugaboo–Rogers Pass traverse, the hut is now a bit dilapidated and has been known to disappear totally under the huge snowpack that falls on this area. A GPS (and strong backs for shovelling) may be vital if heading here in winter. Note that the steep slope between the cirque and the Illecillewaet Nevé can be a serious avalanche hazard.

## LOCATION
*General* In Glacier National Park BC, about 15 linear km (9 mi) S of Rogers Pass on Hwy 1.

*Specific* 82 N/3 Mt Wheeler NAD83 726690.

*Other pertinent maps* 82 N/5 Glacier (for trail between Hwy 1 and Illecillewaet Nevé); *Touring at Rogers Pass*, Murray Toft (replaces the need for the three topo maps).

*Elevation* 1800 m (5900 ft).

*Elevation change from Illecillewaet Campground* 1310 m (4300 ft) gain to the Nevé and then a 759 m (2500 ft) drop to the cirque.

## AMENITIES
*Heat* Woodstove (no wood provided).

*Cooking* Coleman stove; some dishware.

*Lighting* Coleman lantern.

*Sleeping* Loft with foam pads.

*Capacity* 8.

## COST (as of Summer 2001)
*Summer* $10/person/night payable at the park main office at Rogers Pass.

*Winter* Same.

## ACCESS
*Summer* From the Illecillewaet Campground parking lot off Hwy 1 just W of Rogers Pass,

get on the well-signposted Perley Rock trail. Follow this trail up past Perley Rock and then move onto the glacier (noting your access point for the return trip). Cross the long, flat Nevé in a general SSE direction toward the SW side of Mt Macoun, avoiding any temptation to head low to your right. To descend to the cirque, head down along the moraine and slabs alongside the base of Mt Macoun or (longer but more easily) head SW toward the Witch Tower and descend the snow slope and moraine below it. Once down onto the flats, cross the creek and try to find the blazed trail leading SE out of the meadow, but if you lose this, aim generally for the spot where the creek enters the small lake below the Deville Glacier. About 150 m (500 ft) upstream from this point is a well-used log crossing; the difficult-to-locate hut is about 50 m (160 ft) N of the creek amid some huge glacial erratics.

*Time* 8–11 hours.

*Note* Hiking access up the Beaver River is possible, but the trail is thin and the bushwhacking is ferocious.

*Winter* Same, although note that avalanche hazards can be considerable (the Witch Tower descent is less risky than the one from the base of Macoun). The hut may be completely buried in snow and is difficult to locate amid the profusion of snow-covered erratics in the area. The Beaver River route is less onerous than it is in summer, and in bad weather it may be the only exit route.

### GUIDEBOOKS

*Summits and Icefields,* Scott.
*Columbia Mountains of Canada–Central*, Fox.

### INFORMATION & BOOKING

For reservations, contact:
Rogers Pass Centre
*Phone* (250) 814-5232
For general park information contact:
Glacier and Mt Revelstoke National Parks
Box 350
Revelstoke BC V0E 2S0
*Phone* (250) 837-7500
*Fax* (250) 837-7536
*E-mail* revglacier_reception@pch.gc.ca
*Website* parkscan.harbour.com/glacier

# Sapphire Col Shelter

Set on a high col in Glacier National Park, this small shelter is used primarily by skiers and mountaineers, especially those climbing Mts Swanzy and Clarke or doing the Abbot-to-Pollux traverse. Although it is very rustic and has few amenities, this hut provides very snug protection from the wild weather that often blows through here. Note that glacier travel is entailed in reaching the hut.

## LOCATION
**General** On Sapphire Col at the head of the Asulkan Valley, located SW of Rogers Pass in Glacier National Park BC.

**Specific** 82 N/3 Mt Wheeler NAD83 651732.

**Other pertinent maps** 82 N/5 Glacier; 82 N/4 Illecillewaet (may also be needed); *Touring*

*at Rogers Pass*, Murray Toft (replaces the need for the three topo maps).

**Elevation** 2590 m (8500 ft).

**Elevation gain from Illecillewaet campground parking lot** 1340 m (4400 ft).

## AMENITIES
**Heat** None.

**Cooking** None.

**Lighting** None.

**Sleeping** Bunks with foam pads.

**Capacity** 4 comfortably (a few more could be squeezed in).

**COST** (as of Summer 2001)

**Summer** $10/person/night payable at the park main office at Rogers Pass.

**Winter** Same.

## ACCESS
**Summer** See the access descrip-

tion for Asulkan Hut. The route to Sapphire Col departs from this route not far from the Asulkan Hut. As you approach the valley end, cross over to ascend along the SW lateral moraine and then continue up steeply across rock and the Asulkan Glacier to the col between The Dome and Castor Peak. Only experienced mountaineers prepared for glacier travel should undertake this trip. Note that winter travel up the Asulkan Valley entails passing underneath slopes that, in certain conditions, pose significant avalanche hazards. The net distance is about 8 km (5 mi).
*Time* 5–6 hours.
*Winter* Same.

### GUIDEBOOKS
*Summits and Icefields,* Scott.
*Columbia Mountains of Canada–Central,* Fox.

### INFORMATION & BOOKING
For reservations, contact:
Rogers Pass Centre
*Phone* (250) 814-5232
For general park information, contact:
Glacier and Mt Revelstoke National Parks
Box 350
Revelstoke BC V0E 2S0
*Phone* (250) 837-7500
*Fax* (250) 837-7536
*E-mail* revglacier_reception@pch.gc.ca
*Website* parkscan.harbour.com/glacier

# Asulkan Cabin

Located near the upper end of the Asulkan valley near Rogers Pass, this new hut is a popular destination for hikers and especially skiers. The famous steep-and-deep snow of this area can be easily accessed from here; 1500 vertical m (5000 ft)/day of telemarking is not uncommon, and you could spend many days here without ever crossing your tracks. As well, mountaineers and scramblers use this as a base for travel up any of several high peaks that ring this deep valley. By hut standards, this one is quite luxurious, with big, double-glazed windows and propane heating. Owned by Parks Canada, the hut is booked through the Alpine Club of Canada.

## LOCATION

*General* In the Asulkan Valley, about 7 km (4 mi) by trail from the parking area on Hwy 1 near the Illecillewaet Campground BC.

*Specific* 82 N/3 Mt Wheeler NAD27 673737.

*Other pertinent maps* 82 N/5 Glacier; 82 N/4 Illecillewaet (may also be needed); *Touring at Rogers Pass*, Murray Toft (replaces the need for the three topo maps, but note that this hut is imprecisely located on the map).

*Elevation* 2100 m (6890 ft).

*Elevation gain from Hwy 1* 808 m (2650 ft).

## AMENITIES

*Heat* Propane.

*Cooking* Propane stove; cookware and dishware provided.

*Lighting* Propane.
*Sleeping* Loft with foam pads.
*Capacity* 12.

COST (as of November 2000)
*Summer* $20/person/night (Children 16 and under free).
Reservations can be made up to 6 months in advance.
*Winter* Same.

ACCESS
*Summer* Take the Illecillewaet Campground turnoff 3.6 km (2 mi) W of the Visitor's Centre on Hwy 1. Proceed through the campground and park just beyond the Welcome Centre. Follow the clearly marked trail up alongside Asulkan Creek. The cabin is 300 m (1000 ft) beyond the end of the trail; the total distance is 6.5 km (4 mi).
*Time* 3–5 hours.
*Winter* Park at the plowed parking area just W of the bridge over the Illecillewaet River. Ski upstream on the W bank of the river until reaching the old railbed. The route along the valley floor is quite obvious, although good avalanche awareness skills are needed, for the route passes underneath some steep slopes where the avalanche hazard can be very significant.

GUIDEBOOKS
*Summits & Icefields*, Scott.
*Columbia Mountains of Canada–Central*, Fox.

INFORMATION & BOOKING
The Alpine Club of Canada
Box 8040
Canmore AB T1W 2T8
*Phone* (403) 678-3200
*Fax* (403) 678-3224
*E-mail* alpclub@telusplanet.net
*Website* www.alpineclubof
    canada.ca

# A.O. Wheeler Hut

Not far from the site where the CPR built Glacier House in 1897 (and which was the center for mountaineering in North America for the next quarter century), the Alpine Club of Canada built this hut for much the same purpose. Although not a truly backcountry hut, this lovely old log cabin near the highway in Rogers Pass is commonly used as a base for hikes, climbs and ski-tours into the Asulkan and Illecillewaet areas south of the highway and the Hermit Range north of the highway. The hut is large, well appointed and rich in charm and history.

## LOCATION
*General* About 4 km SW of Rogers Pass BC, just off Hwy 1.
*Specific* 82 N/6 Blaeberry NAD27 657791.

*Other pertinent maps* 82 N/5 Glacier (for the Hermit Range); 82 N/4 Illecillewaet (for the climbs of Mts Bonney, Abbott and Swanzy); 82 N/3 Mt Wheeler (for the Illecillewaet Neve and peaks S of the hut); *Touring at Rogers Pass,* Murray Toft (replaces the need for the three topo maps).
*Elevation* 1250 m (4100 ft).
*Elevation gain from Hwy 1* About 45 m (145 ft).

## AMENITIES
*Heat* Woodstoves.
*Cooking* Propane stove and oven; cookware and dishware provided.
*Lighting* Propane.
*Sleeping* Three separate sleeping areas on upper level.
*Capacity* 30 (24 in winter).

**COST** (as of Summer 2001)
An Alpine Club Class A+ hut: $17.50 for members; $24 for nonmembers; $19.50 for group members. (Children 16 and under half price).

**ACCESS**
*Summer* Take the Illecillewaet Campground turnoff 3.6 km (2 mi) W of the Visitor's Centre on Hwy 1. Proceed through the campground and park just beyond the Welcome Centre. Walk up the road to the hut (about 5 minutes).
*Winter* Park at the plowed parking area just W of the bridge over the Illecillewaet River. Ski upstream on the W bank of the river until reaching the old railbed. Follow this left and over the river to the hut (about 15 mintues).

**GUIDEBOOKS**
*Summits & Icefields,* Scott.
*Columbia Mountains of Canada–Central,* Fox.

**INFORMATION & BOOKING**
The Alpine Club of Canada
Box 8040
Canmore AB T1W 2T8
*Phone* (403) 678-3200
*Fax* (403) 678-3224
*E-mail* alpclub@telusplanet.net
*Website* www.alpineclubof canada.ca

# Purcell Lodge

One of the most luxurious backcountry accommodations in British Columbia (with cuisine that has been featured in *Gourmet* magazine), this lodge on a large alpine plateau provides access to a broad array of meadow and ridge hikes, as well as all levels of skiing terrain. With the high peaks in Glacier Park as a backdrop, this is true wilderness-postcard country. The lodge has its own hydro-electric generator and provides a level of comfort on a par with luxury hotels, with amenities ranging from a 24-hour snack bar to balcony access off the bedrooms. The lodge has been selected as Wilderness Hiking Lodge of the Year and Cross-country Ski Area of the Year by two American magazines.

## LOCATION

*General* Near the border of Glacier National Park on a plateau E of the Beaver River, about 21 km (13 mi) W of Golden BC.

*Specific* 82 N/6 Blaeberry NAD27 782788.

*Other pertinent maps* 82 N/3 Mt Wheeler; see small map in *Hikes Around Invermere*.

*Elevation* 2194 m (7200 ft).

*Elevation gain on summer-only hiking trail* Approximately 700 m (2295 ft).

## AMENITIES

*Heat* Propane forced-air and woodstoves.

*Cooking* All meals provided; self-catering is possible outside of high season, with access to a full kitchen.

*Lighting* Electric.

*Sleeping* Private rooms (of 3 different types) with duvets and ensuite vanities.

*Capacity* 20–30.

*Features* Sauna, large living room, library, rooms with balconies, hot showers, flush toilets, 24-hour snack bar, guides/naturalists provided, no heli-skiing or snowmobiling allowed in the area.

## COST (as of Summer 2001)

Prices vary widely depending on length of stay, type of room, size of group, time of season and efficiency of helicopter use. Contact the lodge for specifics. In low season (mid-Oct–January and late Apr–mid-June) the lodge can be booked by groups wishing to self-cater at rates competitive with traditional mountain "hut rental" facilities. Prices start at $540/person for a 3-night stay; this price includes accommodation, bedding, use of all the facilities, use of kitchen equipment, the helicopter shuttle, provincial taxes, national park land use fees and a lodge custodian to oversee systems maintenance. The group is responsible for providing towels, food, cooking, cleaning and guiding services. The group is also required to supply meals and helicopter transportation for one custodian.

## ACCESS

*Summer* Trail directions for hikers are provided upon registration, although the Cameron and Gunn text also describes the trail from the end of the Spillimacheen Forest Service Road. The summer-only trail is 13 km (8 mi) long if you own a high-clearance vehicle—17 km (10.5 mi) long if you don't—after a 1.5-hour drive on a mix of paved and gravel (logging) roads from Golden. The heli-flight from Golden takes 12 minutes, the cost of which is included in the summer package (but deducted if you hike in).

*Time* 5–7 hours.

*Winter* Heli-access only.

## GUIDEBOOKS

*Summits and Icefields,* Scott.

*A Climber's Guide to the Interior Ranges of BC–South,* Krusyna and Putnam.

*Hikes Around Invermere,* Cameron and Gunn.

## INFORMATION & BOOKING

Purcell Lodge
Places Less Travelled Ltd.
Box 1829
Golden BC V0A 1H0
*Phone* (250) 344-2639
*Fax* (250) 344-5520
*E-mail* places@rockies.net
*Website* www.purcell.com

*Hiking through wildflowers at Silent Pass*

*Crossing the Catamount Glacier en route to Olive Hut*

# North Columbias

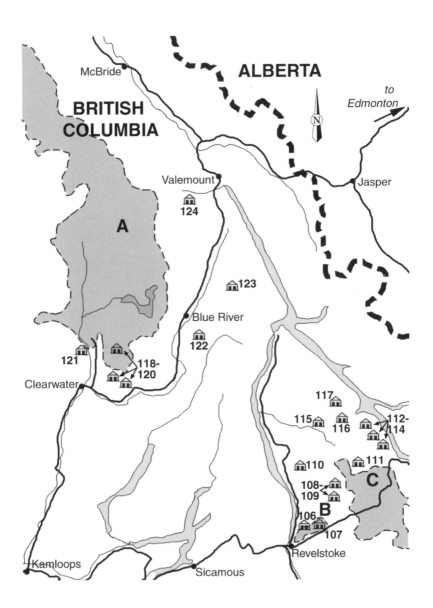

## National & Provincial Parks

*Map
Reference*

A ................Wells Gray Provincial Park

B.................Mount Revelstoke National Park

C ................Glacier National Park

## Huts & Lodges

| *Map Reference* | | *Page Number* |
|---|---|---|
| 106 | Caribou Cabin | 246 |
| 107 | Eva Lake Cabin | 248 |
| 108–109 | Durrand Glacier & Mt Moloch Chalets | 250 |
| 110 | Keystone–Standard Basin Hut | 252 |
| 111 | Sorcerer Lake Lodge | 254 |
| 112–114 | Sunrise, Meadow & Vista Lodges | 256 |
| 115 | Adamants Lodge | 258 |
| 116 | Benjamin Ferris (Great Cairn) Hut | 260 |
| 117 | Fairy Meadow Hut | 262 |
| 118 | Trophy Mountain, Discovery & Fight Meadow Chalets | 264 |
| 121 | Clearwater River Chalet | 266 |
| 122 | Monashee Chalet | 268 |
| 123 | Peter Huser Memorial Chalet | 270 |
| 124 | Cariboo Lodge | 272 |

# Caribou Cabin

The only lodging with amenities in Mt Revelstoke National Park, this cabin is open in winter only and is used primarily by telemarkers taking advantage of the deep snowpack here, or by tourers heading farther up to explore the high country. It is located alongside the Meadows-in-the-Sky Parkway that climbs 1600 vertical km (a vertical mile) from the park gates to the Heather Lake area. There is often a track set along the first 8 km (5 mi) of the road; the cabin is approximately 11 km (7 mi) farther on. A more direct—but steeper—hiking trail also leads to the cabin. The cabin itself is spacious and comfortable.

## LOCATION
*General* In Mt Revelstoke National Park BC.

*Specific* 82 M/1 Mt Revelstoke NAD 27 4**190**34 6**528**51.
*Other pertinent maps* Park map available at entrance to park.
*Elevation* 1527 m (5200 ft).
*Elevation gain from park gates* 1057 m (3477 ft).

## AMENITIES
*Heat* Woodstove (wood provided).
*Cooking* Propane; cookware and dishware provided (sink also).
*Lighting* Propane.
*Sleeping* Three bunk beds with foam pads.
*Capacity* 6.

COST (as of Summer 2001)
*Winter only* $10/person/night (open between Nov 1 and the opening of the roadway for the summer season).

## ACCESS

Turn off Hwy 1 onto the well-marked park access road on the eastern edge of Revelstoke. Carry on for about 2 km (1.2 mi) and park near the park gates. Follow the roadway up to approximately the 17-km (10.2-mi) mark (there is a roadside marker at 15 km); the first 8 km (5 mi) are usually trackset. The cabin is plainly visible along the right side of the road. Alternately, ski up the well-marked Summit Trail, following the signposts and flagging to the cabin.

*Time* Varies widely depending on snow conditions.

## GUIDEBOOKS

*Footloose in the Columbias: A Guide to Hiking Trails in the Park,* available at Revelstoke-area stores (and in Roger's Pass Visitor's Centre).

*Columbia Mountains of Canada–Central,* Fox.

## INFORMATION & BOOKING

For reservations and general park information contact:

Mt Revelstoke National Park
Box 350
Revelstoke BC V0E 2S0
*Phone* (250) 837-7500
*Fax* (250) 837-7536
*E-mail* revglacier_reception@pch.gc.ca
*Website* parkscan.harbour.com/mtrev

For a mail-order catalogue of topo maps of the area, contact:

The Friends of Mount Revelstoke and Glacier
*Phone* (250) 837-2010
*E-mail* fmrg@revelstoke.net

# Eva Lake Cabin

This rustic log structure on the shore of Eva Lake in Mt Revelstoke Park is sometimes used as a base for hikers exploring the area or for climbers tackling the peaks in the Clachnacudainn Range. A bit primitive (it contains nothing except a table and 2 benches), it functions primarily as secure protection from bad weather. Skiers may also wish to use it as a warm shelter, but the 27-km (16-mi) access road to the trailhead is not plowed and may not be fully snow-free until late July. If desired, skiers may overnight at Caribou Cabin, a roadside shelter located halfway up the Meadows-in-the-Sky Parkway.

## LOCATION

*General* On the shore of Eva Lake, about 30 linear km (19 mi) NE of Revelstoke BC.

*Specific* 82 M/1 Mt Revelstoke NAD27 4**222**84 6**591**98.

*Other pertinent maps* Park map available at entrance to park.

*Elevation* 1920 m (6300 ft).

*Elevation gain from end of Parkway* 16 m (53 ft).

*Elevation gain from park gates* 1616 m (5316 ft).

## AMENITIES

*Heat* None.

*Cooking* No stove, cookware or dishware provided.

*Lighting* None.

*Sleeping* Floor only, no foam pads.

*Capacity* 6–8.

COST (as of Summer 2001) Free; no reservations.

## ACCESS

**Summer** Turn off Hwy 1 onto the well-marked park access road on the eastern edge of Revelstoke. Carry on for about 2 km (1.2 mi) to the park gates and then follow the paved road for 25 km (15 mi) to the parking lot. From here, you can walk or take a shuttle bus for the remaining 2 km (1.2 mi) to the summit area and the well-marked Eva Lake trailhead. The broad, well-maintained trail undergoes a couple of moderate drops and gains in elevation before arriving at the lake after 6.5 km (4 mi). The 2 junctions en route are clearly signposted.

**Time** 2–3 hours.

**Winter** Same. The road is not plowed, although a track usually is set for the first 8 km (5 mi). In late season, some of the road will be free of snow.

## GUIDEBOOKS

*Footloose in the Columbias, a Guide to Hiking Trails in the Park,* available at Revelstoke-area stores (and in Roger's Pass Visitor's Centre).

*Columbia Mountains of Canada–Central,* Fox.

## INFORMATION

For general park information contact:
Mt Revelstoke National Park
Box 350
Revelstoke BC V0E 2S0
**Phone** (250) 837-7500
**Fax** (250) 837-7536
**E-mail** revglacier_reception@pch.gc.ca
**Website** parkscan.harbour.com/mtrev

For a mail-order catalogue of topo maps of the area, contact:
The Friends of Mount Revelstoke and Glacier
**Phone** (250) 837-2010
**E-mail** fmrg@revelstoke.net

# Durrand Glacier & Mt Moloch Chalets

Both these high alpine chalets are located in the 80 km² (30 mi²) glacial system comprising 14 glaciers and 25 peaks. The Durrand Glacier Chalet, set atop a knoll just above treeline, provides quick access to superb powder skiing in winter and to hiking through beautiful alpine meadows in meadow. For the mountaineer, both in summer and winter, there are countless routes close by at all levels of challenge. The more remote Mt Moloch Chalet beside the Dismal Glacier is set in the midst of a dramatic cirque overlooking huge icefalls and granite peaks. It is part of the hut-to-hut traverse in winter (for experienced ski-tourers) and is the base for prime alpine rock-climbing in summer. Both chalets offer hotel-like amenities and cooking that are distinctly Swiss in character. All packages include guides and full catering.

## LOCATION

*General* In the northern Selkirk Mountains, 45 km (28 mi) NE of Revelstoke BC (to Durrand Chalet) and a further 8 km (5 mi) to Moloch Chalet.

*Specific* 82 N/5 Glacier NAD27 Durrand 317800; Moloch 365841.

*Other pertinent maps* 82 N/4 Illecillewaet; 82 M/8 Downie Creek; 82 M/1 Revelstoke.

*Elevation* Durrand: 1939 m (6360 ft); Mt Moloch: 2225 m (7300 ft).

*Elevation gain from road to Durrand* N/a (heli-accessed).

*Elevation gain from Durrand to Mt Moloch* 915 m (3000 ft) gain and then 628 m (2060 ft) descent.

## Amenities

**Heat** Both chalets have wood-stoves and propane ranges

**Cooking** All meals provided by accredited chef.

**Lighting** Durrand: 120V hydro-generated electric; Moloch: 12V solar electric.

**Sleeping** Durrand: 10 pine-wood bedrooms; bedding provided. Moloch: 3 pine-wood bedrooms; bedding provided.

**Capacity** Durrand: 20; Moloch: 11.

**Features** Propane heated drying room, sauna, showers, indoor flush toilets, UIAGM/ACMG certified guides.

## Cost (as of Summer 2001)

All prices below include heli-flights, meals, lodging and guides.

**Summer hiking packages** From $655/person for a 3-night stay to $1295/person for a 7-night stay.

**Mountaineering packages** From $1290 for a 7-night beginner course. Prices vary for guided alpine-rock climbing packages.

**Winter ski packages including hut-to-hut traverses** From $930/person for a 4-night stay to $2000/person for an 11-night stay.

## Access

Heli-access only.

## Guidebooks

*Summits and Icefields,* Scott.
*Columbia Mountains of Canada–Central,* Fox.

## Information & Booking

Selkirk Mountain Experience
Box 2998
Revelstoke BC V0E 2S0
**Phone** (250) 837-2381
**Fax** (250) 837-4685
**E-mail** info@selkirkexperience.com
**Website** www.selkirkexperience.com

# Keystone–Standard Basin Hut

This lovely log cabin is reached after a trip through rolling alpine meadows containing some of the most profuse wildflower displays in the Columbias. A good gravel road leads all the way to treeline, so the 11 km (7 mi) trail to the cabin gains little net elevation and thus makes for a hike that even a novice will find fairly easy. There are extensive opportunities for day-hikes in the meadows, and the nearby peaks are easily scrambled. Although not heavily used in winter because of the 27-km (16-mi) trek from the highway, the cabin can be reached by snowmobile. The nearby terrain does not afford great slopes for turns, but the touring can be beautiful. Note that in winter the trail and possibly the hut may be obscured by snow.

## LOCATION

*General* In the Selkirk Mountains, about 45 km (27 mi) by air NNE of Revelstoke BC.

*Specific* 82M/8 Downie Creek NAD27 4**113**37 6**973**03.

*Other pertinent maps* Backroad Mapbook or British Columbia Forest Service Map of Forest Service road access to trailhead.

*Elevation* 2030 m (6700 ft).

*Elevation gain from trailhead* Negligible net difference.

## AMENITIES

*Heat* Woodstove (wood difficult to access in winter).

*Cooking* No cookstove; cookware provided; limited dishware.

*Lighting* None.

*Sleeping* Loft area with foam pads.

*Capacity* 8–10.

**COST** (as of Summer 2001)
Free; no reservations. (There is talk of establishing a booking system if the hut's popularity grows. Check with the Revelstoke or Golden offices of the British Columbia Forest Service for details.)

**ACCESS**
*Summer* Drive N from Revelstoke on Hwy 23 for about 49 km (30.5 mi) and turn onto the road marked as "Keystone Creek Forest Service Road." Follow this good gravel road (suitable for all vehicles) for 16 km (9.6 mi) to the trailhead near timberline. All junctions are clearly signposted, except for one after the 2-km road-side marker—continue straight here. The 11-km (7-mi) trail to the cabin is very clear through open, rolling meadows.
*Time* 3–5 hours.

*Winter* Same, but the trail would be totally obscured and thus would call for some good route-finding skills.

**INFORMATION & BOOKING**
For the British Columbia Forest Service road map, contact:
Columbia Forest District Office
Box 9158 RPO 3
Revelstoke BC V0E 3K0
*Phone* (250) 837-7611
*Website* www.for.gov.bc.ca/nelson/district/columbia

# Sorcerer Lake Lodge

This large, comfortable lodge sits on a rock cliff overlooking Sorcerer Lake with the Nordic Glacier massif providing the view from the front door. The 3-meter, stable snowpack provides great skiing opportunities in both glaciated and treed terrain. A wide array of hikes and mountaineering challenges are close by, including Mt Iconoclast, one of the highest peaks in the Selkirks. However, this steep-and-deep snow and rugged terrain are not suited for beginners in any season. The lodge provides hearty and ample fare at all meals, as well as fully certified guides to get guests to the best spots. Self-guided and self-catered groups may book the lodge but must be experienced and willing to provide resumés.

## LOCATION
**General** Just N of Glacier National Park, about 70 km NW of Golden BC.
**Specific** 82 N/5 Glacier NAD27 513997.
**Elevation** 2050 m (6700 ft).
**Elevation gain** N/a (heli-accessed).

## AMENITIES
**Heat** Woodstoves; propane heater in the drying room.
**Cooking** Propane stove; cookware and dishware provided.
**Lighting** Electric.
**Sleeping** 4 separate bedrooms and a large loft area with bedding provided.
**Capacity** 12–16.
**Features** Sauna, spacious dining and living areas, accredited guides.

## COST (as of Summer 2001)
**Summer** self-guided & self-catered $3500/group/week (exclusive lodge use).
**Heli-flight** $230/person.
**Summer fully guided & catered** $1350/person/week (includes heli-flight).
**Winter** Same.

## ACCESS
Heli-access only.

## GUIDEBOOKS
*Summits and Icefields,* Scott.
*Columbia Mountains of Canada–*
*Central,* Fox.

## INFORMATION & BOOKING
Sorcerer Lake Lodge
Attention Tannis Dakin
Box 161
Golden BC V0A 1H0
**Phone** (250) 344-2804
**Fax** (250) 344-2805
**E-mail** sorcerer@rockies.net
**Website** www.sorcererlodge.com

# Sunrise, Meadow & Vista Lodges

These three lodges in the Esplanade Range of the Selkirk Mountains typically accommodate those on a lodge-to-lodge traverse through high alpine terrain. With Glacier Park to the west and the Rockies across the Trench to the east, the views are spectacular. Although the rock is not suitable for climbing, there are numerous opportunities for hikes and scrambles in the alpine, and the Selkirk powder in winter is unbeatable. With access to runs of up to 760 m (2500 ft), it is easy to rack up lots of vertical in a day. The lodges are all spacious, two-story frame buildings heated by wood and propane.

## LOCATION

**General** In the Selkirk Mountains NE of Roger's Pass BC.

**Specific** 82N12 Mt Sir Sanford NAD83 Sunrise Lodge: 619109; Meadow Lodge: 596133; Vista Lodge: 588155.

**Elevation** About 2200 m (7000 ft).

**Elevation gain** N/a (heli-accessed).

## AMENITIES

**Heat** Wood and propane stoves.

**Cooking** Propane stove and oven; cookware and dishware provided.

**Lighting** Propane.

**Sleeping** Private 2-person rooms; bedding provided.

**Capacity** 12.

**Features** Sauna, guides, women-only packages available, superb cooks for catered trips.

**COST** (as of Summer 2001)

**Summer fully guided & catered**
From $795/person for 3-day/2-lodge trips to $1380/person

for 7-day/3-lodge trips, inclusive of heli-flight.

Prices vary for self-guided and self-catered groups (10-person minimum in high season).

**Winter fully guided & catered**

7-day trips: $1430/person, inclusive of heli-flight.

Prices vary for self-guided and self-catered groups (11-person minimum in high season, with 12th person free).

## ACCESS

Heli-access from Golden area.

## GUIDEBOOKS

*Summits and Icefields,* Scott

## INFORMATION & BOOKING

Golden Alpine Holidays
Box 1050
Golden BC V0A 1H0
**Phone & Fax** (250) 344-7273
**E-mail** goldenalpine@cablerocket.com
**Website** www.goldenalpine holidays.com

# Adamants Lodge

This luxury lodge set deep in the Adamant Range provides a wonderful base for heli-skiing or heli-assisted hiking and mountaineering. The deep powder makes for superb skiing in 1500 km² (575 mi²) of terrain, and in summer the alpine meadows and high ridges provide dramatic hiking. There are many nearby peaks to challenge mountaineers, the most famous being Mt Sir Sandford. As with all the CMH lodges, this one provides all the amenities of a luxury hotel, including a hot tub, sauna, bar, gourmet meals and large common room. Guides for all activities are provided.

## LOCATION
*General* In the Adamant Range of the Selkirk Mountains, N of Glacier National Park between Golden and Revelstoke BC.

*Specific* 82 M/9 Goldstream River NAD83 4**19**084 72**09**98.
*Elevation* 1100 m (3610 ft).
*Elevation gain* N/a (heli-accessed).

## AMENITIES
*Heat* Hot water radiant, thermostat controlled.
*Cooking* All meals provided.
*Lighting* Electric.
*Sleeping* Bedrooms with duvets and private baths.
*Capacity* 10 single rooms, 18 double/twin rooms.
*Features* Jacuzzi/sauna, large stone fireplace, bar, massage, laundry room, climbing wall, exercise room, ski shop, games room.

## COST (as of Summer 2001)
*Summer guided hiking* 4 nights: $1828–$2150/person, depending on season.

*Guided mountaineering* 4 nights: $2430-$2859/person, depending on season.

Both rates are based on double occupancy (reduced rates for children under 15). Rates include transport from Banff, heli-flights, guides and use of all necessary equipment.

*Winter heli-skiing* From $4,409–$7,495/person/week, depending on time of season and single or double occupancy. Rate includes guides and a guarantee of 30,500 vertical m (100,000 ft)/week.

## ACCESS

All transport from Banff is provided. Details provided upon registration.

## INFORMATION & BOOKING

Canadian Mountain Holidays
Box 1660
Banff AB T0L 0C0
*Phone* 1-800-661-0252
*Fax* (403) 762-5879
*Websites* www.cmhhike.com *and* www.cmhmountaineering.com *and* www.cmhski.com

# Benjamin Ferris (Great Cairn) Hut

**LOCATION**

*General* 4 km NNW of Mt Sir Sandford in the Adamant Range, N of Glacier National Park between Golden and Revelstoke BC.

*Specific* 82N/12 Mt Sir Sandford NAD83 392268.

*Other pertinent maps* 82 N/13 Sullivan River (for approach from Fairy Meadow Hut).

*Elevation* 1884 m (6200 feet).

*Elevation gain from Fairy Meadow Hut* Up 670 m (2180 ft), down 120 m (390 ft), up 300 m (975 ft), down 550 (1790 ft) m, up 150 m (490 ft), down 630 m (2050 ft).

*Elevation gain from nearest logging road* Up 1060 m (3500 ft), down 700 m (2300 ft).

Named for a 20-foot-high cairn built 70 years ago by bored Harvard students, this remote stone hut is well worth the rigor of getting there. Mainly used by climbers, the hut affords a good base for rock climbs on the Adamants' renowned granite as well as snow and ice routes up some nearby big peaks, the most impressive one being Mt Sir Sandford, the highest peak in the Selkirks. The views from the hut's front steps are postcard material. While the skiing opportunities are not nearly as extensive as at the nearby Fairy Meadow Hut, this hut is used in winter by ski-tourers and mountaineers.

**AMENITIES**

*Heat* Woodstove (no wood provided).

*Cooking* Coleman stove; cookware and dishware provided.

*Lighting* Coleman lantern.

*Sleeping* Bunks with foam pads.

*Capacity* 6.

**COST** (as of Summer 2001)

Alpine Club Class B hut: $9 for members; $13 for nonmembers; $11 for group members. (Children 16 and under half price.)

**ACCESS**

*Summer* The easiest and fastest way to get to the hut is by helicopter; due to the proximity to Fairy Meadow Hut, you may be able to coordinate flights summer and winter. The three overland routes are very long, very tough and thinly marked. The route from Fairy Meadow Hut entails two major glacier traverses and a lot of steep elevation gain and loss; route-finding is hard and the features on the topo maps are incorrectly named. The other routes entail, first of all, some tricky route-finding on a long, often-forked logging road navigable only by 4x4s, after which things get brutal. Impenetrable bush, steep scree, seriously crevassed glacier-traverses and a total lack of trails highlight this hike from hell. One group in the late 1990s took 3 days to get from their car to the hut. Since the principal visitors to this hut will certainly be mountaineers who presumably will have climbing guidebooks that provide the intricate and pages-long access descriptions, we will not try to reproduce them here.

**Time** Consider yourself blessed if you do it in just one day.

## GUIDEBOOKS
*Summits & Icefields,* Scott.
*Columbia Mountains of Canada– Central*, Fox.

## INFORMATION & BOOKING
The Alpine Club of Canada
Box 8040

Canmore AB T1W 2T8
**Phone** (403) 678-3200
**Fax** (403) 678-3224
**E-mail** alpclub@telusplanet.net
**Website** www.alpineclubof canada.ca

# Fairy Meadow Hut

One of the most luxurious huts in the ACC chain, this comfortable chaletlike building has large windows, two fireplaces, lots of lounging space and a wood-fired sauna. The word *hut* doesn't do justice to this lovely haven. It is set on the edge of a meadow high in the Adamant Range and affords a great array of mountaineering challenges, but it is most highly prized for its proximity to spectacular skiing.

## LOCATION

*General* Near Granite Glacier in the Adamant Range, N of Glacier National Park between Golden and Revelstoke BC.

*Specific* 82 N/13 Sullivan River NAD83 394352. (Note that the hut is not near the words "Fairy Meadow" on this map.)

*Other pertinent maps* Backroad *Mapbook* or *British Columbia Forest Service Map* of Forest Service road access to trailhead; 82 N/12 Mt Sir Sandford (for travel beyond the hut).

*Elevation* 2042 m (6700 ft).

*Elevation gain from end of the logging road* 1006 m (3300 ft).

## AMENITIES

*Heat* Woodstoves.

*Cooking* Propane stove/oven and Coleman stoves; cookware and dishware provided.

*Lighting* Propane and Coleman lanterns.

*Sleeping* Three upstairs rooms with foam pads (no bunks).

*Capacity* 20.

COST (as of Summer 2001)

*Low season person/night* $17.50 for members; $24 for non-members; $19.50 for group members. (Children 16 and under half price.)

**High season person/week (late January to end of April)** $550 for members; $600 for nonmembers; $575 for group members, including heli-transport. Reservations are made for groups of 10 or 20 only.

**Note** Reservations are made by lottery with the draw conducted 6 months before the first day of the requested week. Check the website for details.

## ACCESS

**Summer** Some people fly in (or have their gear flown in) by helicopter; costs possibly could be reduced by coordinating flights with other groups. For ground access turn off Hwy 1 47 km (29 mi) W of Golden on the road signed as the turnoff for Big Lake Resort. Carry on about 65 km (41 mi) and turn left on the logging road marked as 111.5 km on the roadside signs. You may be forced to park and start walking at any point on this road. Note these junctions: after 0.8 km (0.5 mi), bear right; at 1.8 km (1.1 mi), bear left uphill; at 3.7 km (2.3 mi), bear right; at 4.4 km (2.8 mi), the road ends. From here, look for the flagging at the edge of the clearing. For the first few kms, the trail follows this drainage and at times is very close to the creek. After a swampy section, the trail rises high to a boulder field well marked with cairns and flagging. Beyond here, the trail gains the crest of a lateral moraine that leads into the meadows where the hut is located.

**Time** 5 hours; 7–8 if very muddy.

**Winter** Heli-access only.

## GUIDEBOOKS

*Summits and Icefields,* Scott.

*A Climber's Guide to the Interior Ranges of BC,* Krusyzna and Putnam.

*Columbia Mountains of Canada–Central,* Fox.

## INFORMATION & BOOKING

The Alpine Club of Canada
Box 8040
Canmore AB T1W 2T8
**Phone** (403) 678-3200
**Fax** (403) 678-3224
**E-mail** alpclub@telusplanet.net
**Website** www.alpineclubof canada.ca

For the British Columbia Forest Service road map, contact:
Columbia Forest District Office
Box 9158 RPO 3
Revelstoke BC V0E 3K0
**Phone** (250) 837-7611
**Website** www.for.gov.bc.ca/ nelson/district/columbia

# Trophy Mountain, Discovery & Fight Meadow Chalets

This string of chalets in Wells Gray Provincial Park provides an opportunity for a long traverse through some spectacular alpine terrain in this remote, seldom-visited region of BC. Shorter trips based out of one chalet are an option, as are combination hike-and-canoe trips. A similar variety of options exist for winter, including the 65-km (39-mi) traverse or trips based out of any one of the chalets. All three chalets provide rustic comfort and sumptuous meals, with an emphasis on ecological sensitivity.

## LOCATION

**General** In Wells Gray Park, NE of Kamloops BC.
**Specific** 82 M/13 West Raft River

NAD27 Trophy Mtn Chalet: 049386; Discovery Chalet: 046452; Fight Meadow Chalet: 001560.
**Other pertinent maps** Wells Gray Provincial Park Map.
**Elevation** Trophy Mountain: 2153 m (7000 ft); Discovery: 1870 m (1650 ft); Fight Meadow: 1845 m (6000 ft).
**Elevation gain from trailhead** 523 m (1700 ft).

## AMENITIES

**Heat** Propane furnace.
**Cooking** Propane stove/oven; cookware and dishware provided.
**Lighting** Propane.
**Sleeping** 2-person berths in upper story; mattresses and duvets supplied.

(Discovery chalet has open sleeping loft only.)

**Capacity** 10-12

**Features** Large dining and lounging areas, library, sauna, women-only trips offered.

COST (as of Summer 2001)

**Summer** From $360/person for a 3-night, 1-chalet stay to $770/person for a 7-night, 3-chalet traverse.

**Winter** Up to $890 for the 7-day traverse.

All prices above include all guiding, meals, amenities and transportation from Clearwater.

In winter, self-catered and self-guided groups may reserve a chalet on a $40/person/night basis (minimum 8 people and 4 nights, exclusive of transportation). Chalet-to-chalet traverses must be guided.

ACCESS

All transportation (including snowcats and heli-flights, where needed) is provided except for independent groups in winter which may choose to use snowcat or helicopter travel. Full details provided upon registration.

GUIDEBOOKS

*Summits and Icefields,* Scott.

*Exploring Wells Gray Park*, Neave.

INFORMATION & BOOKING

Wells Gray Adventures

Attention Tay Briggs

**Phone** 1-888-754-8735

**Fax** (250) 587-6446

**E-mail** skitrek@wellsgray.net

**Website** www.skihike.com

For the Wells Gray Park map and other information, contact:

Thompson River Parks District

1210 McGill Road

Kamloops BC V2C 6N6

**Phone** (250) 851-3000

**Fax** (250) 828-463

**Website** www.elp.gov.bc.ca/bcparks/explore/distoff/thomdist.htm

# Clearwater River Chalet

chalet has recently been finished elsewhere on the 300-acre property and provides year-round access to the same wilderness environment.

## LOCATION
**General** N of Clearwater BC, close to the point where the Clearwater River flows out of Wells Gray Provincial Park.

**Specific** 92 P/16 Mahood Lake NAD27 032463.

**Other pertinent maps** *Wells Gray Provincial Park Map.* A description of nearby hiking trails is provided upon final payment.

**Elevation** 490 m (1620 ft).

**Elevation drop from parking lot** 130 m (425 ft).

This log chalet in a wildlife sanctuary on the edge of Wells Gray Provincial Park provides access to a broad variety of wilderness activities. There is an extensive network of hiking trails both inside and outside the park, some of which lead to densely flowered alpine meadows. There are also many opportunities nearby for fishing and swimming. Operating from Spring to Fall only, this facility is rented for exclusive use by a group of up to 8. The chalet itself consists of two rooms (a bedroom and a living/cooking room) and is fully furnished. A second, fully road-accessed

## AMENITIES
**Heat** Woodstoves (wood provided).

**Cooking** Propane stove and fridge; cookware and dishware provided.

**Lighting** Solar; propane lamps.

**Sleeping** Bedroom with 4 sets of bunks and foam pads; no bedding provided.

**Capacity** 8.

**Features** Large riverside deck, solar-heated shower house.

## COST (as of Summer 2001)
**Summer high season** $100/night for the whole chalet.

**Summer low season** $80/night for the chalet.

## ACCESS

There is a clear trail leading from the parking area (off the main road leading into Wells Gray Park) down to the cabin alongside the river. A map (and directions on where to pick up the key) will be provided upon final payment.

*Time* About 30 minutes.

## GUIDEBOOKS
*Exploring Wells Gray Park,* Neave

## INFORMATION & BOOKING
Wells Gray Tours Ltd.
250 Lansdowne Street
Kamloops BC V2C 1X7
*Phone* 1-800-667-9552
*Fax* (250) 374-2711
*E-mail* info@riverchalet.com
*Website* www.riverchalet.com
For the Wells Gray Park map and other information, contact:
Thompson River Parks District
1210 McGill Road
Kamloops BC V2C 6N6
*Phone* (250) 851-3000
*Fax* (250) 828-463
*Website* www.elp.gov.bc.ca/
 bcparks/explore/distoff/
 thomdist.htm

# Monashee Chalet

This cozy chalet in an alpine meadow provides access to a wide range of alpine terrain for hiking, skiing and rock-climbing. With an average snowfall of around 5 m (16 ft), the deep snowpack here provides extensive opportunities for tours and turns on the nearby slopes and glades. In the summer, a nearby lake can be used for swimming and canoeing. Hikers and skiers can ascend many of the surrounding peaks (such as Mt Finn), and there are some routes to challenge experienced climbers.

## LOCATION

**General** In the Shuswap Highlands in the North Thompson Valley between the communities of Avola and Blue River BC.

**Specific** 82 M/14 Messiter NAD83 346693 761609.

**Other pertinent maps** 83 D/3 Blue River.

**Elevation** 1820 m (5971 ft).

**Elevation gain from summer trailhead** 244 m (800 ft).

**Elevation gain from Hwy 5** 1058 m (3471 ft).

## AMENITIES

**Heat** Wood and propane heaters.

**Cooking** Propane stove and BBQ; cookware and dishware provided.

**Lighting** Electric (generator-powered).

**Sleeping** 7 sleeping compartments (5 with double beds, 2 with bunks); sleeping bags provided (guests provide own liners).

**Capacity** 14.

**Features** 2-way radio for emergency use, all safety equipment, guitars, canoes, large common room with games area, TV and VCR, and CD player.

## COST (as of Summer 2001)

All prices refer to self-guided and self-catered options. The owners will assist guests in arranging for guides and/or cooks.

*Summer* From $30/person/night for groups of 10 or more to a $210 flat rate/night for groups of 1–5. (Reduced rate for children.)

*Winter* From $40/person/night for groups of 10 or more to a flat rate of $288/night for groups of 1–5. (Reduced rates for children.) Check the website for the extra costs if you require personal or luggage transport.

## ACCESS

*Summer* Turn E off Hwy 5 onto the Foam Creek Forest Service Road 20 km (12 mi) N of Avola. Follow this road (fit for 2WD cars) for 13 km to the summer parking lot and trailhead; watch for the signs at any junctions. A map will be sent to you upon registration. The clearly marked, 3-km (2-mi) trail leads to the chalet.

*Time* 1 hour.

*Winter* Guests are transported in by snowcat or snowmobile (see website for costs). Most guests ski out, but snowcat transport can be arranged.

## GUIDEBOOKS

*Summits and Icefields,* Scott.

## INFORMATION & BOOKING

Interior Alpine Recreation Attention Bernie Teufele
540–1477 Fountain Way
Vancouver BC V6H 3W9
***Phone & Fax*** (604) 736-1477
***E-mail*** berniet@oanet.com
***Website*** www.interior-alpine.com

# Peter Huser Memorial Chalet

If you want to ski or hike in some very exciting terrain (and if you are well experienced in such travel), this chalet slated to open in Winter 2002 in Dominion Basin will provide you with all the challenge you could ask for. Open glades and steep pitches are just outside the door, and traverses across some glaciers provide quick access to a wide variety of slopes and aspects—all on the famous Monashee powder. Mountaineers can access the peaks 1200–1500 m (4000–5000 ft) above the chalet. Use of a guide is recommended; self-guided groups must submit a resumé showing sufficient experience and training in glacier travel and avalanche awareness.

## LOCATION
*General* 35 km (23 mi) S of Valemont BC on Hwy 5 to helipad, then 14 km (9 mi) by air E into Dominion Basin.
*Specific* 83 D/7 Howard Creek NAD27; approximately 710155.
*Other pertinent maps* 83 D/6 Lempriere.
*Elevation* 2000 m (6500 ft).
*Elevation gain* N/a (heli-accessed).

## AMENITIES
*Heat* Wood and propane stove, with wall heaters.
*Cooking* Propane and woodstoves; cookware and dishware provided.
*Lighting* Propane (electrical back-up).
*Sleeping* 8 single rooms; 2 double rooms; foam pads with sleeping bags (guests provide liners).
*Capacity* 12 (separate quarters for guides).
*Features* Big kitchen and dining area, rec area, upstairs sleeping, 2-way radio, books and games, CD player (guests provide batteries).

## COST (as of Summer 2001)
Prices not fixed as yet. Check the website for updates.
*Heli-flight* Expected rate of $250/person return.

## ACCESS

The chalet is accessed by helicopter only in winter, but it can be reached by hiking in summer. This trail is about 12 km (7.5 mi) long and is over difficult terrain. It is primarily to be used as an emergency ski-out trail.

## INFORMATION & BOOKING

Interior Alpine Recreation
Attention Bernie Teufele
540–1477 Fountain Way
Vancouver BC V6H 3W9
*Phone & Fax* (604) 736-1477
*E-mail* berniet@oanet.com
*Website* www.interior-alpine.com

# Cariboo Lodge

The only backcountry facility in the whole of the Cariboo Mountains, this heli-accessed lodge provides quick access to the alpine meadows and glaciers of the Premier Range in the North Thompson Valley. The typical 150-cm (5-ft) snowpack makes for superb skiing, and in summer there are numerous opportunities for hiking in some very remote and scenic high country. As with all the CMH lodges, this one provides all the amenities of a first-class hotel, including a hot tub, sauna, bar, gourmet meals and large common room. Guides for all activities are provided.

## LOCATION
*General* In the Cariboo Mountains, about 210 km (130 mi) NE of Kamloops BC.

*Specific* 83 D/11 Canoe Mountain NAD27 3**331**95 8**440**78.
*Elevation* 1100 m (3608 ft).
*Elevation gain* N/a (heli-accessed).

## AMENITIES
*Heat* Hot water radiant, thermostat controlled.
*Cooking* All meals provided.
*Lighting* Electric.
*Sleeping* Bedrooms with duvets and private baths.
*Capacity* 13 single rooms, 16 double/twin rooms.
*Features* Sauna, hot tub, massage, bar, laundry room, ski shop, exercise room, games room.

COST (as of Summer 2001)
*Summer guided hiking* 4 nights: $1828/person
Rates based on double occupancy (reduced rates for children under 15). Rates include transport from

Banff, heli-flights, guides and use of all necessary equipment.

***Winter heli-skiing*** From $4409-$7495/person/week, depending on time of season and single or double occupancy. Rate includes guides and a guarantee of 30,500 vertical m (100,000 ft).

## ACCESS
All transport from Banff is provided. Details provided upon registration

## INFORMATION & BOOKING
Canadian Mountain Holidays
Box 1660
Banff AB T0L 0C0
***Phone*** 1-800-661-0252
***Fax*** (403) 762-5879
***Websites*** www.cmhhike.com *and* www.cmhmountaineering.com *and* www.cmhski.com

# British Columbia Forest Service Regional & District Offices

Overland access into many of the huts and lodges mentioned in this book is possible only because of the innumerable logging roads that seem to reach into every major drainage in British Columbia. Even in winter, these roads provide snowmobile access where the bush would be otherwise impenetrable. The downside is that while some of these roads are well enough maintained to be navigable by my 1986 Civic, some could stymie even the toughest of 4x4s. And these roads can change from the former to the latter in the space of a 3-day downpour.

Before planning a trip that calls for a 40-km drive along any such roads, you should check with the nearest British Columbia Forest Service office in order to get the most recent information on road conditions. Also, since loaded logging trucks barreling downhill are not the most nimble of vehicles, it's a good idea to find out about current logging operations in the area—you might want to delay your drive in until late evening or on a weekend.

Whether you're heading in to one of the huts in this book or just looking for some new alpine terrain to explore, a great planning tool is the recreation map that each forest district prints. For one thing these maps list dozens of maintained camp-sites that are not otherwise advertised by means of roadside signs. In fact, you've probably driven past many of these inexpensive—or even free—campsites without even realizing it. (For example, there's a wonderful unmarked British Columbia Forest Service camp-site just off the Trans-Canada Hwy about 1 km away from the Albert Canyon Hot Springs.) The maps also list all the main logging or Forest Service roads in the district. To be sure, some care is needed in navigating along these roads, for there are often branch roads that lead off into dead-end cut-blocks, but a bit of common sense—normally, just taking the road that seems most travelled and that seems to be heading in the right direction—should get you where you want to go.

Two cautions about these maps: they are a bit thin in content, not offering much indication of what there is to see or do at any particular destination; and the hiking trails marked on them do not always coincide perfectly with the actual routes.

To obtain these maps, contact the specific district you want (and to see a map listing all 38 Forest Service Districts in BC,

visit www.for.gov.bc.ca/pab/
publctns/getintch/provmap.htm.
Where indicated, the websites
below contain maps of the districts, although none of these
website maps seems to be as
detailed as the print versions
obtainable from the district
office. There now is a small
charge for these print maps.

Alternatively, you can pur-
chase (and have mailed to you)
any or all of these maps directly
from:
Canadian Cartographics Ltd.
Phone 1-877-524-3337
*E-mail* canmap@canmap.com
*Website* www.canmap.com

A good person to talk to at the
British Columbia Forest Service
offices is the recreation officer.
This person's job is to travel
around in the backcountry and
generally keep current with all
that might be needed by recre-
ational users of the forest district—nice work if you can get it.
These people generally are very
agreeable and very knowledge-
able, and if they don't know
something they can usually put
you on to someone who does.

Note that the province is
divided into 6 forest regions,
each of which is subdivided into
districts:

### Nelson Forest Region
518 Lake St
Nelson BC V1L 4C6
*Phone* (250) 354-6200
*E-mail* Forests.NelsonRegion
  Office@gems8.gov.bc.ca

*Website* www.for.gov.bc.ca/
  nelson/nel_r.htm

### Arrow Forest District
845 Columbia Ave
Castlegar BC V1N 1H3
*Phone* (250) 365-8600
*Fax* (250) 365-8568
For a map, visit www.for.gov.
  bc.ca/nelson/district/arrow/
  map/map.htm

Nakusp Field Office
109 6 Ave W
Nakusp BC V0G 1R0
*Phone* (250) 265-3685
*Fax* (250) 265-3067

### Columbia Forest District
Box 9158 RPO 3
1761 Big Eddy Rd
Revelstoke BC V0E
*Phone* (250) 837-7611
For a map, visit www.for.gov.bc.
  ca/nelson/district/columbia/
  dcomap.htm

Golden Field Office
Box 1380
800 9 St N
Golden BC V0A 1H0
*Phone* (250) 344-7500

### Invermere Forest District
Box 189
625 4 St
Invermere BC V0A 1K0
*Phone* (250) 342-4200
For a map, visit www.for.gov.bc.
  ca/nelson/district/invermer/
  District%20Map/index.htm

## Cranbrook Forest District

1902 Theatre Rd
Cranbrook BC V1C 6H3
**Phone** (250) 426-1700
For a map, visit www.for.gov.bc.
  ca/nelson/district/cranbrk/
  map.htm

## Kootenay Lake Forest District

RR 1 S-22, C-27
1907 Ridgewood Rd
Nelson BC V1L 5P4
**Phone** (250) 825-1101
For a map, visit www.for.gov.bc.
  ca/nelson/district/kootenay/
  planning/planning.htm

  Creston Field Office
  1243 Northwest Blvd
  Creston BC V0B 1G0

## Prince George Forest Region

1011 4 Avenue
Prince George BC V2L 3H9
**Phone** (250) 565-6100
**Fax** (250) 565-6671
**Website** www.for.gov.bc.ca/
  pgeorge/pgeo_r.htm

## Robson Valley Forest District

Box 40
McBride BC V0J 2E0
**Phone** (250) 569-3700
**Fax** (250) 569-3738

## Kamloops Forest Region

515 Columbia St
Kamloops BC V2C 2T7
**Phone** (250) 828-4131
**Website** www.for.gov.bc.ca/
  kamloops/kam_r.htm

## Clearwater Forest District

Box 4501
RR 2
687 Yellowhead S Highway 5
Clearwater BC V0E 1N0
**Phone** (250) 587-6700
For a map, visit www.for.gov.bc.
  ca/kamloops/district/clear/
  district.htm

## Salmon Arm Forest District

Box 100 Stn Main
850 16 St NE
Salmon Arm BC V1E 4S4
**Phone** (250) 833-3400
For a map, visit www.for.gov.bc.
  ca/kamloops/district/salmon/#
  click

# British Columbia Provincial Parks District Offices

The following BC Provincial parks either contain huts and lodges referenced in this book or else are easily accessed from such facilities. Each of these parks provides (and will mail out) maps of the terrain and trails and major attractions within its boundaries. Although these maps are not as detailed as topo maps, they often do suffice as fully adequate guides for hikers. At the very least, they're a great aid to general planning. Note, however, that there are plans in the Environment Ministry to update all these maps, and so the ones currently available have not been updated in several years, so any recent changes (such as new or closed trails) may not appear on these maps. The maps always had been free, but this may change.

The websites have been undergoing substantial upgrading in the months before this book went to press. Many of these websites now have good maps for each park, as well as a host of other helpful details. They should be the first place you look for general information about any park.

For more detailed information about trails and backcountry accommodation in any of these provincial parks, contact the district office as indicated below.

Note that the province is divided into 11 park districts, each of which contains numerous parks.

**BC Parks Headquarters**
Box 9398 Stn Prov Govt
Victoria BC V8W 9M9
*Phone* (250) 387-5002
*Fax* (250) 387-5757
*Website* www.elp.gov.bc.ca/
    bcparks/explore/regions.htm

**Kootenay District**
Box 118
Wasa BC V0B 2K0
*Phone* (250) 422-4200
*Fax* (250) 422-3326
*Website* www.elp.gov.bc.ca/
    bcparks/explore/distoff/
    kootdist.htm
Contact this office for maps or any other information regarding the following provincial parks that contain (or are nearby) facilities mentioned in this book:
• Bugaboo
• Cummins Lakes
• Elk Lakes
• Height of the Rockies
• Kokanee Creek
• Kokanee Glacier
• Mount Assiniboine
• Mount Fernie
• Purcell Wilderness
• St. Mary's Alpine
• Stagleap
• Top of the World
• Valhalla
• Whiteswan Lake

## Prince George District

4051 18 Avenue
Box 2045
Prince George BC V2N 2J6
*Phone* (250) 565-6759
*Fax* (250) 565-6940
*Website* www.elp.gov.bc.ca/
   bcparks/explore/pgdis.htm
Contact this office for maps or
any other information regarding
the following provincial parks
which contain (or are nearby)
facilities mentioned in this book:

* Hamber
* Mount Robson
* Kakwa

## Okanagan District

Box 399
Summerland BC V0H 1Z0
*Phone* (250) 494-6500
*Fax* (250) 494-9737
*Website* www.elp.gov.bc.ca/
   bcparks/explore/distoff/
   okandist.htm
Contact this office for maps or
any other information regarding
the following provincial parks
which contain (or are nearby)
facilities mentioned in this book:

* Monashee

## Thompson River District

1210 McGill Road
Kamloops BC V2C 6N6
*Phone* (250) 851-3000
*Fax* (250) 828-463
*Website* www.elp.gov.bc.ca/
   bcparks/explore/distoff/
   thomdist.htm
Contact this office for maps or
any other information regarding
the following provincial parks

which contain (or are nearby)
facilities mentioned in this book:

* Wells Gray

# National Parks Contact Information

### Banff National Park
Box 900
Banff AB T0L 0C0
*Phone* (403) 762-1550
*Fax* (403) 762-1551
*E-mail* banff_vrc@pch.gc.ca
*Website* www.worldweb.com/Parks
  Canada-Banff

### Glacier and Mt Revelstoke
  National Parks
Box 350
Revelstoke BC V0E 2S0
*Phone* (250) 837-7500
*Fax* (250) 837-7536
*E-mail* revglacier_reception@pch.
  gc.ca
*Website* parkscan.harbour.com/
  mtrev

### Jasper National Park
Box 10
Jasper AB T0E 1E0
*Phone* (780) 852-6176
*Fax* (780) 852-5601
*E-mail* See website
*Website* www.worldweb.com/
  ParksCanada-Glacier

### Kootenary National Park
Box 220
Radium Hot Springs BC
V0A 1M0
*Phone* (250) 347-9615
*Fax* (250) 347-9980
*E-mail* Kootenay_reception@pch.
  gc.ca
*Website* www.worldweb.com/
  ParksCanada-Kootenay

### Yoho National Park
Box 99
Field BC V0A 1G0
*Phone* (250) 343-6783
*Fax* (250) 343-6012
*E-mail* yoho_info@pch .gc.ca
*Website* www.worldweb.com/
  ParksCanada-Yoho

# Selected Bibliography

A comprehensive list of all the guides to backcountry activities in the Rockies and Columbias would be many pages long. What I present here is just a summary of the books I use and look on as "the standards." There are, of course, new ones coming out regularly, and there may soon be software available enabling you to print your own map and trail description for whatever specific outing you have in mind.

The texts below, then, are intended mainly for those who have no such guides now and are looking for something that would open up some new territory for them. Needless to say, scanning the book racks at a good outdoor equipment store would give you access to a much broader array of choices.

In this list, we have not bothered to identify the edition number. Many of these books are currently in at least their second edition (one is in its 8th), and I know of a few that will be coming out fully revised and updated within a year or so. Presumably, the only books currently for sale will be the most recent editions.

## HIKING TRAILS

Beers, Don. *Banff–Assiniboine: A Beautiful World*, Highline Publishing.

Beers, Don. *Jasper-Robson: A Taste of Heaven*, Highline Publishing.

Beers, Don. *The Wonder of Yoho*, Rocky Mountains Books.

Cameron, Aaron and Matt Gunn. *Hikes Around Invermere and the Columbia Valley*, Rocky Mountain Books.

Carter, John. *Hiking the West Kootenays*, Kalmia Publishing.

Copeland, Cathy and Craig. *Don't Waste Your Time in the West Kootenays,* Voice in the Wilderness Press.

Llewellyn, Jean. *Trail Riding in Rocky Mountain Country,* HorseSource Publishing.

Neave, Roland. *Exploring Wells Gray Park*, The Friends of Wells Gray Park.

Patton, Brian and Bart Robinson. *The Canadian Rockies Trail Guide*, Summerthought.

Strong, Janice. *Mountain Footsteps: Hikes in the East Kootenays of Southeastern BC*, Bocky Mountain Books.

## SKI-TOURING (OTHER THAN ON HIKING TRAILS)

Holsworth, Trevor. *Ski Touring the West Kootenays*, Kootenay Experience.

Scott, Chic. *Ski Trails in the Canadian Rockies*, Rocky Mountain Books.

Scott, Chic. *Summits and Icefields*, Rocky Mountain Books.

## CLIMBING & SCRAMBLING GUIDES

Boles, Glen. *Rocky Mountains of Canada–North*, American Alpine Club.

Boles, Glen. *Rocky Mountains of Canada–South*, American Alpine Club.

Dougherty, Sean. *Selected Alpine Climbs in the Canadian Rockies*, Rocky Moutain Books.

Fox, John, ed. *The Columbia Mountains of Canada–Central*, American Alpine Club.

Kane, Alan. *Scrambles in the Canadian Rockies*, Rocky Mountain Books.

Krusyzna, Robert and William Putnam. *A Climber's Guide to the Interior Ranges of BC*, American Alpine Club.

## BACKCOUNTRY ACCOMMODATIONS

Barnes, Christine. *Great Lodges of the Canadian Rockies*, W.W. West.

Schmaltz, Ken. *Rocky Mountain Retreats: Recommended Accommodation in the Canadian Rockies*, Points West Publishing.

## BACKCOUNTRY ROADS

Musio, Russel. *Backroad Mapbook, Volume IV: The Kootenays*. Musio Ventures.

# *In Memoriam:* Recently Defunct Huts

## ELK LAKES CABIN
This was an old trappers' cabin that came to be used by hikers and skiers in what is now Elk Lakes Provincial Park. It collapsed in the late 1980s, although a very crude shed still stands (somehow) near the main entrance to the park. The Tobermory Cabin 5 km south now serves the purpose of sheltering skiers and hikers.

## CMC VALLEY SHELTER
This old loggers' cabin in the valley just north of Mt Yamnuska (near the confluence of the Bow and Kananaskis rivers) was restored to good shape in the early 1970s. But, because of repeated misuse, the cabin was officially destroyed and will not be rebuilt.

## GRAHAM COOPER HUT
With perhaps the most spectacular setting of any hut in the Rocky Mountains, this hut on a ridge high above Moraine Lake was a mecca for climbers attempting ascents in the Valley of the Ten Peaks. However, in part because it tempted climbers to reach it via a climb of the couloir right below it—a shooting gallery of rubble that injured many climbers—the hut was replaced by the Neil Colgan Hut across the icefield.

## ECHO BASIN CABIN
This cabin near the Kootenay Pass area west of Creston was erected by some local skiers, apparently without formal approval. And while it has not been removed, it has not been maintained recently and now is used mainly as a day-shelter for snowmobilers. It is not recommended for overnight stays, although such would still be possible.

## OLD RIPPLE RIDGE CABIN
A log cabin built and maintained by Creston-area skiers, this cabin began to deteriorate to such an extent that in the mid-1990s, the BC Forest Service built a new one beside it, for this area is very popular with skiers. For several years both cabins were available for use, but at some point in 2000, the old cabin was converted into firewood for the new one.

## EVANS BROTHERS CABIN
Mentioned in the first edition of *Mountain Footsteps: Hikes in the East Kootenays*, this old but quite habitable cabin in the Meachen Creek drainage west of Kimberley collapsed from snow in the mid-1990s.

## MULVEY BASIN HUT
One of the first huts I ever stayed in, this shelter was always

a rather squalid building in a spectacular setting in Valhalla Provincial Park. Now there is only the setting. In the interests of both aesthetics and hygiene, the cabin was torched by park officials in the mid-1990s.

*The Mulvey Basin Hut*

## NEMO CREEK CABIN

One of the numerous old trappers' cabins in the Kootenays, this building was mainly used by hikers wanting to escape from bad weather while camping in this valley in Valhalla Provincial Park. Parks officials have recently declared it unusable for overnight stays.

## LOWER WEE SANDY CREEK CABIN

With the completion of the new Wee Sandy Creek cabin at the 10-km (6-mi) mark of the hike into Wee Sandy Lake in Valhalla Provincial Park, this old cabin at the 5-km (3-mi) mark became rather redundant. And since it was in quite a dilapidated (and vermin-ridden) state, it has been closed to overnight stays by parks officials.

## FORSTER CREEK SHELTER ("THE GENERAL STORE")

Built by a heli-ski company as an emergency shelter, this cabin was left unlocked for use by hikers or snowmobilers. However, in the winter of 2000, the cabin was badly vandalized. As a result, the heli-ski company has airlifted the renovated cabin to an undisclosed location closer to the Catamount Glacier. A new structure, built as a joint venture between the BC Forest Service and a local snowmobile club, has recently been established a bit farther upstream.

## HERMIT HUT

The first hut ever built in the Canadian West for the sole purpose of mountaineering, this cabin was often used by climbers scaling the big peaks in the Rogers Pass area north of the Hwy 1. It was rebuilt and/or refurbished several times, but by the mid-1980s it had deteriorated quite badly. It was removed before the early 1990s.

# Index of Huts & Lodges

A.O. Wheeler Hut *238*

Abbot Pass Hut *76*

Adamants Lodge *258*

Amiskwi Lodge *94*

Asulkan Cabin *236*

Balfour Hut *84*

Barrett Lake Hut *160*

Battle Abbey Lodge *226*

Benjamin Ferris (Great Cairn) Hut *260*

Berg Lake Shelter *134*

Blanket Glacier Chalet *214*

Bobbie Burns Lodge *222*

Bonnington Yurts *164*

Boulder & Ptarmigan Lodges *168*

Bow Hut *86*

Bryant Creek Cabin *50*

Bugaboo Lodge *216*

Campbell Icefield Chalet *102*

Cariboo Lodge *272*

Caribou Cabin *246*

Castle Mountain Hut *70*

Char Creek Cabin *146*

Chatter Creek Lodge *104*

Clearwater River Chalet *266*

Colgan Hut (see Neil Colgan Hut)

Connor Lakes Cabin *30*

Conrad Kain Hut *218*

Copper Hut *158*

Crusader Creek Cabin *182*

Dave Henry Lodge *128*

Diana Lake Lodge *62*

Discovery Chalet (see Trophy Mountain Chalet)

Doctor Creek Cabin *170*

Duncan Hut (see Scott Duncan Hut)

Dunn Creek Cabin *208*

Durrand Glacier & Mt Moloch Chalets *250*

Egypt Lake Shelter *54*

Elizabeth Parker Hut *74*

Enterprise Creek Cabin *184*

Eva Lake Cabin *248*

Evans Lake Cabin *188*

Fairy Meadow Hut *262*

Fay Hut *64*

Ferris Hut (see Benjamin Ferris Hut)

Fight Meadow Chalet (see Trophy Mountain Chalet)

Fish Lake Cabin *28*

Flint Lake Lodge & Mt Carlyle Hut *178*

Forster Creek Cabin *204*

Forster Hut (see Ralph Forster Hut)

Fortress Lake Lodge *110*

Fryatt Hut (see Sydney Vallance Hut)

Galena Lodge *210*

Glacier Circle Hut *232*

Golden Alpine Holidays Lodges (see Sunrise Lodge)

Grassy Hut *150*

Great Cairn Hut (see Benjamin Ferris Hut)

Halfway Lodge (see Sundance Lodge)

Halfway/Ptarmigan Shelter *78*

Hind Hut (see R.C. Hind Hut)

Huckleberry Hut *162*

International Basin Hut *224*

Island Lake Lodge *24*

Jarvis Lake Cabin (see Kakwa Lake Cabins)

Jules Holt Cabin (see Wee Sandy Creek Cabin)

Jumbo Pass Cabin *202*

Kakwa & Jarvis Lakes Cabins *138*

Keystone–Standard Basin Hut *252*
Lake O'Hara Lodge *72*
Lakit Lookout Shelter *26*
Lawrence Grassi (Mt Clemenceau) Hut *106*
Lloyd MacKay (Mt Alberta) Hut *108*
Malloy Igloo *220*
Marble Hut (see Stead Hut)
McMurdo Creek Cabin *230*
Meadow Lodge (see Sunrise Lodge)
Meadow Mountain Lodge *194*
Mistaya Lodge *96*
Mitchell River Shelter *38*
Monashee Chalet *268*
Monashee Powder Lodge *212*
Mount Assiniboine Lodge *44*
Mt Alberta Hut (see Lloyd Mackay Hut)
Mt Carlyle Hut (see Flint Lake Lodge)
Mt Clemenceau Hut (see Lawrence Grassi Hut)
Mt Colin Centennial Hut *126*
Mt Moloch Chalet (see Durrand Glacier Chalet)
Naiset Cabins *42*
Neil Colgan Hut *66*
North Rockies Ski Tours Lodge *140*
Olive Hut *206*
Peter & Catharine Whyte (Peyto) Hut *88*
Peter Huser Memorial Chalet *270*
Peyto Hut (see Peter & Catharine Whyte Hut)
Police Meadows Cabin *48*
Powder Creek Lodge *172*
Purcell Lodge *240*
Queen Mary Lake Cabin *34*
R.C. Hind Hut *40*
Ralph Forster Hut *132*

Ralph Lake Shelter *36*
Ripple Ridge Cabin *148*
Ruby Creek Lodge *192*
Sapphire Col Shelter *234*
Scott Duncan Hut *82*
Selkirk Lodge *228*
Shadow Lake Lodge *56*
Shangri-La Cabin *122*
Shovel Pass Lodge *124*
Silver Spray Cabin *176*
Skoki Lodge *80*
Slocan Chief Cabin *180*
Snowwater Hilton Hut *154*
Snowwater Lodge *156*
Sorcerer Lake Lodge *254*
Stanley Mitchell Hut *90*
Steed Hut *152*
Sultana Creek Cabin *200*
Sundance & Halfway Lodges *52*
Sunrise, Meadow & Vista Lodges *256*
Surprise Creek Cabin *46*
Swift Creek Cabins *130*
Sydney Vallance (Fryatt) Hut *112*
Thunder Meadows Cabin *22*
Tobermory Creek Cabin *32*
Tonquin Valley Adventures Lodge *118*
Tonquin Valley Backcountry Lodge *120*
Trophy Mountain, Discovery & Fight Meadow Chalets *264*
Twin Falls Chalet *92*
Valhalla Lodge *186*
Vista Lodge (see Sunrise Lodge)
Wates–Gibson Hut *114*
Wee Sandy Creek (Jules Holt) Cabin *190*
West Range Lodge *136*
Wheeler Hut (see A.O. Wheeler Hut)
Woodbury Cabin *174*
Ymir Yurts *166*

# About the Author

JIM SCOTT has been hiking, skiing and climbing in the Rockies and Columbias for most of his life, and has traveled through the Alps and Himalayas. He has published numerous articles in outdoors magazines, and was shortlisted for a National Magazine Award for an in memoriam tribute he wrote in *Equinox* for alpinist John Lauchlan. When not working at his day job as a college instructor, he loves to explore new terrain and sample new backcountry lodgings. Several stints as custodian at Alpine Club of Canada huts prompted him to develop this comprehensive guide for the many wilderness enthusiasts searching for backcountry lodging. Jim Scott lives in Red Deer, Alberta.